MW01006856

TECHNOLOGY, EDUCATION–
THE TEC SERIES

Series Editor: Marcia C. Linn
Advisory Board: Robert Bjork, Chris Dede,
Carol Lee, Jim Minstrell, Jonathan Osborne, Mitch Resnick

ASSESSING
the
EDUCATIONAL DATA
MOVEMENT

Philip J. Piety

Foreword by Allan Collins

Teachers College, Columbia University
New York and London

Published by Teachers College Press, 1234 Amsterdam Avenue, New York, NY 10027

Library of Congress Cataloging-in-Publication Data

Piety, Philip J.
  Assessing the educational data movement / Philip J. Piety.
    pages cm—(Technology, education-connections: The TEC series)
  Includes bibliographical references and index.
  ISBN 978-0-8077-5426-9 (pbk.)—ISBN 978-0-8077-5427-6 (hardcover)
  1. Educational indicators—United States. 2. Education and state—United States.
  I. Title.
  LB2846.P535 2013
  379.1'58—dc23   2012046520

ISBN 978-0-8077-5426-9 (paper)
ISBN 978-0-8077-5427-6 (hardcover)

Printed on acid-free paper
Manufactured in the United States of America

20 19 18 17 16 15 14 13   8 7 6 5 4 3 2 1

Contents

Foreword

In this book, Philip Piety describes how the use of educational data is growing rapidly in schools. He makes clear that over time this is likely to have radical effects on American schooling and could lead to dramatic improvements in what we teach and how we teach—or it could make the schools even more focused on memorization and high-stakes tests than they already are.

I have long been concerned about the way testing has narrowed the school curriculum over the last 100 years. There are a variety of capabilities, which are deemphasized in school because of the emphasis on easy-to-score tests. These are long-standing goals of education, such as:

- Taking responsibility for completing a substantial piece of work
- Working well with others to plan and carry out tasks
- Making persuasive presentations and arguments
- Exercising the body to keep physically fit and healthy
- Finding and deeply researching questions that are worth pursuing

High-stakes tests are not preparing students for the kinds of thinking required by the digital age. Piety's book shows that these types of tests lead to gaming the system by cheating, teaching to the test and its cutoffs, and removing students from the testing pool. They raise critical questions about the logic of data-driven decision making based on test data, which frames education and learning too narrowly.

Another point that the book stresses is the importance of looking at the organizational rather than the individual dimensions of education. Just as learning occurs on multiple social levels and over time, so does the work of teachers and schools. The book urges policymakers to see the value of information ecologies where performance data combine with other representations to help educators respond to their unique circumstances.

Testing used to rate teachers serves to disempower teachers, unlike Lesson Study in Japan, which has empowered Japanese teachers to progressively improve their teaching. The book does suggest how new kinds of data could be used to help teachers improve their teaching, but little is being done in that direction. It also describes how the Knowledge is Power Program

(KIPP) schools are using inventories to help students learn social and meta-cognitive skills that are critical to success. When KIPP schools found that the highest-achieving students were not always the most successful, they looked at the whole system and found that perseverance and determination were even more important. These are not taught in individual classes, but by the students' experiences throughout their whole careers.

I see great promise in the kind of embedded assessment described in the book for undoing the narrowing that high-stakes testing has promoted. If students are learning in computer environments, records of what they do as they learn can be recorded and archived anonymously. Then it is possible to use learning analytics to study which teaching strategies are most effective for student learning by comparing different strategies in these large archives. It is also possible to look at student traits that are critical to success—such as persistence—as Valerie Shute does in the stealth assessments that the book describes. The potential is there for much more effective use of data for improving learning, but there is no guarantee that these possibilities will be realized.

In the final chapter, Piety envisions an integrated design science that is much more situational and allows for variation in the designs to meet different school circumstances. This design science favors design-based research in an approach that is consistent with classroom research and the emergent nature of technology. Let us hope that the design science he envisions can find ways to use data to improve and broaden teaching and learning, rather than focusing on the memorization of facts and skills, which is what current testing emphasizes.

I suspect that if we ever want to use data to improve schooling, we will need to create an agency that has the expertise to collect and analyze data in an unbiased manner, like the Consumers Union that produces *Consumer Reports*. Perhaps some of the new organizations that the book describes will move in that direction by considering the kinds of outcomes that are critical for students living and working in a digital world.

—*Allan Collins*

Preface

This book has been both a personal and professional endeavor. Often it has been hard to separate the two, as preparation for it started long before I began working on this volume for the Technology, Education–Connections series in 2010. I believe it is a project that was only possible for me after a life's journey spent experiencing education, technology, and some of the important ways they can connect. Although this is not a personal story, it is informed by an accumulation of my personal and professional experiences that relate to many issues explored in this book. The stepping stones of my life have provided me with rare vantage points on how data and information are impacting the central activities of education, which I now believe to be one of the most important and misunderstood developments of our time.

How one sees is influenced by where one has been; what is familiar and what is new. A similar principle applies to crossing boundaries. Traversing from one domain to another reveals both a little about each and something about both. Because the boundaries of physical and conceptual places show us how they connect, form parts of larger systems, or are pulled in different directions, the crossing of boundaries can become an act of meaning making. In several consequential periods of my life, I crossed boundaries—inside and outside of educational systems; across different industries; in technical, teaching, and managerial roles; as a struggling and accomplished student; from being a professional to a non-traditional adult student to then a scholar working outside of an academic home; and now as a parent of children in public school—that have helped me provide a more holistic account of the changes occurring in education and some of the forces driving them that until now has not been available.

My road to this undertaking began before I left high school, which I did somewhat earlier than scheduled after living on the border between those who thrive in school and those who become disaffected. I grew up in a traditional middle-class community with educated parents. I loved school from my youngest days. However, by my early adolescence I was being raised in a single-parent household with many of the economic and social challenges that come to children of absent fathers. By my late teens I had stopped attending classes and shortly thereafter became a high school dropout with limited employment choices. At times, the ways I became an adult student and then earned a Ph.D. in education seem random and accidental. This path, however, also became one of the best developmental processes I could imagine for writing this book.

I have seen many sides of education. The institution of public schools I experienced showed me some of its worst: labeling, lowered expectations, and being pushed through the system with little regard for academic development. Many of my primary and secondary school years were marked by occasional interest and marginal performance. School, for me, was often a place of confinement rather than of liberation. It was a place I ultimately sought to escape from and did. I saw then and see now good and dedicated teachers working alongside educators who are more invested in themselves than the children they should be serving. It has been an unfortunate truth across the ages.

I have also experienced some of the best that educators and educational systems have to offer. I remember being profoundly helped by some of the teachers, counselors, and staff at Eastern Junior High School who took time to advise me and make an impact on my life. At one point when the chaos of my home circumstances combined with the confusion of the adolescent years, teachers would pull me aside and offer direct words of encouragement, saying, "you can do it," "you're a good kid," and, "you'll make it through this." These were, as I recall them, regular teachers. They worked in an era when school systems did not look at "productivity" measures. They had been in my school long before I got there and continued for years after I left. In retrospect, their actions seem now anything but random. They are clearly the moves of dedicated educators responding to the circumstances of a student in their care. I never thanked them, but their words and understanding proved transformative even though at that time no change in me or my performance would have been evident.

Educators have a voice and a position that can impress on children. Years later, after working in the technology field I was able to appreciate how those educators used their special role to give one teenager messages that were sorely needed and which other adults had been unable to do. While hard to measure or translate into data, this is the kind of act some educators do every day that does make a huge difference. Not all do this nor do all have students who need it. Education appears simple in that it is an almost universal experience. But, it is one that many experience through diverse paths. To deeply understand the public enterprise of education requires assimilating the fundamental reality of the profound differences that exist in this broad activity we call education.

Shortly after leaving high school, I began my career in the information technology field where I became a computer programmer and worked with emerging organizational software solutions. Much of today's economic reality has roots in what was occurring in those days. That work led me to experience many new boundaries involving different kinds of institutions and fields. After spending some years as a technician, I became involved with a portion of that industry providing consulting, education, and strategic analysis to managers and executives. From week to week or month to month I was immersed in the details of different fields: one day it was military logistics, the next health care, manufacturing, retail, or finance. This experience gave me an appreciation for the different ways organizations use information for improvement. It showed me how information systems can be catalysts for reshaping professions, companies, and fields. It also showed how different endeavors could be in some ways similar while in other ways fundamentally different. Even though implementing these technologies was almost always an arduous process, those organizations that did, were the ones that thrived. I left that field at the beginning of this century to return to school and complete my undergraduate degree. Once there, I reconnected with my love of learning and interest in education.

My adult educational experience was similarly nontraditional and influenced how I approached this book. After many years of work, I completed my long deferred undergraduate degree at the University of Maryland's University College, a school for professionals where classes are often conducted in the evening and with distance technology. I followed this with a master's from Georgetown University, where the scholarship I encountered inspired me to pursue a Ph.D. at a top-tier university. At the University of Michigan's School of Education I studied cognition and learning in the comparatively new field of Learning Sciences. My interest in educational data, however, developed quickly. Through a rare graduate fellowship and combination of administrative circumstances, I was not funded by any particular program and not officially housed within a single department. This is unusual for graduate students, who typically spend much of their time affiliated with a core research program and faculty network. My unusual freedom and the interdisciplinary approach nurtured at Michigan allowed me to pursue those interests across several academic communities and in different public schools and district offices investigating both learning and organizational issues.

My doctoral studies revealed the frequent disconnect between a segmented academy and the complex interconnected realms of practice; how the boundaries of academic fields structure and shape the questions that are asked. These factors converged around the brand new topic of educational data. As early research about this topic appeared, it came tentatively from different communities and almost always equating data with test scores. Those scholars not studying this area often showed trepidation—treating this movement as another ill-conceived reform effort with the potential to harm educators. While waves of organizational technology and ideas were moving into education from other fields, the emerging studies were almost entirely framed in purely educational rather than interdisciplinary terms. Few connections were made across different education communities let alone to other fields that were implicated in these developments. As education scholars looked at these practices it was often as a kind of program or intervention that could be studied with before and after snapshots looking for impact in student achievement. Little of the extant research investigated what I believed were the most important perspectives of this phenomenon: that it is historical process affecting the entire field at the same time and that information of many kinds can be used as systemic resources to connect different organizations in addition to improving productivity. The historical aspect is one that those who work with technology learn by living since the natural evolution of technology and adoption invariably drives rapid changes across systems and sectors.

In the few years since I finished my doctoral degree, the emphasis on educational data has increased, especially in national policy. During this time, I have found practitioners often wondering how to make the best use of limited and imperfect information given to them amid policies that compel them to do so. Advocacy organizations often present simplistic visions that do not acknowledge the serious challenges to using the data in different educational practices. Unfortunately the research is still catching up and rarely actionable. Before leaving my earlier career with information tools and becoming re-immersed in education, I might have seen education as an easy addition to that list of fields that had benefitted from a data movement. Now, after having spent many years with educators, studying what occurs in schools, working with teachers and leaders up close and seeing the work they do day after day, I see that the transformation for education will be special. It is going to be difficult and require a translation of many concepts from industry into the unique practices of schooling. It is not just that education is a social practice, but that it is social across many levels, which complicate this translation. It is also an intellectual area rife with contradictions. Accountability policies that cause data to be collected often have negative side effects at the same time. Although the policies may be from some perspectives necessary they are also not neutral.

The result here is not a typical academic book. It is also not exactly the book I started to write either. As I began this work I too saw this movement negatively impacting, and being resisted by educators and teachers. As well intentioned as the efforts to bring data into education were and are, at the beginning I saw data policies as largely in opposition to those working with children. Not that they should have been, but that the world of educational research that I had spent a lot of time in had reinforced certain stereotypes about educators. I began with a view of data as often inhibiting the work teachers do. And, there are many cases where data-oriented policies do have a negative effect. At the same time, the research for this book has shown that there are many different kinds of educators, why there can be valid reasons for some of the more difficult policies built around data, and how many educators do not resist the idea of using data and information in their work. Rather than educators generally being opposed to the data movement, many are interested and willing, but have not yet seen the promise fulfilled in the tools that are provided them.

There are three things I wanted to convey with this book. First, that what is unfolding now on many levels, often with great difficulty, is bigger than a single program or policy. It is a sociotechnical transition I name the educational data movement. The assessment this book provides is not a concise score or grade. I will not argue here that the data movement has been good or bad or that the field should or should not proceed with it. Sociotechnical revolutions are complex. Like the physiological transitions individuals experience as they mature, these processes fundamentally reshape. They can be trying. They often get better with time. And, they are not optional. Second, I seek to use a wide lens that includes and values different perspectives. As with other sociotechnical transitions, this one plucks cultural chords and brings quickly to the surface important differences in how different people view education. Many of the ideas and tools now being brought into education are from different fields, including business, and often based on different logics and with different core principles than those that have dominated the field of education for a long time. Part of what I want to accomplish in this book is to explain those logics and to reflect as best I can some of particular players and organizations that are part of this movement. Many of them—philanthropies, charter organizations, reform and advocacy groups, the U.S. Department of Education, and even educational researchers themselves—are typically not discussed in educational scholarship. Our research is usually focused on subjects rather than on those funding or conducting the research, let alone on the tools they use to make meaning. In reflecting these different interests and agents I seek to advance a common understanding. This book contains few heroes or villains. I believe the vast majority of those with different approaches to educational improvement share a common concern for children and for those who serve them. The third thing I wanted to convey in this book is the uncertainty of this time. This book is not intended as final word. Because it is dealing with the ever changing nature of technology, it cannot be. Look at the data movement in once place and time and a clear image may appear. Blink and look again and it will almost certainly will seem to have changed.

My hope is that this book can help readers ask good questions in the new era and even consider different perspectives. I firmly believe that education's information practices can and will get better. This is a lesson of history. How quickly and for whom this part of education improves, however, is still unclear. My expectation is that these different perspectives will help develop an appreciation for how information tools might be co-designed in a way that can more fully help those working with children, including those like my own, like others of their generation, and those like the student I once was.

Acknowledgments

The development of this book involved significant research that I undertook on my own and without institutional support. There are advantages to this approach, since every funder and employer has a perspective, and I believed that the book that was needed at this time would have to be able to cross boundaries and represent different perspectives as fairly as possible. I was fortunate to have colleagues who were generous with their time and thoughts, including John Castellani, Kristen DiCerbo, Rich Halverson, Susanna Loeb, Bob Mislevy, Jon Supovitz, and Joan Talbert. Along the way, I met many new people and reconnected with others I had not seen for some time, who were generous with their time and insights, including Sally Askman, Elias Carayannis, Caroline Chauncey, Cheryl Collins, Robert Croninger, Tim Fort, Rolf Grafwallner, Willis Hawley, Rick Hess, Chip Kimball, Mario Morino, Donald Peurach, Bryan Richardson, Andy Rotherham, Nancy Shapiro, Bob Slavin, Tom VanderArk, Ping Wang, Nancy Wilson, and Chris Woolard. I am grateful for these connections and hope to be able to build upon them in the future. I was fortunate to have a special colleague, Linda O'Brien, who helped me think through some of the early ideas in this project. I am especially grateful to Chris Dede, who initially recommended that I take this project on and has always provided advice equal in thoughtfulness to his stature in the field. John Behrens also has been a gift to my work during this time, bringing friendship, insights, and invocations at fortuitous moments.

There are many organizations discussed in this book. None of them provided any financial support for this or any other project I was involved with, other than the time of their staff, who included Ed Dieterle, Don Mitchell, David Parker, Eli Pristoop, Brandt Redd, Marguerite Rosa, and Bill Tucker from the Bill and Melinda Gates Foundation; Luis de la Fuente, Becca Bracey Knight, Erica Lepping, and Nancy Que from the Eli and Edyth Broad Foundation; Lori Fey, Adam Miller, and Joe Siedlecki from the Michael and Susan Dell Foundation; Andrea Conklin Bueschel from the Spencer Foundation; Aimee Guidera, Paige Kowalski, and Elizabeth Laird from the Data Quality Campaign; Patty Diaz-Andrade, Jon Fullerton, and Sarah Glover from the Strategic Data Project; Julie Cruit Angilly, Eugine

Chung, Scott Morgan, and John Troy from Education Pioneers; Ken Frank and Anna Sommers from Education Resources Strategies; Don Hostler and Rick Torres from the National Student Clearinghouse; Brent Maddin from the Relay Graduate School of Education; Courtney Cass, Carrie James, and Annie Lewis from Teach for America; Angela Duffy and Steve Mancini from the Knowledge Is Power Program; Sherri Dairiki, John Danner, and Kristoffer Haines of Rocketship Education; Howard Nelson and Rob Weil of the American Federation of Teachers and Jacques Nacson of the National Education Association; Andres Alonso, Sonja Brookins-Santelises, Tom DeWire, and Kim Lewis of the Baltimore City Public Schools; Anna Gregory and Jason Kamras of DC Public Schools; Sherwin Collette, Donna Hollingshead, and Frank Stetson of the Montgomery County Public Schools; and Jack Buckley, Karen Cator, Richard Culatta, Tate Gould, Steve Midgley, Ross Santy, Jim Shelton, and Joanne Weiss of the U.S. Department of Education.

I am personally grateful to some of those closer to me and this project. The team at Teachers College Press, including series editor Marcia Linn and acquisitions editor Emily Spangler, along with three anonymous reviewers, helped me shape the project and find a path toward completion. This is the first book (hopefully not the last) since leaving Michigan. I am reminded often of the wonderful faculty there who provided me with incredible support and examples. Michael Cohen, Magdalene Lampert, and Annemarie Palincsar were especially generous with their time and advice, for which I am eternally grateful. My doctoral committee was an inspiration. John Swales showed me through his work how a book should be written. Jay Lemke has given me most of the theories and ideas that undergird my work. Joe Krajcik was the ultimate champion and role model. If I have a chance to work in a university, in many ways I would emulate Joe, who makes spaces for others, passes the ball, and encourages those he works with to be their best. Pamela Moss has been both a thoughtful advisor and friend. Her intellectual honesty, ultimate decency, and respect for those she works with have set for me a high standard to which I will always aspire.

Personally, I owe a lot to my family. I have to begin with thanking my brothers and sisters. We all went through a lot together in our school years and their strength helped me write this. My mother has taught me the value of following your vision and always moving forward. My wife, my love, Sarah, has been a constant supporter in this work. She is the most literate person I know and could write several books herself in the time it took me to complete one. And my two sons, Dustin and Thomas, are the best. They are my joys and I have been so proud of the people they are becoming as I write this. They also keep me grounded about what is important in education and in life.

FRAMING THE CONTEMPORARY SOCIOTECHNICAL SHIFT

An uncommon aspect of this book is that it deals with history in the present. It uses a historical frame to look at events that have occurred recently and movements that are still unfolding in an important transition in American education. Much of the focus is on the U.S. kindergarten through 12th grade (K–12) part of the educational enterprise. As a story of sociotechnical change, however, it relates more broadly to the larger world of education and learning and how different kinds of organizations are embracing and adapting technologies.

The two chapters in this part (as with the remainder of the book) do not present a single viewpoint in terms of the value of educational data or argue for a specific direction for American education that will lead to particular results. This is not that kind of forward-looking book. Rather, it argues that the change that is occurring is a *shift*, that through sociotechnical decisions will influence what is possible and easy in the future. The educational data movement is not a policy that might be undone in the future. Parts of it *are* directly tied to federal policies and those policies *do* matter. However, this book argues that the shift toward using data and information transcends policies and administrations. There is little evidence that any field of human endeavor that has embarked on a process of collecting and using information has decided to abandon it, and education is unlikely to be different.

The first chapter lays out basic claims about the educational data movement and its rapid ascension in the years after the 2001 reauthorization of the Elementary and Secondary Education Act, known as No Child Left Behind (NCLB), with which the data movement has a complicated relationship. At certain times the movement appears to be a product of NCLB, but actually is related to many other policies and movements both inside and outside of education. The second chapter explores one area with both important and complicated connections to the educational data movement: business information technology. While there are several ways in which the use of educational data is descended from different lines of educational research, the relationship to business technology is critically important to understand. In some ways, education resembles other fields, but in many ways, as later parts of the book detail, education has unique characteristics. Overall, however, the questions of how to apply ideas and tools proven in business and other fields to education remain unanswered. Much about what is possible in the future is still unclear.

In this part, as with the rest of the book, some of the dark sides of efforts involving educational data are discussed alongside the positives. While the data themselves are inert, the data that practitioners use are often tied to policies like NCLB that guide their use. An example is evaluating teachers or principals based on student test scores, which became popular while this book was being written and is discussed in several chapters. Like NCLB, simple and straightforward data-driven approaches can have complicated side effects and can trigger political tensions. The broader systemic considerations are an important part of the story of the educational data movement this book will tell.

The Educational Data Movement Begins

The first decade of the 21st century was the beginning of immense change in education. If an educator had gone to sleep in the year 2000 and awakened in 2010, like a modern-day Rip Van Winkle, he or she would have found that data—usually about students, but increasingly about teachers as well—had become a central fixture in the field. In those 10 years, the language of education changed as educators became familiar with new businesslike terms such as data warehouses, analytics, outcomes, productivity, performance management, and management science. Our just-awakened educator would find teachers described as "human capital," their work sometimes seen as a commodity, policymakers pushing for more and more reliance on data when making educational decisions, and calls for educators to use data to become more flexible and to continuously improve.

Not everything would have changed. The subjects taught in 2010 were largely the same as they had been for decades. Students faced many of the same challenges from economics, home life, and the nature of schooling as they had in the past. Most of the buildings that students went to every day had changed only slightly. But, unlike those who worked in education in years past, educators of today—from teachers to principals to district administrators—now look to data rather than only their own judgment for evidence of their successes and failures.

Through the first decade of this century, billions of dollars have been spent on data technologies at all levels of the educational system. These investments have come at the same time other areas have been cut back and educators are looking at shrinking budgets and austerity for years to come. While many school districts have reduced positions for librarians and media specialists, it is now common for many schools to have one or more staff positions dedicated to managing student data. The vast majority of these new investments are aligned with test scores and meeting federal special education mandates. The test scores are imprecise and derived from only a few subject areas, but have been used as part of national policy to *transform* education.

Our Rip Van Winkle educator would find much new material to read. Scores of books provide recipes to help districts, school leaders, and teachers develop data-driven management approaches. In some books researchers also discuss how data are being used, misused, or barely used at all. But in the midst of all that is new, our reawakened educator might notice something missing. There is little historical perspective to help explain why the field of education has become so consumed with the use of data in daily practice now, and not in some previous time. There is little discussion of the complex and human dimensions involved in teaching and learning that led many to become teachers in the first place. And there is little that takes a critical view of this period, showing both potential and challenges. There is scant research that shows how the data movement has been responsible for reshaping educational practice or outcomes.

Nevertheless, over time this educator would come to realize, as have most educators today, that the national agenda for data use is now a permanent fixture and growing. Data use, which can mean more than testing, is bigger than any one policy and is infiltrating almost every program and area of practice. I refer to this as the *educational data movement*. The educational data movement is a process of transformation where different kinds of tools are becoming part of the fabric of educational practice. Rather than what happens with a passing fad, the field will not return to where it was before, even though using data to transform education can be complicated and messy.

THE EDUCATIONAL DATA MOVEMENT:
A SOCIOTECHNICAL REVOLUTION

This book frames the educational data movement as a sociotechnical revolution. Sociotechnical revolutions occur when combinations of technologies and social systems evolve together. The printing press; telegraph, telephone, and television; and the Internet have all been parts of sociotechnical revolutions.[1] So have the transitions from steam to diesel in railroads and from analog to digital and mobile phones. Sometimes different social approaches grounded in different technologies coexist for long periods of time before the older one is replaced. However, sociotechnical revolutions only go forward. Once technologies have changed an area of human activity, there are few examples of that process being undone.

The stakes are high for many educators, especially teachers. Sociotechnical revolutions impact lives and change professions. The ways they do so are not always obvious while the revolution is occurring. But with time, it is possible to see the how the types of work people do are impacted by technologies that support that work. Sometimes these transitions are broad, as was the case for email. Sometimes they are local to an industry and a field, as with automated teller machines and self-service gas pumps. Sometimes they affect one type of job and sometimes many. These revolutions often reshape not only the way individual activities are conducted, for example, publishing and communications or teaching, but also organizations, the ways activities are structured, and the different roles and professions that exist. Rarely are any professions untouched.

Theoretically, sociotechnical studies are related to a field of science and technology studies that seeks to understand in the context of science how societies use tools and make meaning out of information. Educational data systems fit into this framework because they involve technologies and evidence that are used to explain what is occurring in districts, schools, and classrooms. Sociotechnical frameworks are powerful ways of looking at change. Because they look at interactions between technology and what people do, they can provide insights that neither a purely social nor a purely technical view can.[2] Dutch sociotechnical theorist Bijker suggests that "[one] should never take the meaning of a technical artifact or technical system as residing in the technology itself. Instead, one must study how the technologies are shaped and acquire their meaning in the heterogeneity of social interactions."

While powerful, this approach carries the risk of focusing on large concepts that can be difficult to analyze in a specific way. Terms such as *society* and *actor*, although conceptually valid, are vague. They can lead to a type of overgeneralization that makes specific actionable findings difficult. A finding, for example, about "school districts" would need to be tempered by the realization that there is great variation among school districts, so that those findings might apply to only a few of the thousands that exist. Rather than general and fuzzy concepts, this book takes an explicit approach. It names specific organizations, projects, and in some cases individuals. The purpose is not to imply that those named are exemplars or problems.[3] Rather, it is to follow real and *observable* organizations and people other than the broad categories that can give an illusion of scientific findings, but also dissipate what can be known about them. Being specific, then, not only is a theoretical approach, but helps demystify organizations and actions that are too easily labeled using simplistic categories. We can't understand what is not discussed. This helps the book track some of the important threads of society and technology that come together at this critical time in the educational data movement.

The assessment of this sociotechnical transition occurs on many levels and dimensions. It does not render a final score, but seeks to deepen our understanding and explain the shape of the educational data movement. It will not cover every aspect of it, nor can it, because each day brings a new set of developments as this area seems to constantly expand. This volume is intended to be a guide and provide perspectives for those who teach, lead, research, and seek to reform education during this transformational time. This book looks across different perspectives, some that are familiar to educators and some that are less so, and tries to connect the dots.

In this book, I make four claims. First, the educational data movement is irreversible and cumulative. Rather than being a discrete policy that might be overlaid with another, using data is like other sociotechnical revolutions in moving only forward. Like other similar revolutions, this one has the potential to reshape professions. And, for better or worse, it is building upon the infrastructures No Child Left Behind created. Second, information tools are operating in education at both individual and organizational levels. Policymakers have focused largely on individual student and teacher productivity. However, history shows that organizational flexibility and responsiveness can be important outcomes of using information tools. Third, educational data have unique challenges. These challenges do not render the data useless. Rather, it is important to be aware of and account for data weaknesses. At the same time, even imperfect data can be useful for understanding educational complexity, supporting collaboration, and enabling new designs for teaching in some situations. Fourth, the educational data movement is still young. New social and technical catalysts are constantly emerging and presenting policymakers and practitioners with design opportunities to balance transparency and local flexibility. As the movement has progressed, it has grown in terms of what counts as data, moving from a focus on testing to a more complex information ecology, in which student performance is central to a range of artifacts that practitioners often are learning to use.

A BUSINESS AND ORGANIZATIONAL PERSPECTIVE

Looking at the social forces behind the use of data in education, there are many ties to businesses. Although not everything in this movement is business-oriented, much is. Before 2008, it might have been easy to consider the federal government's emphasis on these approaches as a product of the administration of George W. Bush, with his pro-business credentials. However, the 2008 election brought a new administration and a change in control of Congress. The emphasis on using data-oriented management principles in education actually increased. Just as the Elementary and Secondary Education Act, known in its 2001 reauthorization as No Child Left Behind,[4] had strong bipartisan support, the push to use data has had broad support from across the political spectrum. Across many important education policy initiatives, including proposals to rewrite NCLB, the Obama administration has continued commitments to develop, integrate, and use data systems to improve the way education works.

Thinking of public education in business terms is not new. The early part of the 20th century also featured efforts to use in education assembly-line concepts that were then being used in manufacturing. Those efforts and the problems associated with them were documented by Raymond Callahan in his 1964 book *Education and the Cult of Efficiency*. Everything from student abilities and intelligence to ratios of teachers to students in subject areas was believed to be reducible to formulas, and through much of the 20th century educational science followed an industrial model. Over time, different movements, from civil rights to educational research, pointed out problems with the industrial model in terms of both equity and effectiveness. The current thrust on using business ideas is based on newer beliefs in performance management combined with new technology for greater personalization rather than a mass-production model as was characteristic of the period Callahan discussed. The principles and technologies being imported into education now also share much in common with what has been successful in other fields.

Although this movement may appear to have come on suddenly, it actually has been in the making for several decades. Throughout the past quarter-century, manufacturing, finance, health care, and many other fields have embraced information-driven organizational change. Tools, technologies, and infrastructures to support organizational data use also have been growing. Some of the foundation for what the Bush administration ushered in was laid in the standards-based reform movement beginning in the 1980s and with the diversification and deregulation of a once-public monopoly that now includes vouchers, charter schools, distance learning/virtual schools, and for-profit universities. Some philanthropic foundations tied to technology businesses also began to focus on education at that time, with specific attention to data. They were not the first ones, as important parts of this movement began in educational research much earlier, but the role of these foundations was timely and catalytic.

In this new era, the business models are applied both externally in the form of incentives and accountability and, increasingly, internally to provide educators with tools to make better operational decisions. NCLB had both elements, with its focus on school performance and press for data-driven decisions. Both external and internal foci continued into the Obama administration, with support for charter schools and a focus on educational *productivity*, as Secretary of Education Arne Duncan described in a speech to the American Enterprise Institute in 2010:

Almost every executive I have spoken with about improving productivity begins the conversation by talking about eliminating waste. We can and should do more to cut costs and increase the bottom line in our schools. . . . I am urging state[s] and districts [to] start to think more boldly about ways to improve educational productivity.[5]

Duncan, like some of his predecessors, frames educational organizations as similar to businesses, where information and data naturally play a role in identifying waste and measuring results.

These new business approaches for education go beyond productivity to new ways of using technology to design organizational practices. As Tom Friedman wrote in his bestseller *The World Is Flat: A Brief History of the Twenty-first Century,*[6] companies have done more than become more productive; they have been able to fundamentally rearrange their ways of working because of what the technology allows. In businesses, changes in productivity did not come as a dividend for all organizations in any formulaic way. Rather, some organizations changed, found new models, and succeeded. Some did not and did not survive. Many businesses today are very different from what they were several decades ago because the tools they use allow them to be more agile and efficient than their competitors.

Other fields, from manufacturing to finance to not-for-profits, have used information to guide daily decisions about the arrangement of resources, from materials to staff. James H. Shelton III, the U.S. Department of Education's assistant deputy secretary for innovation and improvement, commented on a report about American education by the management consulting firm McKinsey & Company, saying:

This is one of the first times that we have seen management science applied to the context for educational performance improvement. Once you start having that kind of understanding of the products and processes involved in making sustained progress, you can use technology to improve the pace at which you actually make improvement.[7]

Shelton, speaking for the administration in 2010, emphasized the need to look operationally at school organizations and to search for new models in education.[8] He himself is a former management consultant and venture philanthropist. Within the Department of Education (DoED) he led a novel program titled Investing in Innovation, or i3, that supports new innovations and organizational models.[9]

At the same time as there is a search for new educational models, there are also pressures on teachers, as one might expect, with a focus on *their* productivity. A seminal evaluation of teacher performance using test data was published in 2008. An important feature in the original design of NCLB revolved around teacher credentials, requiring districts to hire teachers who were "highly qualified." Harvard University professor Tom Kane and his colleagues analyzed test scores of students assigned to teachers with different levels of credentials, including those certified by alternative methods. What they found was that teachers' formal credentials did not influence the growth of their students' knowledge (as measured by test scores).[10] This finding undercut this cornerstone of NCLB using data collected from NCLB tests to do so! The study provided important research grounding to the widely held belief that some teachers can teach well and some cannot. This study and others like it have been influential in a wave of efforts to measure teacher effectiveness through test scores and to link teacher retention and pay to teaching performance rather than seniority and credentials.

As teachers increasingly are being seen in terms of their ability to impact student scores, there are other realignments occurring in what it means to be a teacher. Rather than being at the center of the educational world, information is helping teachers to be viewed as one piece of a larger system. Rather than relying on grades—the way teachers evaluate student performance—others in the educational system are viewing classrooms through many other forms of data and making teaching a more public profession that it was before. And rather than giving teachers autonomy within their classrooms, some are looking for ways to arrange, augment, and in some cases redefine the roles of teachers, with information and many kinds of data instrumental in these efforts.

NCLB AND VALUE-ADDED MODELS: REASONABLE IDEAS, HARD QUESTIONS

Years from now, the first decade of the 21st century might be called the NCLB era, as the law has dominated educational policy in ways that few others have. It was designed as broad legislation with many dimensions that are beyond the scope of this book. As this volume will show, using data in education did not begin with NCLB and neither did some of the core ideas that undergird their use across different educational levels. But NCLB occupies a special place in the educational data movement. The law provided a dramatic boost in the collection and use of certain kinds of data. Many of the tools and systems—*infrastructures*—that were built to support NCLB also are being used in the solutions intended to move beyond it. And, along with NCLB came other federal legislation and programs designed to make education more evidence-based.

Despite its problems with design and implementation, NCLB was based on reasonable ideas, directing schools to meet the needs of all children, including all subgroups. By testing students and holding schools accountable for the results, NCLB had a multifaceted formula for systemic improvement. Both the testing and the use of data from the tests did occur, but NCLB fell short of its goals, and 10 years after it was enacted, it had become damaged goods with few supporters. It also brought unanticipated side effects that made teaching and schooling much harder for many. As a large-scale systemic intervention designed to improve overall student and school performance, NCLB exacerbated inequities and failed to deliver on the promise to broadly improve educational outcomes. It generally is considered to have been responsible for lowering academic standards and creating a situation where many teachers teach to the test, or worse, fabricate results. For many teachers, NCLB, and its focus on data, has been one of the worst approaches to education they have seen.[11] For many, it is synonymous with the data movement and seemed to reduce the richness of education to a few numbers having little to do with what many teachers and educators believe is essential.

Some new efforts to improve education also are based on reasonable ideas. As NCLB has matured and problems with its design and implementation have become better understood, new ways of measuring student achievement and teachers' roles in student performance have emerged. One of the most important developments has been a new way of measuring student progress called a *value-added model* or VAM.[12] NCLB was built on the adequate yearly progress (AYP) indicator. AYP is an *achievement model* that tracks how a school's scores differ from year to year and not how the students themselves have advanced their understanding. AYP compares different groups of students that are in the same grade and same school, but in different years. When the demographics of a school change, when students who are on average more or less advantaged that those in previous years enter, the AYP scores naturally can shift. These shifts, however, have less to do with the teaching and more to do with the characteristics of students who are being tested in different years. AYP is also a school-based indicator. While school leaders may have looked at how the scores from one teacher related to those from another, NCLB did not consider teachers' ability to impact scores. VAMs, conversely, are organized around students and their teachers.

A VAM is a kind of *growth model*. Growth models track individual students and how their scores change over time.[13] They are less sensitive to demographic shifts because the same students are being compared across grades. Simple growth models can show how students have progressed in a given year (with assessments that are linked from year to year). But they are not sensitive to differences in students and the fact that some students, because of home life and/or prior knowledge, could be statistically expected to make certain gains that are different from what statistical models predict other students would be expected to make. A VAM, then, is designed to provide the extra capability to account for differences in students by factoring in characteristics known to affect achievement, including prior knowledge and socioeconomic status. It is designed to show the gains students make because of a specific teacher or school. This is powerful. Because VAMs estimate the growth that can be expected from students with specific backgrounds, these models have the potential to quantify the improvements in learning independent of background so that different teachers and schools that have differing circumstances can be compared. However, in practice they have been plagued by imprecision. A characteristic of VAMs that is widely agreed to is that they can be much less stable indicators in practice than expected. Although intended to be reliable indicators of teacher quality, for a variety of reasons, discussed later in this book, VAMs are—like many educational measures—approximations.[14]

VAMs have both supporters and detractors. The critics of VAMs focus on how they can have a very high amount of variation from year to year. Some teachers ranked in the highest 25% of performers one year may be in the lowest 25% the next, so that looking at any one year's scores can be misleading. The same teachers' scores can vary depending on which classes they are teaching in the same year. Critics also cite multiple data-quality problems and other technical difficulties with equitably using VAMs in real-life settings. Supporters contend that all measurement systems are imperfect and that the benefits of VAMs outweigh their limitations, especially if they are combined with other measures to support thoughtful decisions. At the same time, over several years and along with other related data, a well-designed VAM can help show important differences in teachers' abilities.

Although focusing on the technical details of VAMs is important, especially as people's jobs may be impacted by what the models show, there are significant points about them that can be missed. They are *sociotechnical agents.* Just as with AYP, they are invisible to anyone entering a school. They hold no books, transport no students, and cannot be used to present any instructional material. They are mathematical formulas that have been put into software that often utilizes the same infrastructure used to support NCLB. Yet they have the potential to be instrumental in decisions about educators—decisions that can have dramatic effects for children in many parts of the educational system. This is not to say they are either good or bad, but that they are powerful, and they too are now a part of this sociotechnical revolution. Another important point about VAMs is that they are an example of measuring education more internally than was done under NCLB. Whereas NCLB measured teacher qualifications and aggregate school scores in uniform subgroups, VAM approaches shift the measurement to inside the school and toward the classroom teacher. They align with business and organizational models that consider internal operations of schools, although they provide little detail on what is going on inside classrooms.

As we think about VAMs in historical terms, it is important to understand how they may broaden the role of high-stakes test data from schools, since the models require significant amounts of test data to operate. Although they seem to be a departure from NCLB, they require volumes of test data that accountability approaches such as NCLB provide. Using VAMs across the spectrum of teachers rather than the approximately one-third that are covered under NCLB will entail even more data, which likely will require even more testing. With VAMs and other ways to evaluate teachers more rigorously also come new types of debates about evidence. Is it more important to use a method that may falsely identify a teacher as poor to protect students from all bad teachers, or is it more important to protect teachers from unfair evaluations while maybe allowing some poor teachers to remain on the job?

CONTROVERSY: UNIONS, BUSINESS PHILANTHROPIES, AND NEW EDUCATION ORGANIZATIONS

The data movement has come along at a time of heightened controversy about public education. Indeed, the movement is integral to some of this public tension, and familiar battle lines in longstanding educational debates can be seen throughout it. The data movement didn't give rise to the divisions between those with different perspectives on education reform. However, the movement and different uses for data, including VAMs, play on those tensions—the data can be used as instruments in power struggles that often include teachers unions, business philanthropies, and new education organizations. For example, in 2010, the politically charged documentary film *Waiting for Superman* focused on differences in school and teacher performance, promoted charter schools, and portrayed teachers unions as obstacles to reform. The filmmakers presented data showing student growth and reinforced messages about teacher productivity and credentials that were made possible with studies based on large collections of test data. The question of how education relates to business is implicit in these debates. Traditional educators and their supporters often will use the term *business* as having a kind of anti-education connotation and disparage the "corporate reformers" trying to take over education and transform the character of this human field using ideas and principles from business. For their part, many in the reform community are equally disparaging of traditional education communities that include teachers, the schools that prepare them, and their unions.[15]

The controversies that the data movement traverses include the role of some philanthropies with business connections. Many of the foundations supporting charter schools are also those supporting alternative teacher and leader preparation programs and the use of data. One of the best-known and most powerful is the Bill and Melinda Gates Foundation, endowed by the founder of Microsoft. Bill Gates's views were featured in *Waiting for Superman,* and his foundation has funded many of the charter school organizations that were highlighted in that movie. Consideration of the role of the Gates Foundation and other similar organizations is essential to understanding some drivers and tensions that are part of this shift. The well-known educational historian and former proponent of standards-based reform, Diane Ravitch, writes about these foundations and their influence on American education in her bestselling book *The Death and Life of the Great American School System.* In a chapter titled "The Billionaire Boys Club," Ravitch discusses how "over time they converged in support of reform strategies that mirrored their own experience in acquiring huge fortunes."[16] Without question, these foundations have pursued an ambitious agenda for American schooling. Unlike officials elected or appointed by those elected, they span administrations and provide sustained support for reform, drawing from a vision of education that features performance management and the power of data. The programs and organizations they fund seek to shape policy and influence public opinion.

Ravitch was not entirely wrong in her depiction of collaboration by these foundations. The Gates Foundation, along with the Michael and Susan Dell Foundation (endowed by Michael Dell, founder of Dell Computers), has joined with older foundations, including the Wallace, Spencer, MacArthur, and Carnegie foundations, in spending hundreds of millions of dollars to change education. Others involved in major efforts at school reform, including the Walton Family Foundation (endowed by the founders of Wal-Mart) and the Eli and Edythe Broad Foundation (founded by successful corporate executive Eli Broad), have connections to businesses that have used technology and management science to succeed in the work they have done. What has been rare in discussions of these philanthropies and their efforts to make education more data- and evidence-based is a critical and open exploration of the projects they fund. When we do this, what appears is not simple. There is logic in their efforts to use evidence that is different from the logic often expressed by traditional educators. It is a logic that includes more than the productivity of workers and finding the lowest cost. This logic anticipates organizational and systemic transformation based on the history of such changes in other fields.

To see the work of these foundations as an industrial takeover would be to ignore some important reasons why the use of data is an essential organizational move that often separates those who excel from those who do not. Throughout the 1980s and 1990s, dramatic advances were made in corporate productivity as a result of information technology; by some estimates this technology was responsible for as much as two-thirds of corporate productivity improvements.[17] Bill Gates and Michael Dell saw these revolutions from the perspective of leaders of companies that were successfully providing technology. Eli Broad and the Waltons viewed these revolutions from within companies that embraced technology and greatly profited from it. Many of the types of initiatives around data being seen in education—performance management, management and organizational science, information exchange standards, markets that support innovation—have helped propel not only individual businesses but entire sectors forward. And it is a fact that philanthropies are predominantly the result of business success.[18] At the same time, many of these business and management concepts are still unproven in education. As has been seen before in programs like NCLB and evaluating teachers based on student performance, sometimes really good and simple ideas fail to play out as desired in the varied and contingent world of education. Few people who have had a voice in shaping national education policy have not been moved by how the best-laid plans don't always make short work of or substantive progress on educational challenges. Education and learning are fundamentally complex areas, and the way they are organized and governed in the United States makes them even more so.

This book is ambitious in attempting to synthesize across different fields. Discussing these perspectives—the philanthropies and organizations that they support—is not an implicit endorsement or criticism. Rather, it is to show how they are connected to the educational data movement and connected to one another. Within the data movement, these organizations *are* powerful influences that have an active role in shaping some policies. Their role, as with unions and other national organizations, is central to the story. I argue in this book that one of the characteristics of the educational data movement is that it has been studied and understood in fragments. The fragments are both parts of the educational landscape (classrooms, district offices, etc.) and different worldviews based on different logics. A selective view of the educational world may be easier to read, but probably will make less of an overall contribution. Making sense of this large social process requires understanding many different sectors and how they have or have not been connected. This book attempts a holistic approach, to make some of the complexity comprehensible and to help the reader ask questions about some of these controversial elements as much as to draw conclusions.

HISTORICAL PERSPECTIVE ON EVIDENCE
AND THE EDUCATIONAL DATA MOVEMENT

This sociotechnical story places the educational data movement in historical context. Traditionally, educational programs are treated as a static thing that can be applied to practice and from which a specific kind of result can be expected. This can be called an *intervention model* and it has been used by some researchers as the frame from which to see and evaluate educational data. This view is limited because it does not account for how the world of education may be changing or the relationships between the moving field of educational systems and the often dynamic and disruptive character of technologies.[19] To broaden our view, this chapter discusses three important historical issues that have been at play in the youth of the educational data movement. These issues are early approaches to develop *systemic assessments* that are conceptually aligned with parts of the data movement, but not part of the infrastructures that are used by most states and districts; the general press for evidence in educational practice—called by some education's *evidence movement*—that came along during the early years of the educational data movement; and the level of evidence researchers have been able to develop that using data in education actually is leading to the desired results. Exploring these three issues can help us understand both the effects of the educational data movement and its trajectory.

Systemic Assessments

Educational research has had a complex relationship with the educational data movement. Different researchers, years and in some cases decades before NCLB and the data movement's emergence, have identified important principles that undergird the data movement. Many are presented throughout this book. One area educational researchers began to look at before NCLB was the design of test systems. While the design of indicator and information systems for organizational management decisions is well established in businesses, these principles are not common in education. Since the early part of the 20th century, education has been dominated by traditional testing approaches based largely on discrete test items tied to cognitive definitions developed by the test designers. However, in the years just before NCLB, a few educational researchers started to develop new ways of thinking about testing for *organizational improvement* as well as measuring what students know. These approaches are important in that they foreshadow some efforts now being used to turn test information into a systemic resource.

One of the earliest and most often cited writings about a systemic assessment approach came from psychologist John Frederiksen and computer scientist Allan Collins, who wrote "A Systems Approach to Educational Testing" in 1989.[20] This short concept paper introduced an idea that was radical for educational measurement. These authors were not part of an education school, but a research house that worked on different government projects, of which education was just one. They targeted one of educational measurement's most important concepts: validity. Validity, in a classical educational measurement sense, was defined as how accurately a particular score measures the underlying concept that was tested. A valid score was one that closely represented the true state of knowledge it was designed to test. Validity has become a much more complicated concept in recent years, with many different theorizations of what counts as validity and why it is important.[21] Frederiksen and Collins describe a new kind of validity for tests, which they call *systemic validity*. Systemic validity goes beyond mere indicators of student knowledge, or passive indicators. Systemic validity means that tests will be able to feed back into the system the kind of information that will "induce curricular and instructional changes in educational systems (and learning strategy changes in students) that foster the development of the cognitive traits that the tests are designed to measure."[22] What Frederiksen and Collins described, several years before NCLB, is how educational systems adapt to meet the needs of the tests. They argued that small, abstract, and indirect tasks typical of high-stakes tests offer a false bargain. They are easy to score, but are difficult to connect to authentic student experiences. More direct assessments that measure students in extended and more authentic tasks, on the other hand, have more systemic validity, yet are more difficult to score.

A few years later, Robert Mislevy, a leading expert in psychometrics, and his colleagues Russell Almond and Linda Steinberg at the Educational Testing Service began developing a way of looking at assessments they called Evidence Centered Design.[23] Evidence Centered Design argues that the design of assessment tasks should be influenced by the way the assessment results will be used. They argued that an assessment system should include tasks that cover the different kinds of knowledge, skills, and strategies that are used in the domain being tested. Evidence Centered Design projects frequently use new statistical tools, similar to those used for computational linguistics, that can help collect richer evidence on student cognition and performance based on frequent measuring of tasks that account for prior performance. Evidence Centered Design is independent of Frederiksen and Collins's systems approach to educational testing, but it is just as significant in how it challenges the status quo of educational measurement, where narrow tasks are the norm.

Frederiksen and Collins, and Mislevy and his colleagues, were out in front of much research and policy in the years leading up to NCLB, when most in the very large field of educational measurement were focused on more traditional problems. And when states began to build testing systems to support NCLB, they used traditional models rather than these more progressive approaches.

These researchers were not the only educational researchers who addressed important parts of the educational data movement before it became an identifiable process. In research on school leadership and professional learning communities, special education, and many other branches of teaching and learning research, there were important developments that are relevant for the educational data movement. But these independent efforts did not come together or become identified as related to systemic uses of data until later. Therefore, the movement, in many places, has been identified as something new and something brought to education from the outside. In fact, many elements of the data movement originated at least partly within the field itself, and the movement is a process that is connecting different traditions that are in some cases new and in some cases familiar.

Education's Evidence Movement and the Search for What Works

Along with NCLB came other changes in federal policy around evidence that could be called the *evidence movement*.[24] As with the data movement, the evidence movement began with the standards-based and comprehensive school reform movements in the 1980s and 1990s. Many had noticed that educators often were selecting and implementing approaches that in a few cases were based on *some* research and in a large number of cases the approaches seemed developed with little regard for any prior research and data that demonstrated that the approach actually worked in practice. The argument of the evidence reformers was articulated by Robert Slavin, who wrote:

> At the dawn of the 21st century, education is finally being dragged, kicking and screaming, into the 20th century. The scientific revolution that utterly transformed medicine, agriculture, transportation, technology, and other fields early in the 20th century almost completely bypassed the field of education. If Rip Van Winkle had been a physician, a farmer, or an engineer, he would be unemployable if he awoke today. If he had been a good elementary school teacher in the 19th century, he would probably be a good elementary school teacher today. It is not that we have not learned anything since Rip Van Winkle's time. It is that applications of the findings of educational research remain haphazard, and that evidence is respected only occasionally, and only if it happens to correspond to current educational or political fashions.[25]

It was not until the early part of the 21st century that substantive policy changes began to emerge around this problem of practice. One of those was a restructuring of part of the U.S. DoED to include an Institute for Education Sciences with an emphasis on encouraging studies that could produce strong evidence, principally statistical findings based on random assignment. The administration cemented its priorities in a funded report from the National Academy of Science titled *Scientific Research in Education* that defined random assignment as the "gold standard" of research methods. For many educational researchers—especially those whose work was more qualitative, interpretive, and local—this priority on random assignment was controversial. Many researchers objected to the use of an intervention model in education because of the complex interrelationships between educational elements and because accomplishing random assignment in educational research can be expensive and disruptive to normal practice. Objections notwithstanding, the administration moved forward. A signature element of the evidence movement is a focus on "what works" in education. This has led the DoED to develop a database of evidence-based approaches called the What Works Clearinghouse where the research base supporting each approach is graded and made public. In criticizing this approach, some researchers have pointed out that what works in one situation may not work in others and that understanding *how things work* is equally important.

The evidence movement and data movement share some important characteristics. They appeal to similar logics, as Cynthia Coburn, a professor at the University of California at Berkeley, states: "[a] common sense idea—borrowed from the business world—that people will make better, more efficient, more successful decisions if they carefully weigh the available evidence."[26] Proponents of both argue for greater use of data and information over intuition and individual judgment. In both movements there are those making the argument that education is stuck in another era and that the use of data is key to progress. An important difference in these movements, however, is in the kinds of data they are focused on. The evidence movement is focused on data collected in research settings and analyzed according to specific principles. This evidence can help educators make better decisions about what programs to implement and how to teach. Conversely, the data movement is largely focused on information about specific students and teachers, and on using those data in making near-term decisions about them. Where the evidence movement revolves around the connection between scientific research and practice, the data movement revolves around data-oriented management principles in practice itself.

The Educational Data Movement's Evidence Problem

The educational data movement is full of puzzles and seeming contradictions. None may be more significant than the lack of evidence of its own success. The movement began to develop in parallel with the evidence movement. Since the data movement began, educational researchers often have looked for evidence of impact. Following NCLB, federal and foundation funding began to flow into studies about how educators were using data; the studies often utilized an intervention model to assess the impacts of the data systems. Despite many optimistic claims by educational data proponents, many of whom are funded and/or influenced by the same philanthropies discussed earlier in this chapter, solid evidence of improvement has been hard to find. Some research reported positive impacts of data use, including its role in supporting equity.[27] Others reported the opposite, finding that educators used data to focus on some kids to the exclusion of others in cases where schools were under pressure to make NCLB targets.[28] Many researchers reported that teachers talked more about using data than they actually used it.[29] When we look specifically at what we know about data's role in education during the NCLB era, it turns out that what we don't know about it is far greater than what we do know.

Questions about the research basis for data use were formally stated in late 2009, when the DoED convened a panel of experts to develop a guidebook for practitioners, using the same level-of-evidence framework used by the What Works Clearinghouse. The panel then released five recommendations, along with the level of evidence that existed to support each recommendation, as shown in Table 1.1. While recommending that educators continue to use data, the panel said that the existing "research on using data to make instructional decisions does not yet provide conclusive evidence of what works to improve student achievement."[30]

Further, this new research genre is characterized by uneven quality, with few studies that produce hard evidence and much of it not meeting high standards for scientific rigor. This may render suspect existing reports of data use. Also in 2009, the Spencer Foundation, endowed by the leader of a research organization often associated with practitioner-based research, launched a new program of study into data use. The foundation called the existing research base "fragmented" and inadequate for use in learning how educators should be using data.

> Researchers from multiple disciplines and research perspectives investigate the phenomenon using contrasting conceptual frameworks and different language for similar concepts. More worrisome, a great deal of the research on data use

TABLE 1.1. Recommendations for Data Use and Level of Evidence to Support Recommendation

Recommendation	Level of Evidence
Make data part of an ongoing cycle of instructional improvement.	Minimal
Teach students to examine their own data and set learning goals.	Minimal
Establish a clear vision for schoolwide data use.	Minimal
Provide supports that foster a data-driven culture within the school.	Minimal
Develop and maintain a districtwide data system.	Minimal

> is normative rather than analytic . . . trumpeting the cause of data use, or a particular approach to data use, rather than analyzing what actually happens when people at different levels of the system use evidence in their practice.[31]

While the momentum for data use builds, its actual effects are still not proven or, in many cases, well understood. What researchers have been able to show is that the use of data is multifaceted. Once data systems are built, they need to be incorporated into educational practice and become part of school and district cultures.[32] What researchers have not been able to show is that the data systems developed to support NCLB have made much difference in achieving the intended goal of helping students learn or achieve better.

Should we conclude that the data that flooded the field in the wake of NCLB were not as useful as proponents argued they were or could be? Is it possible that the available data were limited by their design and that if more systemically designed assessments, as outlined by Frederiksen and Collins, and Mislevy and his associates, were used, the results would be different? Could we conclude that the data were as powerful as proponents argued, but educational researchers were unable to find the impact? Neither seems a complete answer. On the one hand, a challenge in developing the needed body of evidence may be that different researchers often are looking at different parts of the educational system. Some focus on schools, others on teacher groups, and still others on district offices. It is rare for educational researchers to cross boundaries that often align with academic communities and research journals.[33] It turns out that there are many overlapping and interacting issues at play in the educational data movement. Unraveling some of this complexity is an important goal of this book.

NO SILVER BULLETS, BUT PROGRESS IN SURPRISING PLACES

As we enter the educational data movement's adolescence, we should have our eyes wide open to the difficulties the movement presents. It is fair to ask why the area is controversial and why gaining a clear picture is difficult. We should be wary of simple recipes for data use and simple complaints about problems with applying data. Each is probably partly right and often wrong. It is important to understand the richness and diversity of educational practice, rather than to encode simple formulas into policies without an appreciation of the different dimensions of the data movement, lest we learn lessons about damaging side effects of simple policies, as happened with NCLB and likely is happening with some teacher evaluation policies that place a heavy emphasis on the same type of evidentiary foundation.

This book peels back the layers of the educational data movement to reveal some of the complexity, contradictions, and changes involved in it. In the chapters that look at national and state, district, school, and classroom data processes, the book follows a search for the important and often promised objective of improving instruction. Almost from the beginning of the movement there has been an expectation that the use of data will lead to better practices of teaching. However important that goal is, it may obscure other effects of the educational data movement. The lessons of how information tools involve effects on multiple levels have helped transform other fields, as Chapter 2 will discuss. Rather than improving only individual productivity, information tools often cross boundaries within and beyond organizations. This is a large part of their power. In so doing, they help reshape pre-existing processes. In education there are many processes in states, districts, and schools, as well as in classrooms, that can be impacted by information. While instructional improvement and, more important, student success are primary goals, they are narrowly focused. There are other ways the educational data movement can reshape the landscape of American education.

This book is not going to provide a simple picture, prescriptions for practice, or a future without travails. Education is complicated and will remain so. The educational data movement, while it is reshaping parts of the educational world, is still full of tensions and contradictions. It is often confusing. There have been large promises and less-than-clear results. There have been different types of communities and different methods used to study it, but still the impact is elusive. This curious situation invites questions. This book compares data, as others have before, to a flashlight or a lens. While not always perfect, these optical aids allow educational practice to be seen in new ways. The educational data movement acts in a similar way on a larger scale. Considering this sociotechnical shift, critically, in all of its many manifestations, also allows the systemic nature of education, with its complexity, politics, and diversity, to be seen. This viewpoint presents stakeholders with some of the decisions that have been made *and can be made* about the future of education.

2

Organizational Information Technology: From Business to Education

Connecting business and education involves crossing one of the most contentious and challenging boundaries in research and practice. In the early 20th century, schools were modeled after the factories of that time and industrial principles were used in school management. Over time, educators and policymakers saw substantive differences between teaching children and factory automation. And for decades the connection between business and education fell into disfavor. Since then, however, education has evolved (and so have businesses). With the educational data movement, this topic again has become part of the conversation. There continues to be considerable disagreement over whether comparing education to business is appropriate at all, with supporters and opponents often drawn from two familiar sides of a political/reform divide. This is partly because the gap between educators and those in business is cultural as well as substantive. Those who choose a career in education and those who choose careers in the generally more lucrative field of business often have different work dynamics and different commitments. Because the educational data movement is steeped in business ideas, understanding it requires understanding concepts familiar, but not exclusive, to the world of business and commerce.

For academics this is a new path. Few educational researchers have studied businesses, and vice versa. Likewise, many who promote business tools in education do not have a deep background in educational practice or research. While there are academic connections between education and several other fields—psychology, anthropology, public policy, finance—the connections to business are less well established, with only a few graduate programs supporting studies across these two areas and few academic journals where serious discussions across these two domains occur. However, it would not be right to draw too thick a line between these two fields, either conceptually or in the different communities involved, because in practice the distinctions are not so clear. This chapter takes on the challenge to build conceptual bridges between these two areas that come together in education's data movement.

COMPARING BUSINESS AND EDUCATION

To begin, if we think about business as one type of social process and compare it to education, a different type of social process, some broad features appear. Both are organized activities involving groups of people. Businesses usually involve adults, with the occasional help of young adults, whereas education involves adults and children in hierarchical roles. In many businesses, materials and products move through the organization, thereby gaining value through what the business does. Other businesses add value by providing services and advice that their clients need. In education, students pass through different institutional territories, but they are not products. They *interact* with the school system and those within it. Over time the students develop in ways that often seem directly influenced by school, while they also develop through interactions outside of formal school settings. Whereas businesses often can define and measure how they add value to their products, the influence of schools is complex, uneven, and contingent. The learning that happens inside and outside of school can be exceedingly difficult to define and measure.

Although many businesses' primary goal is to make money, and schools' primary goals include educating students and supporting their development as productive citizens, these two different goals do not mean the organizations are completely dissimilar. Both employ and serve people. Both can exist across a range of physical and/or virtual spaces. Some businesses are small and local, some large and multinational. Some businesses are profit focused, some are nonprofits, and some are hybrids, such as hospitals, which have both financial and human goals that may resemble the goals of some educational organizations. Significant variation also exists in education. There are different types of school systems: from the small local charter to the large public district to the global online professional schools and virtual universities—all of which are educational organizations. Both types of organizations are designed to support and add value for individuals and groups, whether they are called customers, families, patients, or students.

Despite being organized systems, business and education at first seem largely different because of their essential or core functions. However, if we step back and look at business, we find it is really a broad category that applies to many types of social systems. Education is also a broad category. Rather than being two distinct and opposite types of organizations, businesses and educational systems can be thought of as two extended families. Put them side by side and each family member would have similarities within its own family as well as parallels in the other family. Across both families of organizations are those things they use to add value, which can be labor and/or materials and/or ideas and expertise. Different businesses vary in terms of the types of labor, management, materials, and resources they use. Some are labor-intensive and some are resource-intensive. Some are more physical and some are more virtual. Similarly, different educational organizations use different types of materials and different types of personnel and support structures. Like many businesses, many educational systems are *complex organizations*. While any type of organization can exist on a small scale, as organizations become larger, they gain increased capacity and economies of scale. They also gain organizational complexity, which leads to the need for management and coordination. Large school systems usually include people in different roles across different locations that require coordination. This comparative view helps in understanding the information needs across these different kinds of organizations. For example, the information management needs of the local church-run elementary school may be similar in some ways to the needs of the corner grocery, whereas the large urban school district, with over a hundred thousand students and bus and food operations, may have much in common with large health care companies that have multiple locations and need to allocate people and material among them.

DIVIDING ORGANIZATIONS INTO A TECHNICAL CORE AND PERIPHERAL COMPONENTS

If both businesses and educational systems can be complex or simple, local or distributed, how can we understand what is fundamentally different about them and also what is similar? Organizational theorists and researchers who look at different types of organizations—from those that make things to those that provide services—suggest some ways. Some have used two broad categories: a technical core and peripheral components.[1] I have added a third category of executive management that is responsible for both of these areas and their coordination, as illustrated in Figure 2.1.

This is not a perfect model, but it helps. The technical core involves the main work that an organization does: serving patients in health care, building cars for automakers, and managing money for financial institutions. In education, the classroom and the classroom teacher are central to the tech-

FIGURE 2.1. Dividing Organizations into Executive, Peripheral, and Technical Core

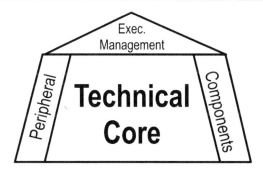

nical core. In this book I also place the school in the technical core, although not all education scholars who use this framework explicitly include school-level organizational elements in its description. The peripheral components are those elements that an organization needs in order to function and coordinate: managing buildings, human resources, payroll, and accounting. The peripheral components are not the reason an organization exists, but they play a big role in how successful it is. Executive management are those at the top who set operational goals for both core and peripheral functions, design the specific organizational structures, and manage to performance targets. The most important difference in the fundamental character of education versus other fields is in their technical cores. The peripheral components are more similar. Human resources and accounting for school systems, while still specific to education, can resemble human resources and accounting in a financial firm or manufacturer. The technical core of teaching, however, is vastly different from financial management or making products. When calls are made to improve teacher "productivity" or to reward the most "productive" teachers, the efforts are largely aimed at the technical core of education.

For those with a business background, the picture of U.S. education at the beginning of the 21st century was one that seemed to indicate problems in all three areas: the technical core of instruction, the peripheral components, and executive management. Student performance was a problem when compared internationally, and within the United States, persistent achievement gaps between social groups had failed to close—both indicating weakness in the technical core. At the same time, many of the school systems that served the most disadvantaged populations had other chronic problems, including decrepit facilities and infrastructures, financial misman-agement, and not having textbooks for students to use. Some districts had high teacher vacancy rates well into the school year and unacceptable building safety and maintenance conditions. In the case of the DC Public Schools, there was a locally publicized case where new textbooks existed, but were locked away in a warehouse when needed by students. These were *systemic failures* likely stemming from breakdowns in the peripheral components and executive management. They affected the technical core in significant ways by depriving the core of the people and resources it needed. Whereas one might accept that instruction is fundamentally harder with students from disadvantaged circumstances, there is little excuse for these failures in the peripheral parts of the system. These views were summed up by the former school superintendent, Senator Michael Bennet of Colorado, who worked in business prior to taking the helm of the Denver Public Schools:

> When I became superintendent our [human resources] HR department was essentially staffed by ex school administrators . . . busily not returning people's phone calls and losing people's paperwork and . . . [having] no idea how to do HR. That's a *systems problem* that matters if you care about getting the most talented teachers into your school district. . . . I use that as an example, but it could be about anything else right down to the most important thing, which [is] teaching and learning. You can't do this systems work *unless you have data* . . . and unless you're measuring what you are trying to do on all kinds of parts of the system.[2]

As a U.S. senator, Bennet became an advocate for investments in education, including the collection and use of data. While Bennet's characterization could have been about many districts, there is no research community that explores the systemic aspects of education where interdepartmental function is realized. The field of education is largely segmented based upon historical roles of teacher, leader, special educator, and so on and educational researchers often focused on particular educational parts—teaching, classrooms, districts, policy—rather than entire organizations and systems. For those who develop indicator and organizational data approaches, whole-systems thinking is essential. In business, organizational thinking frequently involves designing organizational technologies to work across and integrate different groups rather than only one.

FRAMEWORKS FOR TECHNOLOGY

Just as there are many ways to view organizations, there are many ways to think of technologies and how they relate to complex social systems, including organizations. Sometimes technologies can be classified as related to the technical core versus peripheral components. Robots, for example, serve the technical core of a manufacturer, and a digital display whiteboard or tablet computers serve the technical core of a school system. Likewise, payroll and accounting systems could support the peripheral functions of both types of organizations, although with some differences. We can think of technologies in terms of productivity. For example, word processing allows documents to be developed faster than using typewriters. We also can think of technologies as *connectors*. Although some technologies fit into one part of an organization, some cross boundaries and help integrate the work that many people do. For example, database systems allow different parts of an organization (e.g., human resources and managers) to share information and communicate, as well as do their jobs more efficiently. Email is another example. It can be used by people throughout an organization in many roles.

Historically, educational technology research has been directed at just part of the technical core, the part involving classrooms. The idea(s) behind it are that more and/or better instruction can be done with learning technologies and that the arrangements of students and teachers can be altered as well. This optimistic view of learning technologies has been popular since the early 20th century, although at different times different technologies have been highlighted. There was a time when phonographs, filmstrips, radio, and television were seen as able to redefine education. Not too long ago visualization was all the rage. Later interactivity was proposed as a feature that could reshape instruction. Mobility, collaboration, and other technical features have been put forward to reshape learning processes. Each has fallen short. As Larry Cuban has discussed in several well-received books, technology optimists often have hoped for a *teaching machine* that would help in the technical core.[3] Some have cast data systems in education in this way as well, using the term *data-driven instruction*. The role of information tools as organizational integrators often has been overlooked. In this book we look at those other technologies that work across organizations, including, but not limited to, the technical core.

Just as the division of organizations into a technical core and peripheral components is not exact, none of the ways of classifying technologies is really comprehensive, but they help in getting a mental handle on this complex space. This chapter highlights a class of technology called *organizational information technology* (OIT) that can be applied in both peripheral and technical parts of an organization at the same time. These technologies are often systemic in nature and work across organizational boundaries, leading some to call them *boundary objects* or *boundary infrastructures*.[4] Boundaries are important concepts in organizational studies and also in the world of education. They are the places where one group's work and focus should connect to another group's activity. Organizations that have looked for breakdowns in efficiency often have found them at the boundary where one group hands off to another group. Boundary infrastructures, then, often are designed to support a more fluid exchange of information and greater organizational efficiency. When they are successful, by helping different activities become more efficient or even making new things possible, technologies help shift the ways individuals and organizations do things. OIT can be been a *change agent* because of its ability to help reshape practices and structures. In fact, the examples of companies used in this book are largely different from those that would have been examples decades ago, as many large and formerly dominant firms have been eclipsed by more successful competitors that often used technology, including OIT, to their advantage.

WAVES OF SOCIOTECHNICAL CHANGE

In looking at the development of OIT over the past few decades, not only do we see increases in its use by successful organizations; we also see that it is made up of a number of different movements, each with its own trajectory, that have occurred in rapid succession. Those movements followed a pattern common to the adoption of many technologies, called *diffusion*. Diffusion is seen over and over again with technologies and innovations that are now part of daily life. Televisions, personal computers, and cell phones all followed this pattern. With diffusion, there is an initial period of modest growth and early adopters, followed by much more rapid growth and acceptance by a larger population, which often is followed by a small group of late adopters. While many have studied this process, Everett Rogers's approach remains one of the most popular and often is identified with the "s" curve that diffusion typically exhibits. Diffusion of innovations is a way to look at how ideas as well as technologies spread through a social system and also within a large and complex organization.[5]

An important lens onto the history of business OIT was conducted by University of Maryland professor Ping Wang and his colleagues. Wang's study provides a unique and high-level view of OIT from the middle of the 1980s to the early 2000s, the period immediately preceding the educational data movement.[6] Wang studied how management communities—professional managers across industries—consider the same topics at the same time. These topics, which Wang calls "fashions," had a brief popularity in the business literature. After receiving attention, the IT fashions often become projects in large organizations that managers work for, so that the fashion literature can serve as an advance indicator of possible organizational activity and OIT projects. As shown in Figure 2.2, these trends followed the diffusion pattern typical of other technology innovations.

FIGURE 2.2. Pattern of OIT Innovation Fashions Illustrated in Wang (2010)

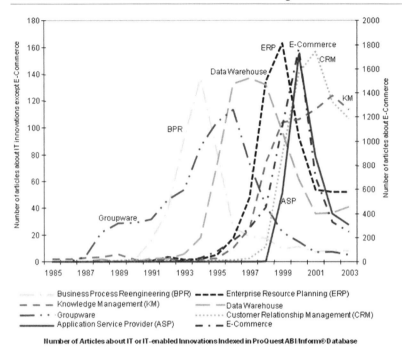

Figure is an adaptation from Wang, 2010. Copyright © 2010, Regents of the University of Minnesota. Used with permission.

Wang's study is important because it begins when many organizations were implementing their first-generation computer automation, which converted paper records into digital systems, and extends into the beginning of the educational data movement. It shows many of the ideas about information-driven tools now being applied to education as they developed earlier within other fields. It provides a way to see how ideas underlying many parts of the educational data movement were evolving and being proven in other kinds of organizations prior to their introduction to education.

Wang's analysis highlights several factors that are important when considering OIT in business as well as in education. First, he breaks down this broad category into subcomponents that can each be discussed. Rather than a single movement with all topics of similar interest, eight distinct socio-technical trends emerged over this period. Each trend tended to cover different organizational goals. Some of these eight are outward-facing toward customers and suppliers. Some are more inward-looking toward the organization itself. Some address logistical operations. Some address analysis and planning. Many have had significant impacts on the ways business is conducted today and the jobs people have or had at one time. And, all bear some relationship to the educational data movement in ways discussed below.

Internal and External Business Functions: ERP, CRM, ASP, and eCommerce

Two related trends form the backbone of American and international business: enterprise resource planning (ERP) and customer relationship management (CRM). For large corporations, those that manufacture and sell products, ERP and CRM are essential parts of the technology portfolio. They are suites of products that together do what many different first-generation computer applications did in the past. While those who do not work directly with OIT (the technical staff and senior managers) usually have little knowledge of the details of these areas, many people benefit from them every day when they buy products (in person or online) and when they interact with the service arms of organizations from banks to manufacturers to hotels. Electronic commerce (eCommerce) and application service providers (ASP) came a little later and are less broad. However, they also are often a part of daily consumer life even though many outside the fields that use them do not realize it.

As Figure 2.3 shows, what makes ERP and CRM different from individual data systems is that they have a *systemic design*. Much of the early, first-generation OIT involved individual departments and functions such as accounting or purchasing. What many organizations found as they invested in automating different functions is that they achieved only limited improvements. Different groups were slightly more efficient, but often were still disconnected from one another. Each had its own collection of information called a "data silo" and sharing information across the organization was problematic. Customers and other business partners such as suppliers found they were not well understood because the organization had multiple sets of records about them. One computer system may have had some information about a customer and its relationship history, and another application would have other parts. Unlike those individual information systems that address one or a few departments, ERP and CRM systems work across many parts of organizations. ERP and CRM integrate that information around a central database. The integration can help connect technical core functions, such as production and merchandising, with peripheral components like shipping and logistics. As ERP and CRM systems unify different information silos into a single architecture, information can flow more freely between parts of an organization, resulting in greater productivity and flexibility.

FIGURE 2.3. Conceptual Illustration of Enterprise Resource Planning and Customer Relationship Management Systems

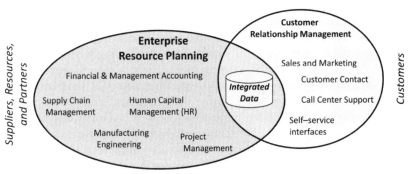

ERP systems are evident when stores have in stock just the right amount of the items that customers want and when they are able to ship new or fresh merchandise as consumers need it. Prior to ERP systems that can track the flow of materials through an organization, many manufacturers and retailers maintained large inventories of products in warehouses. Both the inventories and warehouses were costly. In some cases products could spoil or expire. Large inventories tied organizations, and those buying from them, to those things held in inventory. For many, this has changed. It is common now for companies to have little or no inventory, to acquire just what they need when they need it and sell directly what customers are asking for. Because ERP systems routinely connect suppliers electronically with requirements, companies can plan better. Instead of costly warehouses, these organizations have what are called integrated supply chains that can get products and parts *just-in-time*. Retail giants like Walmart were early leaders in this area and are able to rapidly monitor customer purchasing and communicate instantly with their suppliers and contractors to make sure that the right products arrive where they need to be. Amazon, which began as a bookseller, now sets a retail standard, selling everything from lightbulbs to bicycles, which they have shipped directly by the manufacturers to their customers. Their OIT literally makes this business model possible.

People who call a customer support line and are able to talk to a person in a distant town or country with access to their records and history of previous communication, and at any hour of the day, are experiencing a modern CRM system. CRM systems have become good at tracking not only specific incidents, but also the life-cycle of customers from before they begin purchasing all the way until they need service. Again, leading retailers are using data they collect from various sources, including credit and purchases records, to develop fuller pictures of their clients, what sometimes are called *360-degree views*, that can help them better target advertisements and plan for new products.

Two related trends peaked in the year 2000 after very rapid growth curves. Electronic commerce, or eCommerce, is essential for buying and selling over the Internet, and ASP is a form of outsourcing whereby an organization can have critical OIT systems managed on a remote server. ASP is part of what is now known as *cloud computing* (although cloud computing includes much more than ASP). Rather than organizations operating their own computer applications for human resources or inventory, they contract with an ASP provider. ASP and eCommerce have allowed many small companies to exist based on the Internet, with a combination of eCommerce for retail technical core functions and ASP for functions that support the peripheral components. Prior to the success of the Internet, both of these functions normally would have required substantial investments in buildings and staff.

For many in business, these types of OIT innovations—ERP, CRM, eCommerce, and ASP—have helped reshape the world we live in, much like social media such as Facebook and Twitter have altered personal communication. Not only do these systems allow many companies to function in new and more competitive ways, but they also allow companies to do this with less regard for physical location, as Tom Friedman detailed in his bestseller *The World Is Flat*. From international networks of product suppliers that Amazon and Walmart use to remote call centers, these technologies often have been catalysts that make these global business changes possible.[7]

Educational organizations have much in common with those in other fields that have needed integrated information. They often have multiple disconnected information systems, and different people, from teachers to principals to district staff, can have different views of students. District and state information systems are often disconnected in ways that ERP and CRM solutions address. Today, collecting integrated, 360-degree views of programs, students, or staff across many districts and states is labor-intensive and costly, similar to how it was for businesses and other organizations before implementing ERP and CRM solutions. And virtual web-based education has become commonplace. While there remain significant technical core differences, from an organizational perspective these technologies relate to important parts of the educational world today.

Business Process Re-engineering (BPR)

One of the early trends in OIT discussed by Wang, and one that has been revolutionary in terms of organizations and jobs, is business process re-engineering (BPR). Although the popularity of BPR peaked in the early 1990s, it often is still used by organizations in need of improvement. Beyond automation of individual jobs and integration of different business units, BPR has allowed whole organizations to improve by rearranging the ways they approach different functions. BPR can also involve looking at fundamental business processes to consider how to allocate activities differently among an organization's own staff and/or partner organizations.

BPR can be traced to the work of Michael Hammer, an MIT professor of computer science who also taught at the prestigious Sloan School of Business. In 1990, Hammer wrote a seminal article titled "Reengineering Work: Don't Automate, Obliterate." In it, he argued that rather than taking routine tasks and making them more efficient, organizations should consider the nature of the work they were doing once technology was in the picture. He highlighted an example of Ford Motor Company's effort to optimize its accounts payable department, which employed 400 clerks, when it discovered that the Japanese auto manufacturer Mazda performed the same function with only five clerks. Not hampered by pre-World War II labor structures, Mazda was able to design streamlined processes that required about 1% of the personnel. Hammer challenged businesses to rethink their historical ways of operating, saying:

> We must challenge old assumptions and shed the old rules that made the businesses underperform in the first place. . . . Every business is replete with implicit rules left over from earlier decades. "Customers don't repair their own equipment." "Local warehouses are necessary for good service." "Merchandising decisions are made at headquarters."[8]

Using technology in new ways—often to share information across groups—BPR has become one of the keys to corporate and global competitiveness. It is important to remember that during the 1970s and 1980s American businesses had been losing in competitive matchups with businesses from other countries in the same ways many claim education also has been outpaced. As the comparison between Ford and Mazda illustrates, many American businesses had a lot to learn about how to manage their operations better. While competitors in Japan and Germany began anew after World War II, American businesses largely continued using organizational structures and processes that originated in an era before automation when certain types of paperwork were essential. However, with the advent of OIT and its ability to connect different groups directly rather than by using documents, many historical business functions were not needed or were needed far less. OIT was better than the old-fashioned ways of working, but Hammer suggested it didn't go far enough.

In the years since Hammer's article, management consultants—largely business school graduates—have become important players in BPR. One of the reasons that many organizations need management consultants is that their own management may not recognize opportunities to become more efficient. Many managers are homegrown and have developed professionally within the same organizational structures they would need to change. These same professionals need to see their organizations in different ways through fundamental re-evaluations of long-held assumptions. Management consultants bring that fresh eye that comes from not having built their careers in the organizations they seek to improve. They also bring new conceptual tools based on research from management, information, and organizational sciences about how to leverage technology for organizational effectiveness.

Even though it has been nearly 2 decades since it peaked in popularity as a management fashion, BPR is still very much part of the current business and technology climate. BPR involves challenging assumptions and focusing on the value added by different organizations and positions. The kinds of questions Hammer asked are the kinds that many successful entrepreneurs also consider when they start a new business. Many of the world's largest and most powerful corporations—Amazon, eBay, Facebook, and Google—exist largely as virtual organizations providing information and purchasing value, but without many of the traditional physical structures that many organizations took for granted years ago. These organizations don't simply use technology to make yesterday's activities more efficient; they use technology and BPR principles to reshape the social nature of their business and in many ways alter social patterns around the ideas of consuming, trading, communicating, and getting information. And they did it by thinking in new ways.

Many who look to reform education have experience with this area and see similar needs in the worlds of schools, teachers, and students. Many organizational structures in schools and central offices are based in another era. There seem to be many functions, both peripheral and technical core, that are underperforming while also consuming excessive resources.[9] And, in most cases, the managers of school systems have developed professionally in the education systems they manage or in others similar to them, suggesting to some a need for new perspectives.

Data Warehouses, Data Mining, and Analytics

The data warehouse trend falls in the middle of the critical period Wang studied leading up to the educational data movement. Like other information technology trends, it exhibits a typical diffusion wave pattern with a fast takeoff and then a peak in popularity to be replaced by another shortly thereafter. Data warehousing, however, also sits in the middle of an important continuum of information collection and distribution that goes back many years and extends into the future. During the past several decades, the ways organizations created and shared information have grown as traditional printed reports in first-generation OIT systems have evolved into some of the hottest information technology sectors today: *analytics* and *business intelligence* (also called BI). Data warehousing is a stepping-stone to these more advanced applications of information reporting technology.

Over the course of several decades, from the 1960s and into the later parts of the 20th century, a traditional industrial method of producing management information ended dramatically. At one time, white-collar workers regularly collected data and produced paper reports for management decisions. These middle managers were common in offices of most large organizations. When first-generation OIT efforts in the 1960s, 1970s, and 1980s allowed organizations to print reports directly from computer applications, many of those who performed this function were displaced. Companies did not need to allocate staff to the routine task of compiling information for standard reports when simple computer programs could produce the information faster, more accurately, and cheaper.

Data warehousing represents a paradigm shift, a new way of accessing information. It goes beyond simple reporting to making large amounts of information available for managers and other knowledge workers—those who think and analyze information as their essential job function—to use. Data warehouses usually integrate data from across an organization. Once in a data warehouse, data can be compared and used to answer a wide variety of questions in ways static reports cannot. Data warehouses are used for "what-if" scenarios, to track trends, and one-of-a-kind analyses of specific problems. Just as moving from manual reports to automated reporting was dependent on having computer applications to store information, data warehouses are dependent on multiple computer applications that can each produce data streams to be combined. The ability of a data warehouse to match data from different sources based on common identifiers is critical to analyzing the rich stockpiles of information that most organizations are accumulating with their OIT systems.

The shift from data warehousing to business intelligence/analytics involves several interrelated developments. First, as the amount and quality of data in many organizations increased, new ways of analyzing data became possible. As data warehouses became established, tools developed to search across large quantities of information, look for patterns in the data, and produce visualizations to support analyses. The search for patterns both in highly structured data and, increasingly, in less structured data often is called *data mining*. These tools are important because they help organizations to understand their own world better and to design new ways to meet it.

As the second decade of the 21st century begins, few technology sectors are as busy as analytics. In 2010, a study published in the *MIT Sloan Management Review* showed that those companies that were leaders in their fields were more likely to use data while those that were not leaders were more likely to rely on intuition.[10] The review also ranked the usage patterns for organizations in terms of their application of analytics. The lowest level was *aspirational*, in which data often were used to explain or justify actions. The next level, *experienced*, was marked by data being used to guide actions. At the highest level, organizations are *transformed*, which means they can use data to prescribe appropriate actions.

Like ERP and CRM, analytics are key to many companies' operations and success. Retailers like Walmart use analytics to predict which products will be needed and where. Insurance companies use analytics to identify which small details in different policyholders indicate a greater risk. By using analytics, software companies are able to divide their customer base into segments (e.g., home, business, academic) to maximize revenues. In fact, it is hard to find a successful corporation that does not put these techniques to work today.

Few areas are as important for the educational data movement as data warehousing and analytics. There is a lot of hope and investment in this dimension of data, and also serious challenges. Much of the reporting in education today, from states to schools, falls into the category of regular and static reports. There are considerable numbers of data warehouse projects, but many are in the early stages and are encountering issues with integration of data and basic data quality. There is a new community for applying analytics to education (including the Society of Learning Analytics Research, with support from the Gates Foundation) and a *Journal of Educational Data Mining* that began in 2009.[11] There are even a few publications showing efforts to mine educational data going back to the 1990s.[12] Researchers Behrens and DiCerbo have written about the confluence of different streams of data about students they call the Digital Ocean.[13] However, there is little consensus on which data form the basis for analytics in education today. The high-stakes test data that fill most educational data warehouses have many weaknesses. Most attempts at analytics relate to systemic rather than learning questions, and would be described, at best, as aspirational. Further, most of the contemporary educational data warehouse efforts do not include teachers and frontline educators who are, in many respects, *knowledge workers*.

The Collaboration Story: Knowledge Management and Groupware

Of the eight trends that Wang studied, two of them—*groupware* and *knowledge management* (KM)—are different in that they focus on collaboration rather than transactional information. Compared with the others, these two have broader diffusion curves. Groupware is among the earliest, and knowledge management is one of the latest. In some ways they represent different approaches to the same advanced organizational activity of using information between professionals rather than the record-keeping types of functions that ERP and CRM address. Like BPR, they involve organizations working in different ways, but do not entail eliminating functions or jobs. Like data warehousing, they are targeted to managers and knowledge workers. They may leverage a data warehouse, but are not strictly limited to warehouses or even structured data. Rather, they involve teams that work across functions and departments, coming together to solve problems often using one-of-a-kind reports and special data analyses.

Groupware emerged as a class of tools that allowed professionals to collaborate, often around documents. Unlike invoicing and taking orders, which are routine, clerical functions—easy to outsource or eliminate through BPR—the types of work that groupware supports are special activities and projects that knowledge workers perform. Some functions once supported by groupware products have now shifted to free social media such as Wikis and online project spaces that allow people to collaborate at distances, including sharing files, commenting on documents, maintaining threaded discussions, and tracking open issues. As organizations have collected digital information—data and documents—knowledge management has grown to provide them with different ways of organizing and sharing that information. KM is related to groupware and intersects with data warehousing in that it involves making sense out of different types of information. The field of KM intersects with fields of *organizational learning* and *communities of practice*[14] that consider how individuals arrange themselves and use tools to do their work.[15] It also is concerned with the ways that information, both data and also *tacit* knowledge, is organized and presented for use across potentially wide groups of people in an organization, making it a close neighbor of the information sciences.

In education today, collaboration technologies are one of the least developed and one of the most important areas for the future. As Chapter 6 discusses, collaboration among educators, specifically at the school level, is key to effective educational processes. Collaboration between central office and school staff is important, although not as well researched.

BEYOND INDIVIDUAL PRODUCTIVITY TO TEAMS, MARKETS, AND SYSTEMS

This chapter described some important trends in information technologies and ideas that have helped transform many businesses and other kinds of organizations. It has used a framework that divides the organization into peripheral components and technical core and often used by organizational theorists to make comparisons across different types of fields. This framework helps us to see some of what is similar and what is different about different social fields, including education, and how technology can serve as a connector.

Individual performance has been an important concern in much of the rhetoric and policy related to the educational data movement. Sometimes the productivity focus is directed at individuals—students, teachers, and soon principals—and sometimes it is directed at organizations such as specific schools or school systems. One of the lessons from other fields and their use of information tools is that productivity is only part of the story. During the 1970s and 1980s many American companies invested heavily in technologies and practices to improve their workers' productivity, but economists were not able to measure the increases in performance they expected. Economists debated why this could be. Was it that the investments in OIT were not achieving results or that there were problems with measuring them? This became known as the "Productivity Paradox."[16] Over time, the impact of information investments was seen more broadly. Economists and technology scholars began to see that the benefits of OIT were only partly related to productivity. In 1993, MIT professor Erik Brynjolfsson described four possible reasons why the Productivity Paradox existed and why productivity gains were elusive to researchers, including measurement problems (the gains are real, but researcher methods don't detect them); redistribution (some gain and some lose from the use of technology—Borders Books, for example); time lags (the gains may take a while to be detected); and other problems, including management and organizational challenges with developing and using technologies. Each of these factors may relate to education. By focusing on student test scores, we may be missing how schools are communicating with stakeholders differently and the effects of having these scores on parent and teacher choices. Many other organizations found new ways of doing things and responding to their environment that changed the calculus for some individual workers. Technology was more than a productivity boost. It was a catalyst to arranging their assets differently and supporting collaboration.

The changes from OIT can be bigger than a single organization. For example, Italian professor Claudio Ciborra studied the effect of communication and database technology in the late 1980s, before the Internet, but well into the age of the personal computer and email. In his discussion of these findings, *Teams, Markets and Systems*, he reported that there were several ways in which the information technology was supporting teams working to solve complex problems, including helping them to learn, strengthen social ties, deal with new types of problems, and see the world in different ways. All of this was in addition to doing their work more efficiently.[17] He found the technology also works at the level of markets, allowing different organizations to come together around common issues. These changes can then impact entire systems.

We take these lessons forward in this book with caution. From a broad perspective, educational systems can look similar to other types of complex organizations, with a superintendent analogous to a president, and associate superintendents like vice presidents. But as we look closer at educational practice, as we will in coming chapters, some important differences appear. A fundamental challenge for education will be selecting the appropriate ways to use these tools and translating these principles into the particular practices of schooling. It follows that accomplishing this will depend on understanding how educational practice works in detail—both what it is today in all its many forms and what it can be for different kinds of students, teachers, and educational systems in the future.

PERIPHERAL EDUCATIONAL SYSTEMS AND ADMINISTRATIONS

This part looks at the development of the educational data movement at national, state, and district levels. Using the framework for dividing organizational activity into peripheral components and technical core discussed in Chapter 2, these levels are peripheral. Although they are a complex area, with many interorganizational relationships that need to be understood, they have in common the responsibility for building technology solutions to support both their own administrative functioning and the many organizational components closer to students in the technical core. These peripheral educational systems and administrations then have ownership over the information systems for the technical core, but in many cases are removed from the daily work that occurs there.

There are some common themes that emerge across the chapters in this part and the next, which focuses directly on the technical core. For example, in this part we see how over time there has been a broadening of the definition of data. While early in this movement it seemed data equated to test results, the data discussed in Chapters 3 and 4 encompass information about participants, including teachers, students, and families; about programs and curricula; about relationships at the individual and organizational level; about finance and budgets; and about the movement of students across educational settings, including into college and from teacher preparation programs into classrooms. Variation and the particular form of governance that education in the United States operates within also emerge and frame later discussions. While it has been popular in policy discourse to compare U.S. education with what other countries—Finland, Singapore, South Korea—do in terms of their educational programs, the reality of America's decentralized political and governance structure and the often untidy legislative landscape for education loom large in the educational data movement. These issues complicate the use of data in many ways. This part also explores the role of large philanthropies in the educational data movement, a theme that continues throughout the book. The chapters in this part show how these funders have pursued different projects that are all consistent with a vision of greater data collection, availability, and use in educational decisions. Another pattern explored here is the separation of communities involved in the data movement. While educational researchers have done important research, it often has focused on discrete areas of education, leading to a fragmented knowledge base. This work for the most part has been done independently of other knowledge development undertaken by reformers and those with philanthropic support that also has focused on discrete parts of the educational enterprise. At the levels discussed in this part, as in the technical core levels discussed in the following part, the unions and professional communities representing teachers and other educational practitioners have had comparatively little involvement.

The chapters in this part broadly begin with national and state issues, which lead to a discussion of districts. This leveled approach, while it works in certain respects and helps provide a convenient structure, does not always reflect the systemic nature and interconnections evident in educational data. For example, federal infrastructure efforts discussed in Chapter 3 relate not only to national and state data systems, but to districts as well. Some of the organizations that work with districts discussed in Chapter 4 also work with many state education departments and the U.S. Department of Education. What can be seen through these chapters are some ways that information technologies have affected other fields by functioning not only at the individual level, but also with teams, organizations, markets, and systems.

3

National Initiatives and Building State Data Infrastructures

This chapter focuses on topics that appear to be far removed from classroom practice, but in reality have the potential to help shape how educators do their work: information infrastructures. Infrastructures are an often invisible or little noticed set of resources that make doing certain kinds of activities easier.[1] Infrastructures can be physical, as in the case of a road system, or informational, like the Internet, which is used to transport digital media. When we think of an era that is associated with a technology—the age of rail, the golden age of radio, the Internet era—there is usually an infrastructure that makes that age possible. Shared information infrastructures have been important for many fields in recent years, from health care to manufacturing, from retail to banking. Education is now getting new digital infrastructures that are intended to reshape what is possible with teaching and learning.

Infrastructures are designed things. The design often involves trade-offs. When they are being planned and developed, the designs are more noticeable. Once they are built and in use, their existence and designs may become harder to notice, that is, until something goes wrong or when something can't be done easily. The designs of infrastructures are reciprocal with social practice. They usually are drawn up to accommodate what people do or are expected to do. They also help shape those same human actions and social practices because their designs make some things easier to do than others. When driving on the interstate road system, few of us notice how the roads are configured and how the road signs work together to allow us to navigate efficiently. We simply drive in the same way we use electrical appliances. We rarely think about what a major public undertaking the national interstate system was when it began in the 1950s and how the roads have changed the patterns of transportation of people and products. We don't think about the implication of the decisions made by the designers to route through some locations and not others. Those discussions are history. To think about them as they are being developed is to see history in the making.

When the term *infrastructure* is used in education, it often refers to the tools teachers and students use across sites of learning. For example, in 2007, the National Science Foundation referred to this as a *Cyberinfrastructure for Learning*:

> Cyberinfrastructure moves us beyond the old-school model of teachers/students and classrooms/labs. Ubiquitous learning environments now will encompass classrooms, laboratories, libraries, galleries, museums, zoos, workplaces, homes and many other locations.[2]

This book does discuss learning infrastructures, such as those that the NSF referred to. It also focuses on another kind of infrastructure that can be more meaningful for shaping school practice: administrative infrastructures, including data systems about students, teaching, and educational systems. Although cyberinfrastructures can have an impact on those doing the teaching, these administrative or data infrastructures contain the indicators of achievement and other information about students and teachers that school leaders need to pay attention to. Although they often lack much detail about how learning occurs, these administrative infrastructures are close to national, state, and local decision processes. Their use in policies gives them extra power when it comes to practitioners.

DATA TECHNOLOGY BECOMES A MAINSTREAM POLICY TOPIC

By the end of the first decade of the 21st century, the federal government had taken on an active role in the development of new educational infrastructures, including programs to help states collect data, conversations about exchanging data, and making data infrastructure choices part of federal funding. During this time, in addition to requiring that states and districts report information (as had been the case for some time), new federal initiatives provided significant incentives for states and districts to build specific data structures, including linking student and teacher data. This linking is essential for evaluating teachers based on student test performance, but many states had not done it, and in a few this data linking was against the law. As the decade drew to a close, data technology had moved from the backroom to being a mainstream policy topic discussed by national leaders, including the secretary of education and the President of the United States. As an indicator of the importance that data held by that time, President Obama's announcement of $4.6 billion for the Race to the Top (RttT) stimulus program in 2009 spelled it out:

Success should be judged by results, and data is a powerful tool to determine results. We can't ignore facts. We can't ignore data. That's why any state that makes it unlawful to link student progress to teacher evaluations will have to change its ways if it wants to compete for a grant. That's why the Race to the Top grants will go to states that use data.[3]

In his statement, the President was not only mentioning the topic of educational data. He was also saying what the federal government expected the states to do with the data if they wanted federal funding. The RttT program addressed four reform areas: (1) adopting standards and assessments, (2) recruiting, developing, rewarding, and retaining effective teachers and principals, (3) turning around lowest-achieving schools, and (4) data systems that show growth and can lead to *instructional improvement*. Along with RttT, other federal programs also emphasized the importance of data systems, including the Teacher Incentive Fund (TIF), which required recipients to show how they would integrate their data systems to support merit pay linked to student outcomes.

There are important reasons why the federal government would be concerned with this topic. Historically, the government has been a data aggregator. Over time, a sophisticated apparatus of collecting data from states, districts, schools, and individuals has been built at the U.S. Department of Education (DoED). The DoED uses these data to inform policy choices and evaluate the success of its programs. When Uncle Sam spends money, there are almost always reporting requirements included. What was seen in RttT and TIF, however, was different. It involved the DoED directing educational organizations to implement specific types of data systems to support performance management, and this involvement in how states should manage their data was a new step for the federal government.[4]

The federal focus on data systems began during the Bush administration. An early indicator of the importance of data systems for educators occurred in 2004 when the DoED developed the National Education Technology Plan. This plan described a vision for interconnected information tools that would make a school system an efficient organization that improved student performance, as illustrated in Figure 3.1.[5] This is also when the DoED began funding research into how districts, schools, and teachers use data, which coincided with funding from the National Science Foundation for several projects related to educational data use.[6]

The vision promoted by the DoED in 2004 was bold, systemic, and optimistic. This data management was part of a one-two-three process whereby an integrated system leads to improved instruction, allocation of resources, and continuous improvement. On the left-hand side of Figure 3.1 are different information systems that support different parts of a school system:

human resources, transportation, libraries, and so on. The label given to this illustration, "Improving achievement through student data management," shows a somewhat direct relationship between data and learning. It also resembles other organizations in need of systems integration, the kind that enterprise resource planning and customer relationship management systems discussed in Chapter 2 provide for businesses. Just like many businesses of decades earlier, in 2004 many school systems (and many states) had disparate collections of data that could not be easily used for analysis. Although Figure 3.1 shows many of the elements that are important for the management of schools, it is largely focused on what we would consider education's peripheral components, showing little about the technical core of education: the domain of teachers. Except for a mention of test results, the complex worlds of classrooms, in which more than 60% of educational resources are expended, have little representation.[7] This is striking in light of the commonly stated goal of using these data to improve instruction.

THE STATE LONGITUDINAL DATA SYSTEMS PROGRAM

As the 2004 National Education Technology Plan was being developed and released, another important development in American educational data capacity was emerging from the DoED: the State Longitudinal Data Systems (SLDS) program. The SLDS program was authorized in the Education Sciences Reform Act of 2002. This was the same law that created the Institute of Education Sciences with a mandate to strengthen the quality of educational research, as discussed near the end of Chapter 1.[8] Many policy and research expectations existed for the SLDS program, as this excerpt from the legislation suggests:

> The data systems developed with funds from these grants should help States, districts, schools, and teachers make data-driven decisions to improve student learning, as well as facilitate research to increase student achievement and close achievement gaps.[9]

The SLDS program provided both funding and technical assistance to state education departments for their development of integrated longitudinal data systems. As the SLDS projects build state infrastructures that are more comprehensive than the vision illustrated in Figure 3.1, they have the potential to make one large information network out of independent silos to allow states to track progress of students from preschool to K–12 and in some cases to postsecondary college and careers. They also are intended to provide statistically linked test data that are used to build value-added models (VAMs).

Improving achievement through Student Data Management

On average, there is little aggregation of student data in today's school systems. Information is siloed, redundant and difficult to share. The technologies used — if any — are aging and frequently incompatible. An ideal state has complete aggregation and alignment. It is easier to ensure that students meet challenging standards, teachers target instruction, parents know teachers are helping their children, school districts know how to allocate resources effectively and the government knows how schools are doing.

1 The average state: Isolated silos of information prevent everyone from seeing the "Big Picture."

2 The ideal state: A Total Information Management Tool (Data Warehousing) will aggregate previously siloed data and create a variety of reports for any audience.

3 The Result: These reports inform instruction, resulting in continuous student improvement.

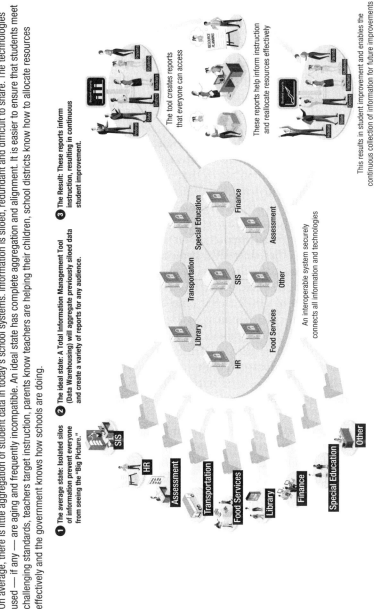

An interoperable system securely connects all information and technologies

The tool creates reports that everyone can access

These reports help inform instruction and reallocate resources effectively

This results in student improvement and enables the continuous collection of information for future improvements

In addition, they can support a range of analyses because connecting student data across years also allows student and program data to be *integrated across programs*. SLDS programs can also include satellite systems to support licensure and certifications, as well as early childhood systems, further broadening their analytic potential. These datasets open up many windows into educational systems quite independent of teacher evaluation.

By federal fiscal standards, the SLDS program is small potatoes. At the time this book was being written, less than $600 million had been spent on it—nowhere near the big-ticket line items such as Title I, which provides nearly $14 billion annually to schools serving low-income students, or the $12 billion spent in some years on special education. However, the importance of the SLDS program is not in its financial size, but in its positioning at a critical information nexus that is key to federal, state, and local policy aims. It is different from many programs that simply provide funding to states. SLDS grants are *cooperative agreements*, where states often commit their own resources in addition to the support they get from the federal government. They often leverage other state investments in data systems and coincide with other state-level projects and become a critical lens to view educational practice influencing many other decisions.

Longitudinal educational datasets—those that use repeated observation of a specific set of subjects over time—are not new. The federal government has managed the development of longitudinal research database programs for studying early childhood, high school, and other parts of education for decades.[10] These datasets are based on surveys plus some student test data. The survey datasets contain information about schools, teachers, and students. They can be used with sophisticated statistical analysis to reveal general patterns in education to help researchers provide evidence-based guidance to practitioners and frame research agendas. They have been used for many a doctoral dissertation and journal article. But, because they are (1) based on samples and (2) do not always use the same test measures used for accountability, they do not support many of the operational decisions that educators face, even though they are powerful research tools. Because SLDS datasets look across years and at all students, they represent a paradigm shift with the ability to track *each student individually* over time; this allows educators to have some information about the students they are responsible for when making decisions about those students rather than having to rely only on what has occurred in the past.[11]

As the SLDS program was getting off the ground in 2006, the DoED funded a research center dedicated to using student-level longitudinal data called the Center for Analysis of Longitudinal Data in Education Research (CALDER). CALDER began with partnerships with some of the states that had already built their longitudinal data systems prior to the SLDS program, including Florida, Indiana, Missouri, New York, North Carolina, Texas, Washington, and Washington, DC. Over the years CALDER has produced a broad array of research using these state datasets. While a small number of these studies dealt with instruction, most focused elsewhere, with teacher effectiveness a common topic in CALDER's work. The center also has looked at labor and career issues, new teacher assignments, experience level of principals in privileged and at-risk schools, potential rewards and risks for states to require teacher performance to be used in licensure exams, finance, resource allocation, and many other subjects. The linking of datasets, for example, about teachers and students, is key to many of these analyses. This type of data can provide meaningful insights into teachers and how they perform in different years, in different schools, and at different times. The same data can provide insights into how schools and educational organizations change over time.

In addition to new understandings of the impact of education policy, SLDS implementations cross and may help redefine organizational boundaries. At the state level, SLDS projects require integrating the work of different districts that historically have been independent organizations. The SLDS then creates a framework—a common boundary infrastructure—for them to work through. Some states that have small rural districts—including New York, Georgia, Colorado, and Oregon—have used the SLDS project to provide web-based access for their districts and schools so that the longitudinal data can be directly accessed. Oregon has specifically engaged state educators, using SLDS funds for statewide workshops and training in a program called the Direct Access to Achievement (DATA) project.[12]

The development of a statewide data system, although beneficial for stakeholders at many levels, brings organizational challenges to the surface. These SLDS projects are more than central database systems. They involve connecting different parts of state governments around common information definitions. In many cases they require changing cultures of independence that have developed inside different parts of a large bureaucracy. In addition, they often require enhancements to state testing systems to show students' progress along common performance scales. Showing growth involves more than comparing scores from different years. In some cases it requires new test items across years that can be statistically related to a common performance scale, which in turn can require expensive development and testing.[13] SLDS projects are multiyear efforts and involve a lot of coordination. It is common for states to be behind schedule and facing many data problems.

However, once completed, the network of 52 SLDS implementations (one for each state, plus Washington, DC, and Puerto Rico) will not be a national data system. Federal law prohibits the creation of any such national

K–12 student-level data system. And at the time the program began, there was no common standard or set of guidelines for states to use; thus, each state launched an independent project and began without clear guidelines on how the SLDS should be built, so that variations in approach from state to state are common.

THE DATA QUALITY CAMPAIGN

As the SLDS program began to make grants in 2004, it was already clear that most states would need a lot of help. Many had struggled with high-quality data. While leaders sometimes were able to answer policy questions using data, it often took excessive staff and time to assemble and compile the results—a description that parallels information reporting in businesses prior to automation in the 1960s and 1970s, as discussed in Chapter 2. Missing and incomplete information was commonplace.[14] Not only had few states integrated their data systems, but many states did not have functioning information systems for all of their departments. In some cases the systems they had amounted to little more than sophisticated spreadsheets. Many in the government and foundations knew there were more than technical challenges to reaching their goals. There was also a lack of awareness and understanding of the issues involved with using and managing data. While the issues of high-stakes tests were familiar to many educational stakeholders, broader data quality issues were not widely understood. Some stakeholders might confuse data with testing and be inclined to oppose or not give support data initiatives. For the SLDS projects to be successful, policymakers in states would need to understand the issues and what benefits there could be for pushing forward to develop robust and integrated data systems.

The Data Quality Campaign (DQC) was launched in 2005, with initial funding from the Gates Foundation. It was billed as "a national, collaborative effort to encourage and support state policymakers to improve the availability and use of high-quality educational data to improve student achievement."[15] The DQC initially was incubated as a project within a small not-for-profit based in Texas called the National Center for Educational Achievement (NCEA).[16] Since its early days as a small group inside NCEA, the DQC has been led by Aimee Guidera, who earned her master's in public policy with a combined specialization of education and business from Harvard. NCEA, also funded by the Gates and Dell foundations, had been deeply committed to using data and had been focusing on career and college readiness, which led it to look across the educational span. In 2004–2005, as Guidera and working groups inside NCEA were meeting to discuss the issues that states and districts were encountering with data, they began to discuss the broader issues with educational data that were emerging nation-wide, leading to the birth of the DQC.

Much like the SLDS program, the DQC addresses issues at multiple educational levels, even though student achievement is listed as a primary reason for its existence. The DQC was designed to be a distinct entity to connect and facilitate around the complex issues of data. It serves a unique role in this space by hosting meetings and webinars that explain how to design and build data systems, how to interpret federal rules related to information privacy, what constitutes effective data management and governance, and educational data standards. The speakers it presents come from state and federal agencies, education reform organizations, and a few academics and researchers. It advocates for data use with policymakers and legislators at national, state, and local levels. The unique role the DQC performs is similar to that of special-interest groups, events contractors, and think tanks. However, the DQC has had little connection to vendors, largely acting as a third leg between the DoED and Council of Chief State School Officers (CCSSO) in focusing on national data policy concerns.[17] Few organizations have a more central role in the educational data movement than the DQC.

To address the confusion in many states over what constituted a viable SLDS program, something the federal government had not spelled out, one of the first steps the DQC took was to promote a common definition known as the *ten essential elements* of an SLDS:

1. Unique statewide student identifier that connects data across key databases across years
2. Student enrollment, demographic, and program information
3. Ability to match individual students' test records from year to year to measure academic growth
4. Information on untested students and reasons they were not tested
5. A teacher identifier system with the ability to match teachers to students
6. Student-level transcript information, including courses completed, grades earned
7. Student-level college readiness test scores
8. Student-level graduation and dropout data
9. Ability to match student records between P–12/higher education
10. A state data audit system assessing data quality, validity, and reliability

The ten essential elements may seem like basic information capacity that states surely would have had in place long ago. Unfortunately, most states were decades behind other kinds of organizations, and each of these ten elements represents a significant step forward. First, a unique and common student identifier is the technical gateway to being able to share data across schools and districts when students move, as they increasingly do. Without this one small feature (which is not trivial to implement), the same student can have fragments of educational history in different systems, making each system less complete for analysis. Second, having demographic and program description information in the SLDS supports analyzing schools and school programs with consideration of their specific types of students rather than a one-size-fits-all evaluation approach.

Half of the DQC's ten essential elements (1, 2, 3, 5, and 9) involve data integration in one form or another. In the middle of this group (5) is the controversial linking of teacher and student data. This is what is needed for VAM-based evaluations of teachers' performance.

The DQC's initial project goal was to help all states complete their SLDS implementation by the end of 2009. However, as Figure 3.2 shows, despite progress toward the goal, not all states had finished as anticipated. Nevertheless, the DQC continued with its work as a new federal administration that supported data use took the reins. Speaking in early 2009 at the launch of a new DQC initiative funded by the Gates Foundation, Secretary of Education Arne Duncan said, "Now that the Data Quality Campaign has put data quality on the map, we need to work together to leverage this work and push it to the next level by using data to drive reform."[18] Shortly afterward, the new administration made data systems a key element of RttT and other funding programs. In addition, the DQC added a new part to its message—*a culture of data use*:

> States have made great progress in building their longitudinal data systems, but now we need a cultural shift to build the political will and take the practical steps needed to ensure that this data is accessed, shared, and used for continuous education improvement.[19]

The cultural shift introduced more criteria that could be communicated to states and then tracked to show progress with *ten essential state actions*:

1. Link data systems
2. Create progress reports using individual student data
3. Create stable, sustained support
4. Create reports using longitudinal statistics
5. Develop governance structures
6. Develop a P–20/workforce research agenda
7. Build state data repositories
8. Promote educator professional development/credentialing

FIGURE 3.2. Data Quality Campaign's 10 Essential Elements by Year

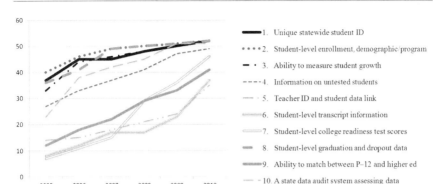

9. Implement systems to provide timely access to information
10. Promote strategies to raise data awareness

Although by 2010 more than 40 states had received grants under the SLDS program and progress was being reported across many of the ten elements and the ten essential actions, much work remained to be done and the DQC continued to be a national voice with strong support from the administration and its original funders. From an initial group of ten founding members, the DQC grew to have over 100 partners. At the beginning of the 2010s, the DQC transitioned to become a fully independent not-for-profit in its own right and is looking beyond the domain of the SLDS to other areas of educational data.

Like CALDER, the issues the DQC focuses on are broad and systemic. They span from teacher performance to program effectiveness to factors affecting success in college and careers. The DQC provides an important source of information for the first decade of the educational data movement. What the DQC reports on and how it does so are different from the way many educational researchers would do this. In fact, the area the DQC focuses on—beginning with state education departments but extending across much of the educational system—is the area that educational researchers historically have not studied. Many CALDER researchers are faculty or senior scientists in some of the best universities, and their studies frequently appear in leading-edge, peer-reviewed publications. The DQC, on the other hand, produces reports and case studies that are freely available on the Internet and consumed by a general policy community in states rather than by academics. But research organizations such as CALDER are able to study only what has occurred in the past. The DQC provides information that is much more current about what is occurring, often before it can be easily studied by traditional methods.

SEEING ACROSS BOUNDARIES:
INSIGHTS FROM CROSS-SYSTEM ANALYSIS

Data, even from imperfect systems, can provide visibility into complex processes. While the various state data infrastructures are still emerging, some educational organizations are finding new ways to look at how students transition from schools to college and how educators transition from teacher preparation programs to the classroom. As with many important features of the educational data movement, some of these efforts began before NCLB and the SLDS program. But through the SLDS program and federal initiatives like RttT that also fund state data systems, there has been a new capacity as more of these infrastructures become functional. In areas where diffusion is occurring, as discussed in Chapter 2, early adopters and leaders can provide examples of possibilities for success and for challenges that those that come later may experience. This section, then, briefly examines three important and early uses of national and state-level data to see across educational boundaries, and introduces topics that likely will emerge in other state and national efforts.

The National Student Clearinghouse

At the end of the 20th century, before the SLDS program even began, there were thousands of digital data collections across the nation with information about students. This hodgepodge of datasets could rarely be used for systemic analysis because the data were inconsistent and disconnected. In the mid-1990s an organization called the National Student Clearinghouse (NSC) emerged to provide confirmation of college enrollment for student loan providers. These lenders needed to know the enrollment status of students with loans, and the NSC started by collecting this information from different institutions of higher education across the country and consolidating it for the lenders. By working directly with colleges and universities, the NSC was able to provide student loan providers with confirmation of the enrollment status of students whose loans depended on their being enrolled. Today, the NSC is a not-for-profit, but is supported through fees charged to commercial entities for background checking and degree verification, collects data covering over 93% of students attending higher education institutions in the United States. This is a business model where the NSC adds value by being a data connecter, providing linkages to data that others have collected.

Already having the records of students in higher education, the NSC has been able to offer K–12 school districts a data service that allows a school or whole district to see what postsecondary institutions their students attended, how far they progressed, and whether they joined other institutions later on. Much as state longitudinal datasets open up new lenses on education, this kind of national cross-system information is a dramatic leap forward for schools interested in understanding the life course impact of the education and services they provide. In 2010, the American Association of School Administrators (AASA) formed a partnership with the NSC around these data. AASA Executive Director Dan Domenech, himself a former superintendent of several large districts, commented that "this is unique information . . . we used to rely on surveys where the response is spotty." [20] Rick Torres, the NSC's executive director, said that "this is real information, and not anecdotal."[21]

Much like longitudinal K–12 datasets, the NSC data provided a new kind of visualization of student progress. They are able to connect student records across state lines, whereas the SLDS implementations are limited to states. This data window is really possible only with data systems that can share and match information reliably. These linkages, however, are limited. They cover only basic enrollment information and nothing about learning. Certainly there is no linking of test scores, as there would be for the datasets used with VAMs. At the same time, the data about college entry, persistence, and changes may be as important, if not more so, from a systems perspective since they show total outcomes rather than the intermediate progress points that tests provide.

Evaluating Teacher Preparation Programs

A more recent move to link data systems occurred around the evaluation of teacher education paths. Historically, states have had oversight responsibility for teacher preparation programs, which are licensed and regulated by states. Many of these programs historically have had low entrance requirements and often used curricula that did not prepare future teachers for what they would encounter in the classroom. This led to two related problems: (1) future teachers who might be missing important subject-matter knowledge, and (2) future teachers without experience in the day-to-day challenges of teaching, with many leaving the field after just a few years. The track record on state oversight of this area was not good. According to a 2011 DoED report:

> In the most recent year for which data is available, states identified only 37 low-performing programs at the over 1,400 institutions of higher education

that prepare teachers—and 39 states identified no low-performing programs at all. Thirty-nine didn't identify a single low-performing program. Over the last dozen years, 27 states have never identified a single low-performing program.

To investigate differences between teacher preparation programs, Louisiana State University psychology professor George Noell analyzed teacher performance using a VAM based on the scores of the teachers' students. Rather than linking students to their college programs as the NSC did, Noell used an SLDS to link data to teacher preparation programs and compare how the graduates of the different programs did in terms of students' growth. This program eventually moved from the university into the state department of education, where Noell published a number of reports showing differences in both the success of teachers from different programs and how long they were persisting in their careers. Like other research, the Louisiana studies showed that some alternative preparation programs were poor performers and some were producing strong results when compared with traditional programs.[22] While these types of test-based evaluations are not perfect, they are a way to compare the paths teachers take that lead to the classroom, paths that have rarely been evaluated with any data before.

While the findings of Noell and his colleagues are potentially important in terms of what they may say about teacher preparation, more important is that they demonstrate a new kind of analysis that is possible using linked data in the SLDS. The science in this area is new, and CALDER researchers working with different state datasets—Corey Koedel with Missouri and Dan Goldhaber with Washington State—have found other results.[23] Goldhaber was able to detect some differences within in-state programs, but not within out-of-state programs. These differences tended to fade over time rather than persisting for years. Koedel, however, found no appreciable difference using different statistical techniques and suggested alternative ways to develop models from these data. While the research on the SLDS themselves is sparse, the SLDS datasets are becoming important resources for new lines of research and important debates about methods and techniques.

The NeXT Project: Supporting Teacher Preparation Across State Lines

While powerful, SLDS analyses are often limited by the fact that SLDS implementations are state-specific. While providing good comparisons for teacher preparation within a state, the process is more difficult when teachers move across states after their preparation program or in mid-career. One recent effort to work with data across state lines was undertaken by the Bush Foundation as part of a teacher preparation initiative. The Bush Foundation was founded by former 3M executive Archibald Granville Bush in 1953 (no relation to the presidents) and works in three states—North Dakota, South Dakota, and Minnesota—that have high rural and Native American populations.

In 2009, the Bush Foundation launched a 10-year effort to improve teaching education called the Network for Excellence in Teaching (NExT). NExT is a partnership between the foundation and 14 colleges of education across these three states to transform the way they recruit, prepare, place, support, and measure new teachers. NExT is ambitious in going beyond evaluating effectiveness of teacher preparation programs, as Louisiana was attempting, to identify specific shortcomings of these programs and look for areas that need improvement. NExT in collaboration with the schools developed a series of survey instruments to administer on all of the 14 campuses to provide more description of the new teacher career process and supplement the value-added data the program will have on the new teachers.

NExT, however, ran into many technical challenges, some due to the different levels of capacity in the various institutions. For example, in some of the participating schools, certain functions were not automated, so that institutions needed to build capacity to do basic data entry or analysis, as well as data mapping across the central systems. The process of trying to link up teacher development practices across these institutions led the project to explore ways of thinking about how to classify incoming students and how to align different categories such as demographics, which are important for reporting and analysis, but about which different institutions have rarely coordinated. NExT also ran into questions about data privacy and intellectual property, since the program will have data across institutions and states that might be used either for program improvement or for research. Although the purpose of the data collection efforts in NExT was to address program improvement, NExT saw, as did many working with student-level longitudinal data, that the same data can be used for both research and evaluation, raising new issues of data ownership and governance.

FEDERAL EFFORTS TO FACILITATE DATA SHARING

Sharing data across states and districts will open up an abundance of windows into the systemic behavior of American education. As the examples of analyses involving college-going and teacher preparation discussed above illustrate, there are important insights to be gained from analyzing connected data across jurisdictional boundaries. Not only would such analyses allow knowledge to be developed from pre-existing data that would take expensive studies otherwise, but allow the same types of questions to be asked year after year without having to repeat a traditional study. With greater linking of data, even more systemic insights will be gained. To support this and to improve the quality of data the federal government collects, there are several federal initiatives ongoing that have the potential to make data sharing more practical than it has been in the past. These include big open datasets, national privacy initiatives, common educational data standards, common curricular standards, and new national assessments aligned to those learning goals.

Big Open Data and Data Privacy

In recognition of the importance of data in government and in education, the federal government launched some initiatives in 2011 both to make federal data easier to use and to protect educational data privacy. One was the Open Data Initiative, put forth by the office of the newly created Chief Technology Officer. This initiative was described as:

> both government releasing general data resources in computer-readable form and also private sector organizations voluntarily giving consumers access to their own data (e.g., utilities allowing consumers to download electronic copies of their own electricity usage data) in a manner that rigorously protects privacy . . . to stimulate a rising tide of entrepreneurship that utilizes these data to create tools that help Americans find the right health care provider for them, identify the college that provides the best value . . . , save money on their electricity bills through smarter shopping . . . , keep their families safe by knowing which products have been recalled, and much more.[24]

The initiative aims to unleash the power of data by making public datasets more available to researchers and entrepreneurs. The proponents use examples like global positioning, weather, and census data that have been collected by the government, or made possible through government programs, to support new tools and information people often use every day. The goal of this work is to put public information in the hands of entrepreneurs and researchers to help solve problems and thereby make activities more efficient and create information-related jobs. This includes allowing people to have access to their own information that the government may have. In 2012 the White House Office of Science and Technology Policy, along with the Department of Education, held a number of events to generate private-sector interest in open data initiatives. These events, named *Data Jams* and *Datapalooza*, allowed organizations that could build new educational data tools to showcase their work. And innovators showed up from small and large software companies with a range of solutions from supporting college advising, to making filling out college and financial loan applications more efficient, to a foundation promoting digital badges that can be used to indicate competence in both in-school and out-of-school activities, to vendors of data warehouses for school districts. This new emerging sector of the field most likely will grow over the next few years as more entrepreneurs are able to find ways to use data to provide value. Much as with other national data initiatives, however, this area was much more focused on peripheral functions, with very little representation of the work teachers do daily or other issues affecting the technical core, as discussed later in this book.

At the same time as there are efforts to make some data more available, there are new privacy issues resulting from proliferation of datasets and their potential to be linked. On the one hand, data provides an ability to look beyond a particular school year and school system to the long-term consequences of instructional approaches. This holds great promise for research, especially in an age when more and more scientific research is based on databases. At the same time, the legal landscape in American education is based on decentralization and safeguards of privacy. In 2011, the DoED created a new executive position, Chief Privacy Officer, to:

> serve as a senior advisor to the secretary on all of the Department's policies and programs related to privacy, confidentiality and data security . . . head a new division dedicated to advancing the responsible stewardship, collection, use, maintenance and disclosure of information at the national level within the Education Department . . . coordinate technical assistance efforts for states, districts, and other education stakeholders, helping them understand important privacy issues such as minimizing unnecessary collection of personal information.[25]

Along with the new privacy officer, a new technical assistance center was created inside the National Center for Education Statistics (the organization that manages the SLDS program) to help provide guidance on the proper use of educational data. The DoED and other organizations, including the American Educational Research Association and the DQC, have been promoting new interpretations of the Family Education Rights and Privacy Act (FERPA) to allow the information to be used for research while safeguarding privacy.

Common Education Data Standards

One key component to being able to use the vast amounts of educational data involves data interchange standards. These kinds of standards have been essential components as other fields, from manufacturing to finance to retail, became more efficient sectors. As with other dimensions of data education is currently far behind in terms of standards. The federal government in recent years has begun to lead efforts to help the field catch up. The federal government often has been involved in standard-setting efforts, generally letting an industry consortium take the lead and providing oversight and guidance. For example, it was federal research that created the initial Internet standards. The Obama administration made the exchange of digital records a priority. Joanne Weiss, the former education technology executive and venture philanthropist who became Chief of Staff to Secretary of Education Arne Duncan, stated in 2012:

> Technical standards do many things. They let different tools communicate. They can help improve the quality and usability of data. They facilitate deep analytics. And they'll allow us to bring to education the kind of personalization that is happening in other industries. As we've seen in countless other settings, technical standards can help move fields forward—they allow industries to become more flexible and efficient.[26]

Standards do, in fact, exist for educational data; the problem is that there are many, and most SLDS and district systems were built without using any standard, because at the time the program launched, the need for standards was not appreciated. According to Jack Buckley, Commissioner of the National Center for Education Statistics, the common data standards are both critically important and late to the game:

> We have funded both through state money and federal assistance the development of student level data systems. But, those systems were built without first setting common standards, without first having a common set of elements or data model. Now in many cases these data systems can't speak to each other horizontally across state lines or even vertically within a state. For example the early learning data often cannot be passed to K–12 data systems that often can pass information to the post-secondary levels.[27]

There are currently three largely independent standards programs outside of the federal government. They all emerged at about the same time and for different purposes. The IMS Global Learning Consortium was founded in 1995 out of the higher education group EDUCAUSE with a focus on media and tools. The Postsecondary Electronic Standards Council (PESC) began in 1997 to meet the needs of university administrators to share financial aid and other information. The Schools Interoperability Framework (SIF) also began in 1997 as an effort to standardize the information required for K–12 school administration. Over time, each of these standards programs has evolved to partially overlap with the others. Each has a community of vendors and technologists that are committed to preserving it. In addition, the federal government itself has several educational standards efforts, including some at the DoED and one at the Department of Defense.[28]

The DoED has taken an active role in a new Common Education Data Standards (CEDS) effort. CEDS is managed by a consortium that includes the CCSSO, the State Higher Education Executive Officers, the DQC, the SIF Association, and PESC. The initial CEDS effort was small and not useful. In addition to the DoED needing to reconcile a number of different internal projects that each attempted to address different parts of the educational landscape, it also needed to sort out how to communicate the difference between a common standards effort and a federal mandate or efforts to develop a national student record system, both of which the federal government is prohibited by law from doing.[29] Later versions of CEDs covered more kinds of data, and the program has high-level support and a broad stakeholder group, although little representation of vendors and practitioners. The CEDS initiative is a voluntary forum for understanding common data issues from early childhood to K–12 education to college and the workforce. Principal funding for the consortium is provided by the Gates Foundation, which has acted as a thought partner and supported CEDS communications.

However, there are challenges facing the federal government in this area. One is that it has more than one role in the educational data landscape. It is an actor through various programs that impact the educational data world, from student financial aid to accountability reporting to civil rights compliance to migrant and native populations to special education. Much of what states and districts collect is driven by federal programs. Many of these programs, like many state educational programs, are managed in separate parts of the federal bureaucracy that have different missions and staffs. The technical challenges that the federal government faces in integrating these perspectives are compounded by its own need to balance its fiduciary role for overseeing a fair and innovative marketplace with its desire to support innovation and the entrepreneurs that often provide it.

The CEDS project also has received some support from the Michael and Susan Dell Foundation, which has developed another standard-based solution named *Ed-Fi* that it presents as also having national potential. Where the CEDS work is just a data standard largely representing areas having to do with federal reporting, the Ed-Fi solution includes both a data standard and suite of tools that focus on district performance metrics with a specific goal of providing actionable information to improve student outcomes. Ed-Fi, which stands for Education Fidelity, aligns with many of the data elements used in CEDS, and the Michael and Susan Dell Foundation has a close working relationship with the CEDS technical working team.[30] Ed-Fi is an example of a foundation identifying an area that neither the federal government nor the private sector was addressing, and developing its own solution to try to fill the gap.

The Common Core State Standards

Equally important for the use of data are learning targets, also called learning standards. Not only must data be able to be exchanged between systems, but when the data are about learning, for example, assessments, they need to be comparable as well. With each state setting its own learning goals, one of the weaknesses of NCLB was difficulty in comparing state programs. One of the signature elements of the Obama administration's educational policy is the adoption of common academic standards for math and literacy called the Common Core State Standards, or *Common Core*. A parallel effort is under way for science. With the National Governors Association and the CCSSO as partners, the Common Core initiative has been endorsed by 41 of the 50 states and the District of Columbia. These standards are technically voluntary, but have been integrated into other federal incentives, including the RttT program, which required states to adopt the Common Core as well as enhance their data systems.

The Common Core is a significant move forward for interoperability because the standards not only will increase comparability of the results across states, but will enable technology developers to build a range of digital media and tools that can be used in larger markets than was possible when each state had its own unique standards. The learning standards, combined with common data standards, will lead to educational product developers building tools designed to work together. For example, one might build math presentation materials, and another could build data and analysis tools. Because the content standards provide topical alignment and the data standards allow interchange, both products would have a larger market.

Race to the Top Assessments

State test systems are a major expense, with some costing tens of millions of dollars per year as new items are always required. Another portion of the RttT funding, some $650 million, was set aside for the development of two common test systems aligned to the Common Core, called by some the RttT assessments. One of these programs is the Smarter Balance Assessment Consortium (SBAC), with 28 member states that are responsible for almost half of American K–12 students. The second is the Partnership for Assessment of Readiness for College and Careers (PARCC), with 23 states that also represent just under half of the students. Since some states belong to both consortia, the participating states do not represent the whole nation. But the products of these consortia will be available for all to use, and most states are involved in at least one of the consortia. SBAC is building both summative assessments and interim tools that can be used periodically in schools. PARCC also has summative assessments, but has a diagnostic assessment designed to be given at the beginning of the year. In addition to sets of items that align with the Common Core, these projects are full information systems with delivery mechanisms and data tools for use by practitioners. The idea behind these programs is to harness new technologies and build tools that can be used in schools to monitor progress toward common goals. Both programs use computer-adaptive testing and natural language processing and/or artificial intelligence. Both have been developed with some Evidence Centered Design principles. Since many of the assessments are delivered only with technology, these programs will either drive wider technology purchases in the schools or face challenges if schools don't purchase the additional technology that they need.

In addition to the two RttT assessment programs, three other multistate assessment consortia were funded by the DoED. One was the National Center and State Collaborative partnership (NCSC), a consortium of 18 states, the District of Columbia, and several territories led by the University of Minnesota and funded for $45 million. Another was the Dynamic Learning Maps (DLM) Alternate Assessment System Consortium, which includes 11 states led by the University of Kansas and funded for $22 million. Both of these grants were to create *alternate assessments* for students with disabilities. The term *alternate assessment* is used primarily for students with disabilities who are unable to use the standardized assessment tests. The same term is also used to indicate more authentic assessment methods, including portfolios and other natural tasks. One of the NCSC's important design elements is that it supports professional learning communities (discussed in Chapter 6), while the DLM is designed to have many curriculum-embedded assessments and an adaptable sequence that supports tracking student progress. The third contemporary program, involving 29 states, is the Assessment Services Supporting English learners through Technology Systems (ASSETS) and funded for $10 million, also from the DoED.

These programs have the potential to provide state-of-the-art assessments and reporting tools that can feed information back to the states and districts that use them in ways discussed in Chapter 1. These types of programs, with their massive investments and new sets of tools, likely would not be possible if it were not for the Common Core. As states yield some control over standards, they also have access to greater technology that can provide richer assessments and information reporting. These new assessment consortia, because they use newer technology and theories such as Evidence Centered Design, hold promise for better assessments in the future. They are designed to provide more systemic validity by including reporting systems and mechanisms for sharing information with practitioners, including in one case for teacher learning. If these programs achieve even some of their aims, they will provide new assessments for many states and likely will produce new tools that will move the field forward. However, they are dominated, as NCLB was, by math and literacy, with little to offer other subject areas or innovations for authentic problem-based approaches as might be required for science, technology, engineering and math (STEM) and 21st-century skills. Further, just as the field of special education was early to the educational data movement—*decades before NCLB*—so are some of the important innovations in these consortia limited to special education programs. This gives some reasons for optimism, but also reinforces traditional separation of mainstream and special education.

A DECADE OF PROGRESS, HARD QUESTIONS

In the years since NCLB was enacted, dramatic progress has been made in terms of national data capacity. In 2001, most states had outdated data systems. Many did not work together, and the different agencies and departments using them often did not communicate. As a result, many important areas for policy analysis were essentially dark because there was little or no data to use to evaluate them. What did exist was often of questionable quality. Since then there has been broad but partial progress in states' capacity and appreciation for the potential of integrated information. Despite this progress, there are some reasons for concern. Three of them are the dominance of NCLB and what NCLB excluded, the focus on institutional interests with little perspective from educators and those closest to students, and a lack of a solid research base or oversight to guide these efforts.

NCLB's Legacy in Its Infrastructures

The data that are available for educational decisions at the state level include many different forms, from test data to other demographic and programmatic details. But the predominant ones have been those represented in NCLB. Because NCLB required testing in math and language arts, those two subjects are at the center of the SLDS datasets. Many states have included other scores, especially science, which NCLB required to be tested, but have not used them in accountability calculations. But the growth models and longitudinal data are based largely on just these two parts of the curriculum, which represent about a third of the classrooms. Many areas—social studies, much of science, art, music, and more—have been left further behind. Also, special education, which is addressed by different federal programs, has been largely a separate area in state data systems (as it is in many districts). Although many special education students take alternate assessments, many others are in mainstream settings some or all of the time. These students are often the ones creating the greatest challenges for meeting accountability targets. And yet, for a variety of practical and historical reasons, special education data remain largely separated from mainstream data even though many students receive special services.

Predominantly Institutional View

Just as the picture of education shown in Figure 3.1 was accurate but reflected only part of the education picture, so does much of the work that went into developing educational infrastructures represent largely state, district, and sometimes school views, but not often much about teaching and learning. To date, there has been little involvement of organizations representing educators in the design and development of SLDS infrastructures or programs. It was only recently that the American Federation of Teachers (AFT) became a DQC partner. The National Education Association (NEA) has had less involvement.[31] This gap is striking given that almost every public statement and policy document about the use of these data mentions their use in improving instruction. The DQC has included teachers in its forums and highlighted the role of sharing data with parents. However, the infrastructures themselves are largely weak in matters related to teaching. Similarly, efforts to develop data exchange standards have been largely in the hands of a select group of organizations that represent institutional rather than instructional perspectives.

Major Investments Without Research and Oversight

While millions of dollars are spent on national initiatives and state data systems, little of it has been guided by research or by public input. Although there are research programs looking at how districts and schools use data, there are precious few studies that look at the state data systems programs and how the design choices different states make might impact their schools and ability to use data. While data quality is known to be an important issue, there have been few studies that actually explore the prevalence of specific data quality issues and their root causes or solutions. The work to develop common data standards to allow for the exchange of information between different state systems is the foundation of national data infrastructures. But there has been little research to guide it. Part of the reason for this may be the shortage of educational researchers with the knowledge to be able to advise these projects. Part of it may be that the research funding has been directed at uncovering the effectiveness of data using an intervention-oriented and "what works" model, as discussed in Chapter 1, rather than a sociotechnical lens and studying these efforts as a national infrastructure process. Part of it may be that research often can take time and give the appearance of slowing down progress where progress is needed. For whatever reasons, this work represents a major national investment, and much of it has occurred without oversight or guidance.

Districts:
Data Warehouses and
Teacher Evaluation Systems

In some ways, the era of educational data becomes even more complicated and varied in districts than at the state and national level. While states are developing longitudinal data systems, each with some unique characteristics, districts are the ones that hold much of the other data that are used in practice. The districts also create the policies and intermediate technology systems that shape what is possible for a district's schools to do with data from its own systems or its state's systems. The district is also where the research into educational data use begins because most studies of educational data use are organized around either a district data system, district staff, and/ or school staff grouped by district. Although it is a gateway into educational data, the district is by no means a simple unit of analysis. There is no typical district, and students in the United States attend many different kinds of districts with varied technologies, capacities, and orientations toward data.

While this chapter looks primarily at districts, and organizations and research that have focused on districts, the issues in it often relate to other levels of states and schools. The first topic discussed in this chapter involves district variation, which can be geographic, political, or demographic. It provides a caution for any views that attempt to describe districts or other educational structures in general terms. The chapter also covers the roles of researchers and those from outside of education, how district-based data technologies developed on a broad scale, along with teacher evaluation, which is a responsibility of districts but relates to many educational levels simultaneously.

FROM HUNDREDS TO HUNDREDS OF THOUSANDS: DISTRICT VARIATION

As we turn to the district, we enter unusual terrain from an organizational perspective. The school district, also known as the local education agency, often is treated as a specific kind of entity, just as a teacher, student, or classroom are often treated as easily comparable. Unless one works with different kinds of districts or has reasons to look across districts to analyze them, the extent to which U.S. districts vary may not be apparent. It turns out that few entities in the educational world vary as much as districts do. This variation is an important part of understanding the educational data movement. It is important in terms of understanding districts' capacity to implement policy, because district size, location, and political organization influence what information they need to have and how they are able to utilize it. Variation in districts also relates to issues of equity with data practices. This variation impacts the knowledge base, as most research is conducted in large districts even though only about half of the students in the United States are educated in a district with more than 30,000 students. These differences complicate what we can know or assume about a district, and make the district both fascinating and challenging to study.

To understand district variation, it is important to step back to a larger building block of the educational data world: the state. States, like districts, often are treated as unitary and easily comparable entities. From state to state there are important differences in governance that flow down to districts. For example, Maryland has a district for each of its 24 counties plus one for the City of Baltimore. They range in size from one with 4,000 students to several with more than 100,000 students. In contrast, in Michigan there are more than 800 districts, some with as few as 100 students and one with more than 100,000. Even though Michigan has a little more than one and a half times the population of Maryland, it has 33 times as many districts. In Maryland, the school districts are aligned with political boundaries. In Michigan, many of them cross county lines in a way that seems designed to make them incoherent with other political systems.

Like Michigan, many other states with small rural districts—such as Ohio and New York—augment their districts with intermediate support organizations that operate in some ways like a super-district to support the small local districts. These super-districts often have their own elected boards and funding. They can be called intermediary school districts (ISDs), regional education service agencies (RESAs), or boards of cooperative educational services (BOCES). While the names vary, these organizations often perform similar services for many districts, including developing curricula, operating classes in special subjects or for disabled students, and collecting and managing data. While a typical view of a state as being made up of districts is correct, it is incomplete. Hawaii has one only one public school district in addition to charter systems. In the District of Columbia, which is considered a state from a policy and accountability perspective, only slightly more than half of students are taught by a single public school district—the rest attend charter schools.

Charter schools represent another complication. Each charter organization, which can be either a single school or part of a network of schools operated by a charter management organization, also can be considered a district. Some charter management organizations cross state lines, including the Knowledge Is Power Program (KIPP). In 2011 KIPP operated more than 100 public schools in 20 states, enrolling more than 32,000 students. The SEED School is a residential school system that is chartered to operate in several states. Rocketship Education, focusing on primary grades, began in California and is branching out to Wisconsin and Tennessee, and there are dozens of others. In some areas, school districts and charters work together. In other areas, they compete. In Baltimore, for example, the public school district provides its charter schools, including several KIPP schools, with tests and data. In other areas, there is less coordination.

DISTRICTS DISCOVER DATA WAREHOUSING

For decades, districts have been collectors and holders of data. They have had records on student registration and grades; on teachers, their professional development, and their employment history; and on buildings, equipment, and transportation. Like many organizations over the past several decades, many districts built and purchased database applications to help manage this information. As with many other types of organizations, these data systems accumulated one at a time with little integration.

During a time when competitive pressures were driving other organizations to integrate their data systems, many educational organizations were just beginning to focus on common academic standards and were developing new programs to support them rather than developing state-of-the-art data tools to provide integrated information. There was little motivation in the 20th century for districts to develop integrated data systems because few policies required it. Unlike corporations that need to adapt to what their competitors are doing to survive, and public utilities whose costs are monitored, there were no market forces guiding school systems to become more efficient and better informed. As a result, by the time NCLB was enacted, with its emphasis on data-driven decision making, most school systems were where many other organizations had been 10 or 15 years earlier—with disconnected collections of data silos and programs. While most district administrators and school staff I spoke with felt that their organization was particularly unprepared, the reality is that few districts possessed the robust integrated data infrastructure they wished for, although some were farther behind than others.

A shift was evident in 2001, just a few months after George W. Bush took office and sketched out his educational agenda. In April 2001, the magazine for district leaders, *School Administrator*, had its first issue dedicated to the topic of data, titled "Data-Driven Decisions: New Ways to Get Answers: The 'Drill Down' and the 'Walk-Through.'" The issue included some of the earliest writings about data in education, including from Phillip Streifer, who drew upon his experience as an administrator to show how districts could benefit from student performance information.[1] Also included was Theodore Creighton, who focused on data used inside school buildings.[2] Interestingly, while much of the attention on educational data that occurred in the following years focused on test scores, this early issue included discussions of broader forms of information that could be meaningful for districts, such as student interviews and the knowledge that could be gained by walking through buildings and talking to students and staff. This combination of test scores with other information is a pattern that repeats throughout the development of the educational data movement in districts and at the finer levels of practice discussed later in this book.

After NCLB made the use of test scores an important topic for school districts, more data warehouse projects began to emerge in districts across the nation. As the first decade of the 21st century progressed, just about every large district began to develop a data warehouse or advertised that they had one. In New York, an $80 million project to build the Achievement Reporting and Innovation System (ARIS) began in 2007. In Milwaukee, the Integrated Resource Information System (IRIS) received millions in federal and foundation money.[3] In 2008, the Metro Nashville Public Schools (MNPS) began to build their Longitudinal Educational Analytics and Decision Support System (LEADS) system with federal and local funding, and affluent Montgomery County Public Schools (MCPS) in Maryland built their own MY-MCPS data warehouse.[4] During my own dissertation research in Michigan, I found a similar pattern of data warehouse construction. However, in Michigan, where many districts are small, only a few large districts took on the job themselves. In many parts of that state ISDs and RESAs were building these systems, and some individual districts even worked with the Michigan Department of Education to develop a data system.

A NEW AND UNCERTAIN RESEARCH LITERATURE

While data warehouses proliferated in districts, educational researchers began to study them. Following NCLB, research funding started to flow for looking at how educational data can be used to improve outcomes. With it emerged a new and uncertain research literature. From the beginning it wasn't clear where these studies belonged. They didn't easily fit into most established research programs. The vast educational research community often can seem like a giant schoolyard where different groups cluster. There are learner-focused studies that look at how some instructional approaches or materials work with individuals; classroom studies that show how teachers and students work in a particular type of subject and grade, such as explaining fractions in 3rd grade or literacy in middle schools; principal and leadership studies that look at the jobs of leading schools and districts; and policy-oriented studies that look at how different programs and regulations play out on the ground with educators. And for each of these types of studies, there are typically one or more dedicated journals where researchers can publish their work. Data use was the new kid. Some early studies were built around a district data initiative, in many cases focusing on just one or two parts of those districts' organizations. Others focused on individual teachers, teams of teachers, school administrator-led activities, or district staff. There was no typical data study, and no journal emerged as the natural home for the particular issues raised by educational data.

Early Research

The early literature varied in the framing and methods used. One of the earliest books about educational data use, Streifer's 2001 *Using Data to Make Better Educational Decisions*, used an informal case study narrative approach featuring three schools, a K–8 school, a middle school, and a high school, and showing how a range of information, including the state performance test, a ranking of instructional materials by level of difficulty, student ranking against state measures, and grades, can be used together to identify possible instructional issues in schools. He placed information use into a systemic context so the reader sees why it is important to get new information or use the information at hand to address basic educational concerns. In one of his analyses, district administrators diagnosed systemic breakdowns and set performance targets for English language arts. In another, they identified possible interventions for middle school mathematics. In two other analyses, he used a university study of school data to identify possible problems with textbooks and possible grade inflation in high school science. Streifer also included several discussions that look at information longitudinally.

Later, researchers from the University of Pittsburgh's Institute for Learning (IFL) school reform program teamed with RAND Corporation to study three large urban districts.[5] They reported that two of the three engaged in data-driven decision making to a much greater extent than the third and largest one. They found that those that did invest in using data did so in different ways using a variety of data sources, including both state and district tests. Of these two data-oriented districts, one used the school improvement process as a vehicle for change, while the other focused on a data system technology and the development of *interim assessments* linked to this system. Interim assessments, which we discuss in more detail in Chapter 6, are midway between accountability tests and classroom assessments. For the school improvement program, the district encouraged the use of state test results and a structured program to allow it to focus on specific instructional goals. The researchers also discussed how the staff understanding and technological infrastructure were both critical to the district's ability to use data, a finding that occurs with great frequency across this new literature.

Looking deeper into district cultures and different approaches to data use, Coburn and Talbert studied four organizational levels (upper and front-line district administrators, principals, and teachers) within one California district to see how research and evidence were perceived.[6] They show that beliefs of the staff varied in this district by organizational level. The district staff had a stronger faith in research than the school staff; top-level district administrators and principals favored evidence with psychometric tests, while lower-level administrators and teachers favored assessments that exposed student thinking. They also showed how multiple measures were important, especially for principal decision making. However, one of the most important findings was how similar ideas about data and evidence were shared by individuals in a given organizational unit and how those shared beliefs were related to the history of reform messages the people had experienced. The authors wrote, "We found that individuals who were connected to particular reform movements—because of their organizational division and/or their professional network—tended to hold a similar cluster of conceptions as those promoted by that movement."[7]

These three different glimpses of district-related research, along with many others, show some of the different ways we can think about data use in school systems. We see districts using data to evaluate schools in Streifer's work, different districts approaching data differently in the IFL/RAND studies, and how pockets of beliefs occur at different organizational levels and units in Coburn and Talbert's work. This variation from some of the earliest research in the educational data movement shows some reasons why developing a common theoretical explanation or model for educational data use at the district level has eluded researchers: The attitudes and approaches to data use can vary within districts, and the technological dimensions of many district data systems are constantly changing.

Later Research

As the first decade of the 21st century progressed, there were larger studies that looked at developing data capacities in more districts and in other regions. In 2004, with funding from the Heinz Endowment and the Grable Foundation (named for Errett Grable, a founder of Rubbermaid,

Inc.), researchers at RAND looked at data use across southwestern Pennsylvania, an area with over 100 districts of different sizes.[8] These researchers combined superintendent surveys in 26 districts with more in-depth case study research in six of them. Their surveys showed widespread interest by educators and reports of data use for administrative, school improvement, and instructional purposes. Although interest was strong, the researchers reported varying capacity for effectively using data. They also found, as others had, different management styles related to data. Within the case study districts, some utilized a *centralized* approach to data analysis, having staff in the central office review data, whereas some featured a *decentralized* approach, with data analysis in schools led by principals or groups of teachers.

One of the largest and most important research programs about educational data in practice came in 2006 when the DoED launched the *Study of Education Data Systems and Decision Making*, conducted by the Center for Technology and Learning at SRI International, a research organization that has worked extensively with education technology. This was larger than any previous study. It looked at multiple levels of the educational system from states to classrooms, although the state-level information was largely contextual and the study of different levels often was done in separate parts. It had bigger samples of districts, schools, and teachers, and was conducted over multiple years with ample funding to allow looking across state lines. This study also drew on a number of data sources, including national surveys and focal case studies of districts that were nominated for their exemplary data practices. The researchers drew on existing National Educational Technology Plans and the National Educational Technology Trends Study that SRI also had supported. This study found more evidence of the growth in data systems across American education, indicating more than a dozen different types of data being used in districts:

1. Student demographics
2. Student attendance
3. Student grades
4. Student test scores on statewide assessments
5. Student course enrollment histories
6. Student graduation status
7. Student behavior data
8. Student participation in educational programs
9. Student special education information
10. Teacher qualifications
11. Student test scores on district-administered assessments
12. Student test scores on school-administered assessments
13. Teacher professional development records

As with much of the early literature on data use, this study frequently uses the term *data* to indicate test results, but then often described many other forms of information that districts used. Whether this study shows each and every type of data that districts were maintaining or would maintain is less important than that it indicates the range of evidence active in districts during this time. This study also showed how larger districts tended to have more data capacity than smaller ones, and how integrating data systems, even for the large districts, involved technical as well as organizational challenges. Like the other educational data research, the study made little mention of intermediate districts or those other organizations, like Teach for America (TFA) or KIPP, that both intersect the traditional hierarchical educational system and are continuing to expand their share of the American students they interact with.

It is reasonable to expect that the research into educational data use at the district level might parallel research into information systems generally. In many studies that look at districts, there are mentions of multiple departments. Where most of the educational research stops, however, is at any *systematic inquiry* into data practices across these different units.[9] For example, the research is thin on the different ways that curriculum departments, operational reporting structures (e.g., assistant superintendents), special education, and human resources and professional development offices in districts use data and how data of different kinds work across them. There is also little in the history of educational research that compares different district departments independent of data. As Columbia University professor Alex Bowers has pointed out recently, the research base on what makes an effective district also is only beginning to develop.[10]

Only a few researchers looked at how information might be impacting inter-institutional relationships, as experience from other fields would suggest. As Chapter 2 explained, improving individual productivity is often only one benefit of technology. In many cases, there are also benefits to changing relationships between internal teams of an organization or across organizations in terms of markets. There are a few examples, including University of Texas professor Jeff Wayman, who looked at how districts can use data centrally to prompt schools to act in certain ways, specifically around issues of special education. University of California at San Diego professor Amanda Datnow and her colleagues looked at how data can be used within a framework of school-based management (also called site-based management.[11] University of Pennsylvania professor Jon Supovitz looked at how data were integral to the evolution of a district reform process. And at the Harvard Business School, Stacey Childress and her colleagues traced some of the ways data were used to divide a county into different zones for services and attention. However, these are exceptions, and the educational data use literature rarely connects with broader literature on organizational change. There is little in the evidence base to show whether the increasing availability of data is causing school–district relations to be stronger, weaker, more centralized, or more local.

Even after more than a decade of increased data use and many different studies, there has emerged a realization that educational data represent something different and difficult to study. In 2007, Pamela Moss said that "evidence based decision making" is "a relatively recent construct and the boundaries of the 'field' are still very much under construction."[12] In 2010, the SRI team led by Barbara Means, a national leader in education technology, stated, "The data systems themselves, the assessment data that populate district data systems, and school and district practices around data use are all changing rapidly."[13] In 2011 Cynthia Coburn said, "In many ways, the practice of data use is out ahead of research. Policy and interventions to promote data use far outstrip research studying the process, context, and consequences of these efforts."[14] What has been rare in any of the studies into educational data use is much connection to disciplines outside of educational research. Even though there is recognition that the data movement has relationships to other fields, specifically businesses, educational researchers have focused on this area from largely within the confines of their own communities. Despite frequent mentions of the importance of technology, there have been few connections to researchers who study technology in organizational systems and how technology movements reshape fields of human activity.

PERSPECTIVES FROM OUTSIDE OF EDUCATIONAL RESEARCH

As researchers sought to understand the data movement as it was unfolding, another movement was occurring involving new people entering educational organizations with management, policy, and government or military experience. They usually entered educational organizations as a career move and often through some support from large foundations. A few months after the 2001 special issue in *School Administrator* about data warehouses, there was a special issue on superintendents with military and business backgrounds. It said that these new leaders were used to working with data and metrics in their management of large, complex organizations in a way that could benefit schools.[15] The decade then saw an influx of new professionals working in district offices and charter management organizations in ways that parallel the alternative teacher programs begun by TFA in the 1990s.

The four programs discussed in this section—the Broad Academy and Residency, Education Pioneers, the Strategic Data Project, and Education

Resource Strategies—are all different, but I present them together because each brings new people and analytic methods into education. They also are deliberately forming professional networks for reform in which the use of details are an important element. These organizations hold meetings, retreats, and webinars to keep the communities active and interconnected. Their work has been focused largely on organizational and peripheral aspects rather than directly on instruction.

Broad Academy and Broad Residency

One of the most well-known pathways for new talent to enter district management began in 2001 when the philanthropist Eli Broad launched a training program to prepare senior executives from both inside and outside of education to become superintendents and districts leaders in large urban school systems. Historically, central offices in districts have been staffed by people who either joined school systems as teachers or began in administrative support jobs. In businesses, it is not uncommon for senior managers to be brought in from other companies, or even fields, to bring new perspectives and help energize large stagnant organizations. Over time, large organizations can develop closed-group thought processes, and new people and perspectives can open things up. However, prior to the start of the 21st century it was rare for districts to employ professional managers with experience from outside of education. In its announcement, the Broad Foundation said:

> Superintendents are in charge of our nation's greatest investment—our children. However, many have little training or background in complex financial, labor, management, personnel and capital resource decision-making. In fact, 98 percent of superintendents are trained as teachers—not managers.[16]

The program was called the Broad Superintendents Academy, run by the newly established Broad Center for the Management of School Systems. About 70% of the program graduates, called Fellows, have some education or education-related background, with the rest from military, business, social services, and government. By 2011, the program had filled 71 superintendent positions and 101 senior school district executive positions in the country, including more than a third of the major urban superintendent positions nationwide.

In 2002 the Broad Foundation began a second program to provide graduates from other fields (law, business management, public policy) opportunities to work in the management ranks of education. Named the Broad Residency, it involves a 2-year tour of duty during which the Broad Foundation shares the cost of the Resident's salary with the organization the person works in. According to the foundation's website (and not independently verified), Broad Residents made many types of contributions to the districts in which they worked, including eliminating 25% duplicate central office staff in Miami-Dade and moving 400 positions to the classroom; securing $32 million in grants for Long Beach, CA; creating a data-driven approach in Fresno, CA, to identify the root behavioral causes of student suspensions/ expulsions, which allowed staff to preemptively reduce incidents by 10%; reducing the deficit at the Boston Public Schools by $3.2 million by tightening food-ordering processes; saving the Denver Public Schools over $2 million by negotiating lower interest rates and increasing vendor competition; developing a model to forecast principal vacancies in Chicago with 97% accuracy; and reducing unnecessary New York City central office reporting demands, saving time for principals.[17] Although the Broad Residency began with a focus on traditional school districts, it later expanded to provide support for charter management organizations, state education departments, and the DoED. The Gates Foundation also has invested in this program, which by 2011 had placed 253 Residents in 39 school districts, 30 public charter management organizations, and 8 state education agencies.[18]

Education Pioneers

In 2003, an organization called Education Pioneers was founded to provide early-career professionals job opportunities in education. Like many education reform organizations, Education Pioneers recruits those with nontraditional backgrounds, often with MBAs and Masters of Public Policy, but some with education degrees. These fellows serve a 10-month tour in school districts, charter management organizations, state agencies, and education nonprofits. This program has been strongly supported by large foundations, including many of the big names that have supported the data movement. By 2011, the organization had placed more than 1,000 fellows, with a goal of reaching 10,000 placements by 2023. In 2010, Education Pioneers piloted a new Analyst Fellowship program specifically focused on attracting into education and preparing leaders and managers with data and analytic skills and expertise. The program has received so much demand that Education Pioneers expanded to new locations and increased the number of Analyst Fellows from 10 in 2010 to more than 60 in 2012, with an expectation to recruit and place more than 200 by 2014. This new track was specifically supported by the Broad, Gates, and Michael and Susan Dell foundations.

The Strategic Data Project

Another important development in district data programs occurred in 2008 when the Gates Foundation funded a new multimillion-dollar initiative called the Strategic Data Project (SDP). The SDP is managed in a research center at Harvard University led by Professor Tom Kane, the educational economist whose work on teacher productivity highlighted problems with teacher credentials as a reform lever, discussed in Chapter 1. As the name implies, the SDP is focused on data analysis. Whereas Broad Residents are taught to use data and have professional backgrounds where data analysis is important, the SDP Fellows have a core competency in quantitative analysis and program evaluation. In their assignments, SDP Fellows report to senior district leaders who have demonstrated a commitment to having new talent to work on challenging and substantive problems. They get guidance from faculty in Harvard's education, business, and economics schools. The SDP Fellows also come together every 2 to 3 months for professional development to share experiences, and there has been some presentation of their work in educational research meetings.

The SDP teaches its fellows that it is important to look across district departments and data systems for holistic answers to big issues, and they are trained to see the importance of an integrated view that a data warehouse provides, as illustrated in Figure 4.1. The program also has developed some tools to support two kinds of common district analyses that align with the Gates Foundation's strategic initiatives. The first is the *Human Capital Diagnostic Pathway*, geared toward helping districts and agencies understand their teaching workforce at critical points in a teacher's career, including recruitment, placement, development, evaluation, and retention/tenure. Similar to what Louisiana did, SDP researchers have explored differences between teachers from different types of preparation programs as expressed in test scores. Similar to CALDER researchers, SDP analysis has shown patterns of assignment where the newest teachers often work with the hardest students and in the hardest schools.[19] Both of these types of analyses have become more possible with linked data. The second SDP focal area is a four-step *College Going Pathway* that looks at the transition from 9th to 10th grade, application to colleges, college enrollment, and then college persistence. The SDP also has used data from the National Student Clearinghouse to help in these analyses.

In the spring of 2011, the SDP held an annual meeting to discuss its progress and challenges. It was joined by representatives from the Eli and Edythe Broad and Michael and Susan Dell foundations, as well as by staff from Education Pioneers and the Data Quality Campaign. At this meeting, SDP Fellows presented some of their accomplishments, including a program for Fulton County, GA, to investigate the "summer melt" (where students who had been accepted into college in the spring did not enroll in the fall), which utilized six different non–test–data sources to identify patterns and craft an intervention program;[20] support for a teacher development program in Delaware around data use involving more than 1,000 professional learn-

FIGURE 4.1 Strategic Data Project Vision Illustrating How Integrated Data Support Deeper Analysis

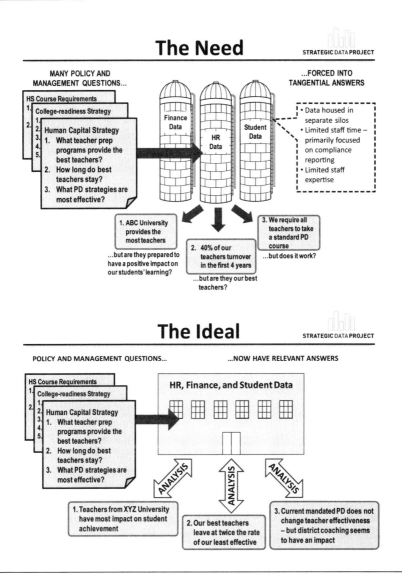

Figure drawn from Strategic Data Project materials. © 2012 The President and Fellows of Harvard College. Used with permission.

ing communities with over 7,000 teachers across 200 plus schools;[21] and development of multiple measures for teacher evaluation in iterative consultation with groups of teachers in Charlotte-Mecklenburg schools. The measures included teachers' knowledge of content pedagogy, contributions to the professional communities, student surveys, student work, and classroom observations.[22] These are just a subset of the projects that SDP Fellows undertook and they show the range of information and practice areas they work in. Like those samples from the Broad Residents, these projects involve a number of forms of data and different aspects of the educational organization, with teacher performance one of many areas they look at.

Education Resource Strategies

As the first decade of the 21st century progressed, many districts began to look at their finances in new ways. Educational funding often has been formulaic and allocated according to the federal and state program structure. In 2002, two management consultants, Karen Hawley Miles and Stephen Frank, former members of the prestigious business consulting firm Bain & Company, formed the nonprofit organization Education Resource Strategies (ERS) to "change the way people, time, and money are used in urban education so that all students receive the support they need to succeed."[23] They have partnered with many districts to focus on financial reform, with support from large foundations, including Broad, Gates, Carnegie, and others. Part of what ERS does is to look across data systems at spending in school, program, and classroom levels. In 2008, Miles and Frank wrote *The Strategic School: Making the Most of People, Time, and Money*, in which they contemplate schools reducing labor costs by configuring teachers and aides in different ways to accomplish the same instructional goals.[24]

ERS's work provides an important example of new uses for data that have become more common during the educational data movement. ERS uses district datasets to support financial and cost-effectiveness analyses. As more data become integrated and data are classified more specifically by grade, subject, and learning goals, it will be possible for financial analysts to look deeper into specific student needs and how a different combination of labor and technology can work to satisfy them. This analysis will have the potential to specifically target teachers and different teacher labor options. Is it more cost-effective for a district to use fewer senior teachers who have longer tenure in the system, or to use more inexperienced teachers with lower costs, but with a greater possibility of turnover? These analyses also might look at how effective one arrangement of staff is versus another, or how effective one approach to professional development is in terms of providing value.

The True Believers

The first three organizations discussed—the Broad Academy and Residency, Education Pioneers, and the Strategic Data Project—are active in creating a network of believers in educational data. As with TFA, some who enter through one of these programs stay in education a short time. Many, however, stay longer. Some progress from being Pioneers to Broad Residents or SDP fellows. Some Broad Residents ("Broadies") have worked in senior staff positions and then become executive officers in school districts. Several have filled senior positions at the DoED and worked in leadership positions of large foundations, including those involved in the educational data movement. Many have gone on to work in positions in other foundations. Across these groups, the use of data is central. It is featured in the groups' training and mentoring. These networks are filled with believers—both in their own ability to make an impact on educational challenges and also in the power of data in that work. In some ways, they are reminiscent of the Peace Corps and the social justice volunteers from the 1960s. In fact, it is not uncommon for those who pursue these paths to have some Peace Corps, TFA, or similar social action experience. In these new roles, the reformers travel to urban centers of poverty and blight to work for better educational outcomes. They also are paid competitive professional salaries and gain access to professional opportunities through their work. They are producing new kinds of findings about the use of data in large educational systems. But their projects and their findings have been largely separate from the research into data use and from the educational research community. And, like most other research at this level, the connection to the technical core and instruction is distant.

TEACHER EVALUATION: WIDGETS, IMPACT, AND PAR

Moving into the second decade of the 21st century, many districts had transitioned into a focus on measuring teachers through their contributions to student test score growth, principally through VAMs. Teacher evaluations are systemically quite complex because they occur across several levels of the system. Many state education departments are involved because states control licensure and because federal programs, such as Race to the Top, are committed to the states. At the same time, teachers work for the school districts that are responsible for the human capital function and hold important data on teachers and students. The evaluations that rate teachers' classroom practice are conducted largely in schools and often led by school principals.

Teacher evaluations were not always such a big deal. In 2009, after the field had seen several years of studies questioning the value of teacher credentials, the New Teacher Project produced an important policy report titled *The Widget Effect: Our National Failure to Acknowledge and Act on Differences in Teacher Effectiveness.*[25] The report exposed the fact that teacher evaluations could be suspect because, in all but very few instances, districts were rating all teachers as excellent or very good, even though the quality of teaching was widely understood to vary significantly from classroom to classroom with many average and poor performers. While research into high-quality teaching had been occurring for decades, most districts had not committed to robust evaluation systems. In the years following this report, pressure mounted to fix a perceived teacher quality problem, and there was a dramatic interest in using test data for evaluating teachers.

Teacher Evaluation Methods

By the time of the *Widget Effect* report, there were already a number of ways to evaluate teachers based largely on observing how they taught. These methods of observing teacher work and ranking teachers' performance all involve structured protocols and rubrics that are used by one or more observers to rate a teacher in the classroom. These approaches can be called "classroom observations," "teacher observations," or "principal observations" (because principals conduct them). These systems, all of them, entail breaking down instruction into discrete categories, although there is no consensus in research or practice as to what those categories should be. One of the oldest, developed by researcher Robert Marzano in the 1990s, has five dimensions of teaching that research has shown effective teachers do well.[26] While the number of dimensions in the Marzano approach has grown to 12, all the current evaluation approaches are in some ways related to Marzano's work in that they focus on a set of activities that teachers should be good at, evaluate teachers on those dimensions, and then try to connect teachers to professional development to help them improve on those areas they are rated weak in. Also in the 1990s, Charlotte Danielson developed her Framework for Teaching (FFT), often considered to be the most popular in use. Danielson worked with the Educational Testing Service on its PRAXIS tests of teachers and wrote about tasks and rubrics in her *Teacher Evaluation to Enhance Professional Practice* (2000), co-authored with Thomas McGreal. Her approach has become a mainstay of the maturing teacher observation movement.[27]

As the first decade of the 21st century drew to a close, initiatives developed in the Obama administration and from many supporters of test-based accountability to evaluate teachers based on their students' test scores. Many districts began to use VAMs to rank their teachers. Some developed their own, many contracted for a model, and a few used models developed by their state. These models are dependent on the data that are collected in the district and also on some critical items, such as class rosters, that are managed in schools. Different districts had to deal with how much emphasis to give the VAM for teachers. Race to the Top required that grant recipients give substantial weight to student growth, but exactly how different districts and states chose to implement their evaluation requirements varied. There are practical considerations for the districts. On the one hand, using a VAM based on existing state test data is a short path to meeting the requirement. On the other hand, VAMs often produce results with high levels of error and are usually unpopular with teachers.

Across the nation, the two dominant methods of evaluation—VAMs and observational rubrics—began to be used, although in different proportions, to build teacher and in some cases human capital systems that are used with many type of staff. Many of these systems are built around integrated databases so that they represent a *new kind of data system* that is not well represented in the literature on data use. Even though they are not considered instructional systems, these teacher evaluation systems are technologies that have the potential to greatly influence what occurs inside classrooms and who stays in which classrooms.

Case Study: IMPACT

One of the most advanced and also one of the most controversial teacher evaluation systems was developed by the DC Public Schools (DCPS) starting in the 2009–10 school year. The system, named IMPACT, was established under the leadership of the polarizing chancellor Michelle Rhee, with cooperation of the local teachers union (which later sought her ouster). DCPS received more than $75 million in private foundation funding, including from the Broad and Walton Foundations, in support of teacher improvement efforts.[28] While IMPACT often is identified with Michelle Rhee, two senior staff—Kaya Henderson, who succeeded Rhee as chancellor, and Jason Kamras, who became the chief of human capital—were the system's architects. Both Henderson and Kamras had been TFA teachers. After teaching in the Bronx, Henderson worked in several leadership positions for TFA and then with Rhee at the New Teacher Project. Kamras was educated at Princeton before coming to Washington, DC, in 1995 to teach in a DCPS middle school. In 2005 he was named National Teacher of the Year. Later, he served on the Obama administration transition team.

IMPACT is important for several reasons. It is one of the first large-scale systems using a VAM to be operational, and its results have been discussed in the press. The evaluations using these VAM scores have been used to provide bonuses to teachers for whom these test-based results showed student growth and termination for teachers whose test-based results were poor. It is also a comprehensive system with many technology components that may represent an example for others in the future. It is a broad staff evaluation system that covers more than teachers, as it also is used to provide expectations for 26 different job categories, including library media specialists, counselors, school-based psychologists, social workers, and even custodians. It is also one of best-documented systems, with a library of guidebooks that detail expectations and what will contribute to an evaluation. It also is built on a technology platform that includes a data system and video library of exemplary teaching.

The development of IMPACT included an extensive consultative process that included many focus groups with teachers and parents. The result was multifaceted with an individual teacher VAM for tested subjects and a school-based composite VAM score applied to all who work in a school, combined with other measures, including an observational protocol called the Teaching and Learning Framework. The IMPACT classroom practice component includes five separate observations for each teacher per year, as well as conferences around those observations. Some are conducted by principals and some by trained master educators with relevant subject knowledge. The conferences—structured around the master educator's observation report and scores—allow master educators and teachers to discuss a recent lesson observation and the strengths and areas for growth demonstrated by the teacher. These meetings allow teachers to alert the evaluators to factors that may not be obvious, and that influence the way the teacher teaches, as well as to seek content-specific guidance and resources.

Figure 4.2 shows five different jobs that are covered under IMPACT and the relative weight of different evaluation components for the 2010–11 school year. For a teacher in a grade and subject that had accountability tests, the individual value-added (IVA) score accounted for 50% of the evaluation, the Teaching and Learning Framework evaluation for 40%, and the school's value-added score (SVA) and commitment to school community (CSC) for 5% each. For a teacher in a nontested subject, the IVA score was replaced by a smaller percentage of a student growth measure based on the teachers' own assessments (10%), and the Teaching and Learning Framework-based observation was weighted more heavily at 75%. For special education teachers, this pattern is continued, but with the addition of new evaluation areas for the timeliness of eligibility processing for a special educator's caseload, and for the completion of the Individual Education Program (IEP) reports. Two other school personnel areas—office staff and custodians—used both the SVA and CSC scores plus specific detailed expectations that included attending to data quality for office staff, and completion of paperwork for supervisory custodians.

FIGURE 4.2. Different Components of Five Different Jobs Rated Under IMPACT

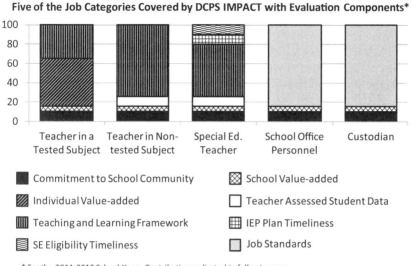

Five of the Job Categories Covered by DCPS IMPACT with Evaluation Components*

■ Commitment to School Community   ⊠ School Value-added

▨ Individual Value-added   ☐ Teacher Assessed Student Data

▥ Teaching and Learning Framework   ⊞ IEP Plan Timeliness

▤ SE Eligibility Timeliness   ▢ Job Standards

* For the 2011-2012 School Year. Contributions adjusted in following year.

While there has been little published research on IMPACT or the other teacher evaluation systems being developed nationwide, *Inside Impact*, a report issued in 2011 by Pulitzer–Prize–winning author Susan Headden at a think tank named Education Sector (often funded by leading data-oriented philanthropies), provides some insights.[29] Headden interviewed teachers, principals, master teachers, and administrators. She described the evaluation process, reporting how master educator ratings can vary and that discussions with evaluators did allow for some modifications of scores based on information the observers might not have had when they initially rated the teacher, although those cases were "rare."[30] Not surprisingly, teachers who rated well tended to have a better belief in the system. Perhaps surprisingly, she also found that many teachers appreciated the detailed feedback they got as part of the evaluation process—*even when they were not rated highly.*

IMPACT is like a first-generation automation effort, as described in Chapter 2. According to Kamras, "In years past the evaluations were on paper forms in filing cabinets all across the school system."[31] With IMPACT, he says, senior leadership can use the database information to look across the district and across different components of the evaluation system as they investigate patterns in teaching and areas needing improvement, and plan for future human capital needs. Kamras described some of the features of IMPACT:

Because all of the IMPACT information is captured in our online platform, we can now make data-informed decisions about our people. For example, we now know who needs help and in what pedagogical areas. That, in turn, allows us [to] tailor our professional development offerings in the most strategic way possible.[32]

IMPACT has met with opposition. Some have questioned its fairness[33] and some have claimed it is biased because teachers in the more affluent parts of the city were far more likely to be rated as highly effective than teachers in poor sections.[34] A *Washington Post* article in 2012 described how a teacher who had scored well on observations of her classroom practice was terminated because of low student growth as calculated by the VAM.[35] On the other hand, there have been reasons that a school system like DCPS would want a strong system that both rewards the good teachers and helps eliminate the poor ones. Large urban districts often have been less attractive places of employment for teachers, and many have used them as a stepping-stone to positions in other, usually suburban, school systems where the circumstances can be easier and pay often better.

While still controversial, the IMPACT system is evolving. As it evolves, it also becomes more established. In order to get the bonuses, which can be as much as $25,000 in some cases, teachers give up some of the security that their contract afforded them. In its initial year, IMPACT evaluations were used to justify performance bonuses for 636 (16%) of teachers and to dismiss 75(2%) of teachers. The next year, IMPACT was used to offer 663 bonuses, and 206 teachers were terminated for performance. By the third year, 988 bonuses were offered, and only 98 teachers were terminated for performance.[36] In 2011, DCPS introduced new tests into 2nd grade and 9th grade to allow it to evaluate more teachers with a significant value-added component.[37] At about the same time, DCPS relaxed the requirements for teacher observations for teachers who had been rated as highly effective. For the 2012–13 school year, DCPS reduced the contribution of the IVA score from 50% to 35% in tested subjects. Chapter 5 discusses a major study into the reliability of different teacher evaluation components that suggests a possible motivating factor in this reduction.

Case Study: Peer Assistance and Review (PAR)

For teachers, IMPACT began as a system with a high reliance on student test scores. Other districts also use student test scores at varying levels, including many as low as 20% of a teacher's total score. Some do not use student test scores at all. The Montgomery County Public Schools system, which borders DCPS, does not. Instead, they use a Peer Assistance and Review (PAR) approach. PAR was developed in 1971 by a teachers union leader in Ohio and has been used by many districts nationwide. PAR at MCPS is a component of a larger Professional Growth System that covers staff as well as teachers. The idea behind PAR is that once a teacher is identified as needing support—usually a first-year or veteran teacher—the teacher works with a master educator to either improve his or her instruction or be counseled out of the field. *The New York Times* called PAR a national example. According to Jerry Weast, the MCPS superintendent until 2011:

> In the 11 years since PAR began, the panels have voted to fire 200 teachers, and 300 more have left rather than go through the PAR process. . . . It took three to five years to build the trust to get PAR in place. . . . Teachers had to see we weren't playing gotcha.[38]

MCPS did not join the State of Maryland in its application for RttT, which would have required evaluating teachers based on student test scores. One of the most affluent districts in the nation, MCPS declined to participate in the process, citing concerns about the use of test scores in gauging teacher quality. According to Weast: "We don't believe the tests are reliable. . . . You don't want to turn your system into a test factory."[39]

Just as IMPACT and PAR are different approaches to evaluation, so are their districts different. It would be easy to conclude that one of these programs is better than the other, while ignoring the differences between them. While both DCPS and MCPS have affluent and poor student populations, DCPS has higher concentrations of poverty, whereas MCPS has a more privileged student spectrum. These systems have different histories. For decades, MCPS has been a highly sought-after place of employment, where the salaries and benefits have been among the best in the nation and the relationship with the teachers unions historically has been collaborative. DCPS has a legacy more similar to other large urban systems, with many management and staff difficulties and a relationship with the teachers union that has been contentious. Not surprisingly, teachers often have used DCPS as a training opportunity and then transitioned to MCPS.

Many important questions remain about teacher evaluation and also about the systems that districts use for it. Among the most important is whether they actually help keep the teachers a district needs while helping eliminate those they do not want. Do these tools identify the differences between teachers *independent* of the conditions they teach in? Are they fair? Do they work as designed? Fundamentally, these difficult questions require a kind of information that has yet to emerge as reliable as these questions require. But, there has been some new research. In 2012, The New Teacher Project conducted a study on teacher retention that produced a report titled

The Irreplaceables: Understanding the Real Retention Crisis in America's Urban Schools.[40] The study was funded by several philanthropies, including the Gates Foundation, was advised by CALDER researchers, and produced a case study of the DCPS IMPACT system. The study found IMPACT helped DCPS remove their lower performers while maintaining retention rates of higher performers comparable to other large urban districts. The financial incentives seemed to make a difference, as fewer teachers cited compensation as a reason for leaving, although still many more top performers left DCPS than left MCPS. As to one of the most important issues surrounding IMPACT, *Washington Post* reporter Emma Brown wrote:

> The TNTP report confirmed a fact long debated among District educators and politicians: Highly effective teachers are less likely to teach in schools with large numbers of poor children. That either means that few of the city's best teachers are working in needy schools, or — as many teachers contend — the IMPACT evaluation system is unfair to teachers working in the most difficult environments.

DCPS's Jason Kamras, one of the designers of IMPACT, acknowledged that with the progress there was more work to do. As to the question Brown posed about why the system shows fewer good teachers working in high-needs schools, he said, "I think, at the end of the day, we'll find out that it may be a little bit of both." In terms of large and expensive systems like IMPACT designed to reshape instructional performance, fundamental questions remain as the role of social context continues to loom large.

As the limits of teacher-performance focused policies became better known, some school systems, including DCPS, have begun to focus on school leadership. *The Irreplacables* study showed the importance of building a culture that makes teachers want to stay, and the observations of teachers required by IMPACT were helping to create a mechanism for these conversation at the level of the school. These school-level and cultural issues are topics that are discussed in the next several chapters. What is also discussed is the role that different artifacts—from student test scores to examples of student work to observations of teaching—play in these collaborative conversations.

DISTRICT DATA SYSTEMS IN THE MIDDLE

Districts are very much in the middle of the educational data movement. They are between state agencies, which in many cases are still building integrated longitudinal systems, and their schools, where the responsibility for delivering instruction lies. They are, like states, evolving technologically, and many of their data systems are plagued with quality and integration challenges. They have built information systems and collected many forms of data, but have seen only glimpses of how these systems are changing or improving. Culturally, many central offices continue to operate as they have for decades, as separate organizations. What is remarkable given the important role that districts play in this movement is how thin the knowledge base is about how different districts are progressing through this period. There are over 15,000 districts nationwide, and only a small number have been studied in terms of their data use. Of those that have been studied, usually it was in the form of brief case studies and snapshots rather than in-depth treatments that describe the process of change.

Districts also fall in the middle of different forms of evidence. On the one hand, there are communities of researchers who often use traditional approaches to understand how districts operate. On the other hand, there are new communities of business-oriented analysts who have less grounding in educational research but have been able to make some inroads into using data to identify waste and improve organizational performance. These communities are largely separate, and neither community has made much progress in connecting district data systems to instructional improvement.

Important questions about data and equity also occur with district data systems. One of the weaknesses of NCLB was the way in which it accentuated equity gaps through a design that treated all schools the same and used the same set of subgroups independent of a school's population and resources. In the area of district data systems, there are also issues of equity and design worth considering. Many of the districts that have received the most attention from funders and district-based interventions to promote data use are those with disadvantaged and at-risk populations. When a large data-focused foundation or one of its projects enters into an arrangement with a district, the odds are good that the district is large, urban, and with a high dose of poverty. As the DCPS IMPACT and MCPS PAR comparison illustrates, the districts with the harder working conditions also may use evaluation systems with stronger sanctions and rewards. It likely will be many years before the systemic impacts of these types of approaches are appreciated.

III

THE TECHNICAL, INSTRUCTIONAL CORE

This part deals with those areas of educational systems that are closest to students—those that could be called the technical or instructional core of education. Others who have used the term *technical core* in education often limit its use to students, teachers, materials, and classrooms, which is also a traditional view of instruction. This part begins with a chapter that draws on this traditional perspective of schools comprising of instructional classrooms. However, those familiar with schools and education know, and research documents, that a school is more than a collection of classrooms. It is also a critically important factor in student learning. Many consequential decisions for students—including the teachers students are assigned to and what extra supports they receive—are made in the school with the active involvement of school leaders and specialists. School leaders are instrumental in building staff, cultures, and local tools that have an important role in student development. The second chapter in this part discusses schools as collaborative structures and how data have and can impact learning across classrooms. These two chapters support a discussion in Chapter 7 about how new technologies can both make the traditional technical core more productive and possibly reshape it.

One could draw a conceptual line at the school, as University of Wisconsin professor Richard Halverson has done, and locate some reform policies, such as NCLB, as external to the school and others as internal. External policies aim at fixing a school from the outside, while internal approaches are less coded in policy and focus on empowering school leaders to develop their own solutions.[1] This boundary is not pure and clean. Some reform efforts are designed to restructure the relationships between individual schools and their districts. A few researchers exploring educational data—including Coburn, Supovitz, Young, and Wayman—have tried to work across that boundary.[2] However, if we look at the data systems of today, that conceptual line around a school has a lot of merit. Most of the infrastructures for formal educational information exist as part of, and are managed by, districts and state organizations, not schools. And the work with students—the work that data systems are intended to support—happens within the schools and is led on a day-to-day basis by school staff. This book, then, uses the line Halverson sketched as a way to identify the beginning of the technical core.

Chapter 5 is focused on understanding some of the knowledge base around data and the traditional role of teachers. Some of it relates to teachers as the consumers of data in their classrooms. Some of it relates to the discussion of data about teachers and teacher evaluation from Chapter 4. Chapter 5 explores this traditional role of teachers and how that role is intermeshed with a traditional design of schools. Chapter 6 expands the technical core discussion with a look at schools and teachers in teams. It illustrates the distributed and collaborative nature of schools, explains how the research on educational data use intersects with other research on school effectiveness, and addresses students with different needs—central issues involving information's power in education. In this school view, we see some of the issues that are central to the technical core, but are not always limited to traditional classrooms. These elements include cultures of success, student differences, and distributed leadership. One of the lessons from other fields that have used information is how digital information has allowed some organizations to rearrange and redesign staff roles for greater efficiency and effectiveness. Finally, Chapter 7 looks at some new technologies that have emerged in recent years, with the promise to make the technical core more efficient and possibly help reshape traditional roles and organizational structures.

Schools, Classrooms, and the Classical Model of Teaching

One of the greatest challenges for researchers studying data use is to understand how it impacts what occurs in schools. This often has been targeted at instruction and the work of teachers in classrooms. Schools are more than teachers and classrooms, however. Schools are cultural entities. While Chapter 6 will explore schools more fully, this chapter will look at the data movement with a limited view of schools as comprised of teachers and classrooms. It uses this more traditional frame to establish some foundational concepts that at first might seem disconnected—schools responding to NCLB, formative classroom assessment, reform organizations, a large study into teacher evaluations, and a conceptual discussion of the role of teachers—but that come together through the chapters that follow.

SCHOOLS AND TEACHERS RESPOND TO NCLB

At the end of the first decade of this century, school buildings often looked very similar to the ones that existed a decade or several decades before. However, there are some important changes, much a direct response to NCLB, and some more visible than others. For example, many schools have data walls in public hallways to let staff and visitors know how the school is performing and what the leadership considers important. Some schools have data rooms where staff meet and plan. These rooms usually have walls covered with information about individual student performance on various tests and in some rare cases how students' performance has changed over time. In many schools new personnel, including literacy and math coaches/specialists, have become established along with data specialists. These coaches make professional development more local and school-based and they often use data analysis in their work.

A knowledgeable visitor who spent some time in the school watching how the teachers, leaders, and other staff interacted also might see some differences. Where a school from several decades ago typically would have had a principal who delegated instruction to the teachers, some principals today are more involved in their teachers' work. This likely would be the case even where principals were not engaged in teacher evaluation, as many are today. It also would not be uncommon to have groups of teachers meet to discuss test scores and other issues that relate to their instruction. However, teachers working this way and principals taking ownership of instruction are by no means universal. Many schools still operate with very traditional separation between what one teacher does and what other teachers do, and between the teachers and the leadership. What would be hard for the observer to know, as it has been for researchers and evaluators in recent years, was the extent to which these external and internal uses of data are making the school a better school and for whom.

In the years after NCLB was enacted, it became hard to disassociate the data movement from the law that had such a large role in making practitioners look at data. Some of the initial research on NCLB's effects was not so positive. Researchers reported some teachers were likely to put on more of a show about using data than actually integrating data into their instruction. One of the most widely reported examples of gaming—practices where educators try various strategies, which may include cheating, to get better scores—involves focusing on "bubble kids." Bubble kids are students whose scores put them close to a proficiency cutoff, for example, in the high end of the basic range. Bubble kids may be able to reach the next proficiency level with a modest amount of growth compared with students who are further behind. Northwestern University professor James Spillane and his student, future Harvard professor John Diamond, compared two elementary schools at risk for being labeled failing under NCLB with two schools that were not at risk.[1] In the at-risk schools they found that there were deliberate attempts to focus instruction and opportunities toward the bubble kids in the hopes of getting them over the bar to the next proficiency level, meaning that those further behind got less attention. While the accountability system was theoretically the same for all students and schools, in practice the same types of data were being used in very different ways depending on the circumstances of the school.

In *Test Driven*, University of Maryland professors Linda Valli and Robert Croninger provide detailed evidence of the introduction of district data policies, data systems, and support staff focusing on data that were emerging in schools just after enactment of NCLB. They found that the connection between test data and student learning was far less powerful than had been anticipated by NLCB. The test data were usually out of date and associated with high-stakes policies that caused schools to adopt test-taking cultures at odds with cultures of universal learning and educator responsibility. They state that "in test taking cultures learning is supplanted rather than supported by assessments. Schools participate in gaming strategies to avoid adverse consequences and teachers reshape instructional activities to mirror standardized tests."[2] These issues and more were detailed in *Collateral Damage: How High-Stakes Testing Corrupts America's Schools* by Sharon Nichols and former American Educational Research Association president David Berliner, who detailed many of the negative systemic impacts of NCLB and its emphasis on tests and test data.[3]

BROADER RESEARCH ON SCHOOL AND TEACHER DATA USE

As the decade continued and some larger and deeper studies were conducted, the picture of data use in the schools included more detail. RAND researchers began to report on some of the reasons that data use is resisted, including timeliness and availability of the data. Data about the previous year's kids often had little value to teachers. Also, many educators perceived test data to be faulty and unreliable indicators of student success, a topic discussed in more detail in Chapter 8. Teachers (and other educators) often did not have sufficient knowledge of statistics to properly use the data to make appropriate inferences.[4] As the preceding chapters discussed, researchers looking at data use have searched with difficulty for appropriate research frameworks and solid findings that can help build deep understandings of how data operate in educational systems. This research is weakest when it comes to describing how teachers actually use data in practice. Even though teachers seem largely impacted by the push for data use *and* there are many ways to see how the data movement is affecting teachers' environments and work, much remains unknown about how teachers use the data they are provided.

The DoED *Study of Education Data Systems and Decision Making* was a rich source of survey and case study data pointing to success and barriers with school data use, and from it a more complex picture the relationships between test-dominated data and practice emerged. The study found that schools increasingly had access to data and were using them in practice. It found that there were growing organizational supports from districts to help schools integrate data into their work. It also found that "data from student data systems are being used in school improvement efforts but are having little effect on teachers' daily instructional decisions."[5] The study included case studies from districts considered to be exemplary and found a range of uses for the data, with classroom and instructional purposes being less common than school-level uses (see Table 5.1).

This study is important. It occurred after NCLB and the educational data movement had been established for some time. It is the only study of its scale conducted on the data movement and showed that:

TABLE 5.1. Frequency of Data Use in Schools, 2007–2008

Data Use	Frequency
School improvement planning, including setting of quantitative goals	35
Curriculum planning based on item or subscale analysis	25
Student placement in classes or special services	22
Grouping or regrouping of students within a class	21
Tailoring instruction to the skill needs of individuals or small groups	15
Deciding whether or what to re-teach	13
Identifying teachers with successful strategies to emulate their approach	11
Referring students from classroom for supports or services	9
Determining what aspects of your teaching are working well/poorly	8
Evaluating teacher performance	7

Table based on U.S. Department of Education, Office of Planning, Evaluation, and Policy Development (2010).

1. Schools are dependent on the type of data available from their districts and many districts lacked fully integrated data systems and assessments for schools to use.
2. Schools progress through stages of data use, initially using data for accountability and improvement planning, later for more directly student-related purposes, and still later for instructional purposes.
3. Teachers use data more when led by their principals and there is variation in the way different principals approach data in their schools.
4. Training and support are important for helping practitioners both to use the technology they have and to understand the meaning of the data they have.

This study showed how there had been a steady march forward in data capacity and use in schools, stating in its conclusion that "educational data systems are improving, but the combination of technical and human resources available in schools has yet to constitute a capacity for routine use of data to support instructional decisions."[6] It isn't just that practitioners need to learn how to use the data, but that they need certain kinds of data to be able to engage in meaningful activities, and in many cases those kinds of data are not yet available.[7]

FORMATIVE ASSESSMENTS IN THE CLASSROOM

One aspect of teachers' use of data for which there is a solid research base to show impact on learning is the use of formative classroom assessments. Formative assessments contrast with summative assessments, which are designed to measure learning from outside of instruction. Formative assessments sometimes are called short-cycle assessments because they bring information to the teacher that is more immediate and allows for more rapid decision making than is the case with less frequent kinds of assessments.[8]

When policymakers began pushing the data-driven, decision-making agenda early in the 21st century, educational researchers had been working on instructional uses of assessments for several decades. NCLB, however, most likely highlighted its importance. Beginning in the 1970s and 1980s, the term *formative assessment* began to appear in educational research literature. It had a simple proposition that was new for many teachers: assessments in the classroom could both help teachers teach *and* help students learn. Over the years, through the 1990s and into this century, formative assessment became an active research movement. In a seminal review of the research titled *Inside the Black Box: Raising Standards Through Classroom Assessment*, British researchers Paul Black and Dylan Wiliam showed how in study after study, across grades and subject areas, teachers' use of assessments can account for important gains in student learning, often by as much as half a grade or more.[9]

It is important to remember that from a teacher's perspective, formative assessments may be embodied in things the teacher already does: asks questions, gives quizzes, and have students work on projects. An important component of formative assessments involves feedback. Knowing that formative assessments can improve learning does not translate into changed practice. Because teaching can be so demanding, developing assessments and giving feedback seem to add to the teacher's workload. Formative assessments also can be called by another name that is important to consider for several reasons: *curriculum-embedded formative assessments*. Assessments that a teacher can give in the process of working through a lesson are embedded within the curriculum, regardless of whether those assessments are developed by the district, teacher, publisher, or another source.

There is still fragmentary evidence about which teachers are using formative assessments, how they are using them, and under what circumstances. Further, what research does exist often is disconnected from the research on data use. While researching formative assessment practices on a large scale is costly and difficult, teacher evaluation programs can provide a window on this because evaluators are inside teachers' classrooms and often rating them on those practices. The Measures of Effective Teaching study involving thousands of teachers, which is discussed later in this chapter, showed that just under half of the teachers observed scored good or great in their use of classroom assessments, whereas just over half scored fair or poor.[10] This finding—that roughly half of teachers do this well—was consistent when the same lessons were rated using different raters and observation frameworks.

The *Study of Education Data Systems and Decision Making*, conducted from 2006 to 2010 for the DoED, described the need for more formative assessments to be developed by districts to support teachers, indicating that many teachers still need tools to help assess students. In many cases today the assessments teachers give are informal and nondigital. They include short written tasks, asking questions of the class, and/or having students come to the board to explain something. These assessments, while useful, do not create data streams for later analysis. This could be changing, however, because of digital technology, as discussed in Chapter 7. New technologies, including both free and fee-based, web, PC, and handheld-based assessments are becoming commonplace, especially in the early and tested grades. Teachers now have many more tools at their disposal. Increasingly, textbook providers have been including assessments within their products so that teachers who use commercially published materials are increasingly able to use assessments that are aligned to them and can integrate easily with data analysis platforms the publishers also sell.

TFA AND KIPP: REFORMERS OF THE TECHNICAL CORE

While the data movement proceeded through its early and challenging stages in the years following enactment of NCLB, organizations that in many cases began before NCLB were expanding their role in American education and using data as integral parts of their "reform" approaches. This includes alternative teacher preparation and charter schools, both of which have received much support from the same foundations and policymakers promoting educational data. One of the most visible and successful of these is Teach for America (TFA). TFA started in 1989 when Princeton University undergraduate Wendy Kopp decided to design a service program for teaching in high-need American schools. She modeled her corps after the Peace Corps, which TFA is now larger than. TFA teachers sign on for a 2-year commitment and receive their training in teaching from TFA, which also coaches and mentors them as they work. Fueled by philanthropic support and contracts with school districts that regularly employ TFA teachers, the organization has grown dramatically. In 2012, TFA had more than 9,000 teachers (corps members) in classrooms and a national staff in excess of 1,500.

For some, TFA has been a symbol of unwanted interference that threatens teachers and the quality of education. One of the main criticisms is that it undercuts traditional teacher communities with lower-cost labor and uses narrow definitions of teaching aligned with tests. For others, TFA has represented a type of can-do spirit to tackle some of America's most pressing educational challenges: finding teachers for the most disadvantaged areas, developing leaders who have a commitment to results, and building education leaders who share a commitment to student success. TFA has had a curious relationship to the educational data movement. It was not founded as a data organization and would not be characterized as one. At the same time, the educational data movement's story has multiple interesting connections to TFA. Understanding them is important for developing a fuller understanding of the changes occurring in education related to data.

TFA's extensive mentoring and coaching process often involves looking at student performance data. Much of these data are test-oriented. Annie Lewis, Vice President of Teacher Preparation Program Design, has said, "Student achievement is non-negotiable."[11] As a national network that logistically supports teachers across a range of institutions, TFA helps its corps members develop and share classroom assessment tools. The data TFA collects, however, are broader than assessments. The organization also is concerned with how to engage students and deliver instruction, which corps members and regions are most successful, and understanding characteristics about candidates that can predict why some perform better than others in the classroom. TFA was also one of the earliest collectors of data about teaching. It has been looking at different ways to measure teaching and has used data to help identify characteristics of future teachers for years, although for the most part these data have been used only internally. Only part of TFA's connection to the educational data movement is in its actual classroom work. Now with over 24,000 alumni, TFA's ideas and influence have spread beyond those in classrooms.

Many charter schools have strong connections to TFA. Some were formed by TFA alumni, including the Knowledge Is Power Program (KIPP), founded by two TFA teachers in 1994. Like TFA, KIPP also has received both criticism and acclaim, with much criticism coming from traditional sectors and acclaim from funders. It has gone on to become one of the most successful charter networks by repeatedly demonstrating that its students can perform well on tests. While they are separate organizations, TFA and

KIPP share important connections. The president of the KIPP Foundation is married to Wendy Kopp, and many KIPP organizations draw from TFA corps members and alumni. Like TFA, KIPP has received continued financial support from major foundations with business affiliations. With more than 100 schools, KIPP also uses information across its different regions. KIPP has developed its own sets of metrics that include achievement, school culture, leadership and organization, where its graduates go, climate, and many other factors that could indicate good or poor quality in the system.

Although KIPP is committed to student achievement and is a strong proponent of data use across its network of schools, it also has been developing alternatives to traditional high-stakes tests. In 2005, Dave Levin, one of KIPP's co-founders, began to look seriously at issues of student character.[12] KIPP had always stressed both academics, including test performance, and personal traits, such as empathy and determination. Its slogan, and the title of a 2009 book about KIPP by *Washington Post* writer Jay Mathews, is *Work Hard. Be Nice.*[13] Levin and KIPP discovered that students who did well on tests were not always the ones who succeeded in college. In many cases, those who did well after leaving KIPP had other character traits, such as determination and perseverance, that were not tested or even well understood. While doing well on tests was important, it was not sufficient. Levin joined with another school leader in thinking about this issue. They then connected with professors from the psychology departments at the Universities of Michigan and Pennsylvania who had done work on the psychology of character. This collaboration resulted in a *character report card* for KIPP students. This report card has 11 dimensions and allows the schools to track the personal development of their students as a complement to achievement.[14] The idea of focusing on perseverance and reliance in students was not new. Many traditional educational researchers had been exploring this issue for a long time. What was new was that these ideas were formalized into a codified data type used in practice rather than a concept that appears in a research literature.

As the educational data movement continues to develop, TFA and KIPP, and many organizations with connections to them or modeled after them, will play a role. Alternative teacher preparation programs are continuing to gain support, and charter school systems are growing beyond their original locations to span states and become in essence a new category of school district, although one that often works outside of traditional educational research. This sector may be able to experiment and innovate with new, technology-rich educational approaches more easily than traditional school systems and likely will continue to have access to foundation funding to help it do so.

MEASURING EFFECTIVE TEACHING

As strong performance evaluations of teachers entered the American educational scene at the end of the first decade of this century, it became essential to define what teachers do, so that they can be measured and graded, given feedback, and connected to appropriate professional development. With evaluation systems such as IMPACT, discussed in Chapter 4, and the many others being developed using combinations of test scores and classroom observations, the stakes were raised for teachers. In many cases, their careers will be tied to these evaluation instruments, and important questions emerged about the validity of those instruments. Would better evaluations according to one or another framework be more strongly associated with student outcomes or would they have little or no relationship? The stronger the association, the more easily teachers can be held accountable for test-based results because those outcomes would align with how evaluators rate their work. The weaker the association, the more questions can be raised about the prospect of measuring teaching using test scores.

To describe something involves interpretation. To define something adds an expectation of precision, but does not require it. *Measurement*, however, is a more difficult and exacting process. It helps define and describe, but further structures with specific kinds of evidence. Evaluation systems require specifying the exact dimensions that teachers are judged on. While there is a broad recognition that teaching is complex, there is no consensus on what elements should be included in teacher evaluations or at what level of detail. As Chapter 4 discussed, there are dozens of different approaches to classifying this work, each defining teaching in a slightly different way.[15] Most address general teaching characteristics, while a few are specific to domains such as math, science, and literacy. One of the most widely used is Charlotte Danielson's Framework for Teaching (FFT), which includes 22 elements (e.g., providing feedback to students, demonstrating flexibility and responsiveness) organized into four domains. Another nationally recognized approach, the Classroom Assessment Scoring System (CLASS) developed at the University of Virginia, uses 11 dimensions (e.g., concept development, quality of feedback) organized into three major domains. CLASS began with early childhood education, but expanded. When it was used in later grades, the dimensions evolved to reflect different things teachers do with older students.[16] While there has been little attention to teachers' use of data in the major teacher observation frameworks, some have categories for "classroom assessment" and "keeping records." Note that the DCPS IMPACT does, however, make the use of data an explicit job requirement for teachers and others.

Measuring and comparing these qualitative frameworks with the quantitative, test-based, value-added models (VAMs) is very difficult to do well. A rigorous study that would have the statistical heft to allow the comparison of different observational systems would need a huge investment in terms of teachers, students, and researchers. It could require the ability to randomly assign teachers to classrooms and collect research-quality evidence about what was occurring in those rooms. It would need trained raters who could observe instruction and reliably score it. And it would need a large management infrastructure.

To explore this issue of reliable teacher evaluations, the Gates Foundation launched the Measures of Effective Teaching (MET) project in 2009 with an initial investment of $45 million, which grew to over $50 million. MET was at that time, and likely will remain, the largest research program on teacher evaluation.[17] The project was intended to "provide an accurate and reliable picture of teaching effectiveness."[18] The study was looking beyond a simple quality metric toward "understanding what great teachers do and by improving the ways teachers gain insight into their practice, . . . help[ing] more teachers achieve success for their students." The MET study was significant not only in its scale, but also in what it found and did not find in terms of reliable indicators of teaching.

The MET project was led by Harvard professor Tom Kane, whose work several years earlier had shown how teacher credentials bore little relationship to student performance.[19] It included research partnerships with Dartmouth College, Harvard University, Stanford University, the University of Chicago, the University of Michigan, the University of Virginia, the University of Washington, the Educational Testing Service (ETS), RAND Corporation, and the New Teacher Center. It was conducted in seven large urban school districts: Dallas Independent School District, Denver Public Schools, Hillsborough County Public Schools, Memphis City Schools, New York City Department of Education, Pittsburgh Public Schools, and Charlotte-Mecklenburg Schools.[20] MET combined five different types of measures of classroom performance:

1. Student achievement gains on assessments, including standard accountability assessments and several alternates;
2. Teacher knowledge of how to teach their subjects (pedagogical content knowledge);
3. Classroom observations using six different classroom observation protocols that were rated by professional raters;
4. Student surveys of perceptions of the classroom instructional environment; and
5. Teachers' perceptions of working conditions at their school.

MET included over 3,000 teachers who volunteered to be part of the study and have their teaching recorded using innovative technology that allowed the entire room to be captured as a motion panorama. The technology allowed those evaluating the teaching remotely to see much of what the teachers saw as they were teaching, as well as what the students saw of the teachers and the whiteboard. The study resulted in over 7,500 recorded lessons that included over 48,000 students. Each lesson was scored three times, for more than 22,500 observation scores. ETS managed the scoring of the observational rubrics by training over 900 different raters. A significant component of this research involved rating the same lessons according to more than one rubric, so that observation rubrics can be compared with other forms of evidence and also with one another.

MET did find that it was possible to measure teaching, although with considerable imprecision. It found the observational rubrics were positively associated with student test score gains. They did not find the scores from observations of instruction showing one thing and the test scores showing the opposite. However, the statistical relationships between observations and scores were not strong. When a rater observed a single lesson, less than 40% of the variance was accounted for. As the number of observers of teaching increased, so did the relationship to student outcomes, reaching almost 70% with four observers. Accounting for two-thirds of the variance in student performance was good, but not nearly as strong as many hoped and not very strong by research standards. The value-added scores did help predict student achievement, although unexplained variation remained, indicating that using these measures on their own was risky. While these findings don't show an upper limit in terms of the reliability of these measures, they show that even with ample resources and a very strong design, there remains significant imprecision. In their final report the MET project stated, "Teaching is too complex for any single measure of performance to capture it accurately."[21]

Also, across different observational instruments, more teachers scored well on classroom management aspects and less well on deep instructional practice. This could be an important sign of how often teachers are engaging in deep practice versus delivering orderly, but maybe less engaging, content. Also, across the different observational frameworks, those that were based on general teaching practice, for example, CLASS and FFT, tended to cluster together, while the subject-specific teaching characteristics also clustered together, indicating that viewing teaching from a subject perspective and a general perspective could produce different kinds of ratings.[22] What MET showed about the reliability of evaluation instruments is only part of the story. Consistent with information reported on the DCPS IMPACT system that teachers valued the feedback and explicit expectations from the system, MET provided teachers with ways to view their teaching.[23] This could be an indication of just how often teachers work in isolation today. MET also found that surveys from students that were structured to reveal specific classroom actions that affect students (e.g., asking questions, working in teams), rather than simple satisfaction surveys, seemed to be meaningfully associated with student outcomes.

Sometimes a single study or series of studies can make a lasting imprint on policy. For example, in the years after the studies that began in 2006 showed how teacher credentials had little impact on their effectiveness in raising student test scores, there was a move away from focusing on teacher credentials in federal policy that provided momentum for outcomes-based evaluations of teachers. It may be interesting for historians to look at MET's findings at the end of 2011 and a shift in policy afterwards. In 2009, the *initial* expectation in Race to the Top and other federal programs was that teacher evaluation *could* be effectively done with test scores. The information that emerged from MET was that the imprecision in these scores was hard to eliminate. In 2010, researchers at CALDER came to a similar conclusion.[24] In 2012, just after MET results were known, the DoED began granting NCLB waivers using less strict approaches involving student growth. The policy discourse also shifted to be more inclusive of a broad range of evidence about teachers' contributions rather than the test dominance from a few years earlier. The shift in DCPS to a 35% weight rather than 50% of VAM scores occurred around the same time, and many public statements by DoED officials recognized that a mixture of measures should be used, with test scores being given a primary, but limited, role. This position also was aligned with what teachers unions had been saying in their support of evaluations for several years.

In terms of improving the young knowledge base on what great teachers do and helping gain insights into teacher practice, MET probably will be considered a landmark study. Its size and robust statistical design make it a standard, and its wealth of data likely will bring up new questions and research agendas in the future. MET also extended the range of what can be considered evidence about teaching quality. In a time when there were two dominant competing approaches to evaluating teachers—test scores and observations—MET made new types of measures, including surveys of students and teachers, a larger part of the research conversation. MET also produced a library of recorded video for use by researchers that will join several of the other large video collections researchers can use for in-depth study. The project also produced some guidelines that address the logistics of the evaluation process, considerations for managing raters of teachers, and the high levels of training required for classroom observers and principals. MET showed that these raters need to understand bias, interpretation, and evidence; the instructional philosophy behind the classroom observation instruments used to make high-stakes decisions; the value of a rich media library with multiple examples of every possible score; and the importance of practical and authentic observations in the training.[25]

THE CLASSICAL MODEL OF TEACHING AND ITS INFLUENCE ON THE KNOWLEDGE BASE

One of the greatest challenges of our time—of research, of school leadership, and now of measurement—is to define teaching or what teaching should be. The educational data movement occurs at time when there is great uncertainty about what it means to teach. The types of changes that education is going through, as other fields have before, impact jobs and roles and organizational structures. During this time, there has been a quest to describe the job of teachers in ways that can be used to compare teaching with other types of professions. The definition of teaching is an important factor in how we consider teachers' use of data in their jobs. Is their work mechanical—to transmit knowledge—or are they knowledge workers and knowledge creators? These are the kinds of questions that highlight what makes education different from other fields.

People with different backgrounds often see different things when they look at these adults who spend their days with children. Teachers are seen alternatively as caretakers, agents to deliver instructional content, low-skilled service providers, craftspeople, artists, managers who perform complex creative work, and experts to guide students and model for them what it means to be a user of language or pursuer of questions. Some have drawn comparisons of teachers to athletes, who combine talent and practice, play on teams, and perform better some years than others; to doctors and therapists, who are highly trained professionals and help improve the lives of their clients; to authority figures like ministers and clergy; and to public servants. Teachers also become like family members for some students who need emotional support and encouragement scarce outside of school.

While a teacher might be able to describe how he or she approaches the job, many teachers struggle with a broad and generalized definition of teaching. Having been with teachers many times in my education and work, I have found that often they can adequately describe only what *their* teaching is like, the tools and techniques *they* use, and what *they* believe guides their actions. Ask them to define *teaching generally* and the conversation is far less specific. Many defer to a belief that their teacher colleagues should have the ability to approach teaching in different ways with autonomy. Autonomy often has been the recommendation of teachers unions. It is part of many school cultures to think of classrooms as self-contained and to trust that teachers will manage their classrooms without others needing to know the details about what goes on inside.

Almost all of what we know about and expect from teaching is influenced by how we have seen teachers work in front of a group of students and in a classroom. I refer to this as the *classical model* of teaching. Unlike 30 years ago, there is now a research base that describes the kinds of classroom actions that teachers take in many situations. There are large video libraries of teachers in the United States and around the world that provide examples for study, including the MET study. However, most of the large-scale datasets, whether video records or other forms of data, are built around this classical model.[26] It is a lens that is easy to apply to education when framing research, policy, and advocacy agendas. However, this model should not be viewed as the totality of either education that exists today or what education can be in the future. One of the most important lessons from how other fields have used technology is that it can help change organizational structures as well as improve individual productivity. So while there is great interest in teachers using data and in data about teacher performance, these questions leave unaddressed the fundamental nature of the role of teachers and the designs of schools. Chapter 7 will revisit this issue.

STILL SEARCHING FOR INSTRUCTIONAL IMPROVEMENT AND TEACHER CONTRIBUTIONS

The data movement began with high hopes for improvements in the technical core: Student assessment information would help teachers and other educators see gaps in student knowledge that they could address. Later there was a hope that student test data would be able to be used to target strong and weak teachers. By the end of the first decade of the data movement, a more complex picture had emerged. Educators might use these same data to game the system and narrow their approach in an effort to escape sanctions, thereby undermining the credibility of the data-based accountability scheme. Research into the accuracy of test scores for teacher evaluation showed that while the scores can be indicative of quality teaching, the correlation between student test results and other measures was modest—not strong enough to conclude that a reliable teacher quality formula had been found. As with many parts of the educational data movement, there was progress and much had been learned, but the path for a data-driven transformation of the technical core of education seemed rocky and full of challenges.

As with other areas of education where data are used, there has been a broadening of the general conception of what educational data are, from almost exclusively test scores to an array of information types—video, surveys, student work, observational rubrics—among which test scores remain prominent. The MET study provided insights into both observational rubrics and what it takes to reliably score students according to them, as well as the value of student surveys. These new species of data are now only beginning to be explored. The data movement also intersects with the tradition of formative assessment: the use of questioning and information from assessments as instructional tools. While this area had been explored by researchers, the extent to which it has been widely practiced has not been well studied. As a practice and research area, formative assessment has been located narrowly at the intersection of two communities: measurement and teaching. As part of the educational data movement, formative assessment fits into a broader set of communities.

As much as has been learned thus far about teachers and data, there is still a major gap in the knowledge base: *the ways teachers might develop or adapt data systems for their own purposes.* Similar to the infrastructures built at the state and district levels, which are advertised to support teachers yet have little involvement of real teachers in their design, data use at the classroom level has been constructed almost completely by those outside of teaching. There are scarce examples of data use from the perspective of teachers, and little research conducted by teachers about their practice and how different kinds of data fit into it. The next two chapters will attempt to address these questions.

The School as a Collective, Teaching as Collaboration

This chapter revisits the world of schools and teaching from the perspective of professional collaboration. This is where the capacity and character of a school are different from the sum of their individual parts. Schools are communities. Rarely democratic and sometimes autocratic, each school has a character and approach to students that come from its leadership and shared values. The leaders in a school can be those with formal authority: the principals and assistants. They also can be distributed leaders: teachers who are respected by their peers.[1] These characteristics—culture, distributed leadership, values—are not easily captured in data. When they are, it is often through surveys and other forms of evidence that do not have the same status as test scores. Still, while the data do not always show it, practitioners working in schools know that these factors matter regarding what kind of teachers and staff choose to be in the school and how they go about their jobs.

Each school is different in its circumstances as well. Although the data often present schools as comparable in the same way that data can show bank branches or retail outlets as comparable, in this way the data can be misleading. While there are over 15,000 districts in the United States, there are over 120,000 public and private schools. Schools range in size and circumstances from small rural institutions to large urban facilities. Some schools have served stable communities and student populations for decades with low staff turnover. Some serve an ever-changing and often transient population where students come and go, where families have many configurations and economic/social circumstances that make supporting their children difficult, and where staff turnover is an annual event. These schools are more likely to be urban and have new and inexperienced teachers; and to be in greater need of programs such as Teach for America (TFA) and other alternative preparation programs.

Within schools, especially in large districts, there can be programmatic variation. One school may have a special science program and another have a special education program that draws from different school zones. In some areas of the country where districts are small, these specialty programs may be regional or managed by an intermediate district or even by the state. Some high schools provide day care for their students' children and focus on community college transitions. Other schools have science clubs and routinely produce large numbers of students who enter elite universities. While bank branches differ in their size, clientele, and physical structures, those differences are minor compared with the differences between some schools. The same is true for retail outlets, grocery stores, and car dealerships. They all vary, but the variations are minor compared with education. As a result, many of the differences in schools are hard or impossible to see through the data. While these differences are not a reason students cannot succeed, they are nonetheless real factors in how different schools organize and operate.

EQUITY, COLEMAN, AND THE EFFECTIVE SCHOOLS MOVEMENT

While NCLB made school performance much more important for many educators, questions about school effectiveness predate NCLB by decades. In the aftermath of school desegregation in the 1950s and 1960s, questions about the relationship between school performance and student circumstances, including poverty, began to be asked. This launched a major movement toward educator self-accountability.

The *Coleman Report*

In some ways the middle of the 20th century was a different era than today for American education. It was a time when *behaviorism*—a field identified with training animals through repetition—was dominant in educational psychology. Segregation of schools only recently had been outlawed. Back then, teachers had almost unquestioned responsibility for what occurred inside their classrooms. It was a time when many educational inequities could be cast as a White/Black issue, since Hispanic immigration was not nearly the factor it is today. But many people asked some of the same questions about the role of schools that they do today. They began to ask whether the amount of money spent on education was having any effect on altering social inequities. Part of the question then, similar to questions now, was: *How much can a school overcome the circumstances of its students?* To investigate this issue, a study was commissioned by the U.S. Department of Education in 1966 called *Equality of Educational Opportunity*.[2] This study was one of the largest ever undertaken and involved over 150,000 students across the nation.

Because of its popular impact, many people, including many educators, still consider its findings valid. It was led by sociologist James Coleman and the report became known to many as simply the *Coleman Report*.

In looking at the critical issue of how well schools could educate students of different backgrounds, the *Coleman Report* said basically that schools individually, and collectively as a social institution, had very little effect on student success compared with student background. Coleman's findings were powerful: *Social circumstances trumped schooling*. It was an argument that resonates in our culture today. Following the logic of the *Coleman Report*, the urban low-income school will never match the affluent suburban school in terms of helping students. A generation of rationalizations for the failure of schools as being attributable to their students was born. While the *Coleman Report* was powerful, it was also *critically flawed*. There are important parts of the story that the report was not able to show. While the Coleman study was wide-ranging and contained many important findings, it systematically underestimated the impact schools can have on student achievement. One of the most important, but little-discussed, sociotechnical twists of 20th-century education involves the technology the Coleman research group used.[3] The computing power available for that time was limited and so Coleman's team was not able to use in their analysis all of the data they had collected. In addition, the statistics they used were limited because they did not separate the impact that could be attributed to schools specifically from the impact that was attributable to students. The statistical models Coleman used compressed both levels of variation into one, which made school differences less apparent in the results. In time, new insights emerged.

The development in the late 1970s and 1980s of new, more powerful and multileveled statistical models that also were able to take advantage of stronger computing resources allowed researchers to quantify the differences that schools made with students while also factoring in the student circumstances.[4] These new statistical tools allowed researchers to show clearly that given the same characteristics, some schools could produce significantly better results than others. These new statistics helped find what Coleman did not: *school effects* that show differences in how different schools work with kids. This is an important policy finding, perhaps as important as the findings a quarter-century later that the ability of teachers to produce student growth was not influenced by credentials.[5] It showed that schools could, in fact, perform very differently from one another given the same types of students. This has been replicated in study after study using the right data and statistical techniques. This research shows that there are things some schools do that seem to help them outperform others with similar students. These differences can include leadership, culture, academics, and an emphasis on achievement.

Effective Schools, Instructional Leaders, and PLCs

Even before evidence began to accumulate that schools differed in how well they performed, an influential research program emerged related to school organization, instruction, and evidence called the *effective schools movement*. This movement was led by not only evidence, but ideology. Harvard and later Michigan State University professor Ron Edmonds put a stake in the ground in 1979, saying educators could not use student circumstances as an excuse for educational failure:

> It seems to me, therefore, that what is left of this discussion are three declarative statements: (a) We can, whenever and wherever we choose, successfully teach all children whose schooling is of interest to us; (b) We already know more than we need to do that; and (c) Whether or not we do it must finally depend on how we feel about the fact that we haven't so far.[6]

More than 20 years before the enactment of NCLB, Edmonds, along with many other educators, was promoting very similar principles that schools must meet the needs of all students, that they actually could do it, and that failures were failures of commitment. One of Edmonds's findings was that those schools that were effective, even with challenging student circumstances, generally had strong principals who saw their role as more than building managers: They were *instructional leaders*.[7] Important research and reform movements around principals began about this time also, and some of the early writing about school data use came from scholars, including Michael Fullan and Lorna Earl from the Ontario Institute of Educational Studies, who also were focusing on instructional leadership.[8] NCLB took this idea further by placing sanctions on schools that did not improve, including leadership changes and restructuring. This compelled many school leaders to care more about instruction, or at least how it was measured on the NCLB tests, than they otherwise might have. But the ideas are bigger than NCLB and are based on a serious research literature. Some researchers focus on principals acting as clinical supervisors for their teachers.[9] Some focus on how principals need to become leaders in learning by understanding what the kids are learning as much as what the teachers are teaching.

Another important movement that has been intertwined with both the instructional leadership and effective schools movement and also relates to educational data involves teacher collaboration, called professional learning communities (PLCs).[10] PLCs also have a diverse and rich literature, including pioneering work by Robert Marzano. There are many books and programs available for schools to help them with this approach to reform. While the principal-as-instructional-leader movement involves breaking down barriers between school leaders and instructional staff to help improve learning, PLCs involve breaking down barriers between teachers. PLCs often are organized by grade and/or subject and can be used in conjunction with principal leadership efforts. They frequently focus on responding to situations when kids do not learn as teachers expect, and often involve groups of teachers reviewing different types of material and evidence, including video records of teaching and examples of student work.

The Role of Data

While none of these programs was developed as a data program, they all can draw on student data while looking at student work, teaching practices, or other classroom issues. Both principals in the role of instructional leaders and PLCs are likely to be sociotechnical activities built around evidence. Instructional leadership and the ideas behind effective schools are critically related to the data movement at the school level. Because school leaders are not in all of the classrooms all of the time, instructional leadership requires some type of independent metric or information. Being an instructional leader will require the principal or a designee to evaluate and track the performance of teachers. A principal who is not an instructional leader might tend to accept the grades his or her teachers give students as the best indicator of their success and potential. Conversely, an instructional leader is more likely to leave his or her office to see the classroom and look at student performance, student work, and other forms of evidence, including test data. Similarly, a PLC could be an opportunity for teacher commiseration and general philosophical discussions, but become more grounded in specific students when student data are included.

Given the sheer amount of work that would be required to implement either program in a school compared with the easier and less time-consuming path of letting each teacher teach as he or she felt was right, these are both areas where information can be an important resource in helping to connect organizational practices. However, when NCLB came along, what initially seemed to occur was a new set of initiatives built around *data-driven instruction* based on the idea that test scores, rather than better professional collaboration on instruction, would drive better teaching. As a result, principals had instructional leadership thrust upon them, but PLCs had no similar emphasis.

THREE SCHOOL PROGRAMS CONNECTED TO DATA: KEYS, SFA, AND DATA WISE

From the preceding discussion, it is possible to see two archetypal ways that school reform can be led: by principals or by groups of teachers. These two approaches also can be used in combination, and they differ chiefly in where the center of control and leadership comes from: those in formal leadership roles or those in the faculty who often exercise distributed leadership. There is a third and common path for school reform: from outside programs that bring techniques, designs, experts to consult and coach, and often materials that are used to support teaching and staff development. These programs come in a variety of types and configurations. In this section, I highlight three of them related to the educational data movement that present important contrasts in approach and results.

Keys to Excellence for Your Schools

Keys to Excellence for Your Schools (KEYS) was developed in the 1990s by the National Education Association (NEA), the largest union representing educators. KEYS focuses on school culture and climate, both of which have been shown in research to be important dimensions in how effective schools are. KEYS draws much of its inspiration from the effective schools movement and is designed as a synthesis of Edmonds's principles with the Total Quality Management concepts that were popular in business in the 1990s.[11] KEYS is then one of the earliest efforts to cross the education–business divide using school-level data. In its delivery, KEYS combines surveys with consultative services, including coaching and training designed to build collaborative staff cultures by focusing on seven research-proven school reform areas:

1. Clear and focused school mission,
2. Safe and orderly environment,
3. High expectations,
4. Opportunity to learn and time on task,
5. Instructional leadership,
6. Frequent monitoring of student progress, and
7. Positive home–school relations.[12]

Schools using the KEYS model adopt a cyclical continuous improvement approach in which the school collects data from staff about focal areas and collectively develops goals, strategies, programs, and professional development. The school then monitors the changes in the school's effectiveness as shown on its surveys. KEYS, however, did not include student performance data in its conception and did not use those data to measure its success.

While KEYS has a following of supporters, it made a modest impact on the data movement. KEYS was still active in 2012, but several people questioned the NEA's long-term commitment to the program, although there were some efforts to expand it. Why would such a promising program not thrive while the data movement was expanding and when collaboration and community-building were emerging from the literature as important benefits from collecting and using data? There are several possible reasons. One may be the organization itself. The NEA, as a labor union, may not be seen as a partner in data-driven reform efforts. It is also possible that by focusing only on surveys and school culture rather on achievement data, KEYS was not able to tap into expectations for data use when NCLB came along. Also, KEYS has a very thin research base on its own success. While KEYS was designed based on solid research, and the NEA produced a book about the KEYS process with chapters by leading educational researchers, the evidence documenting the success of KEYS itself is anecdotal.

Success for All

Another education program that intersects the educational data movement is Success for All (SFA). SFA shows how the data movement can be found in programs that did not begin as specifically identified with data, but where the moniker of data-driven provided focus for programmatic design and communication. SFA was founded by Johns Hopkins University researcher Robert Slavin and his wife, Nancy Madden, based on the beliefs of the effective schools movement. SFA began focusing on interventions for struggling readers in one Baltimore school in 1987. By the beginning of the 21st century, SFA was being used in nearly 1,500 schools.[13] SFA itself is not constructed as a data program, but its design uses data to track student progress. It also uses techniques in its material and programs that have been proven in research aligning with principles of the evidence movement, discussed in Chapter 1. The comment below comes from the SFA launch of a Goals-Focused Improvement Process in the 2001–02 school year that shows both its evidence and data principles:

> Student achievement results drive the process. The primary feature of the Goal-Focused Improvement Process is that it is data-driven. Student-achievement data are used to determine where schools are currently performing relative to where they want to be, to identify interventions that are most likely to have the greatest impact on achievement, and to evaluate if selected interventions have been successful.[14]

SFA saw dramatic growth in research funding and became an organization with at one time over 200 staff members. It was also the focus of a book by University of Michigan professor Donald Peurach, who details how its growth attracted both supporters and critics.[15] Supporters can point to a research literature in peer-reviewed publications that highlights its success in raising student achievement. Critics charge that it is highly scripted and regimented, that not all schools or staff were able to implement it, and that its founders have become a kind of corporation with success uncommon for academics. In discussing the complexity of sustaining a large, mission-driven school improvement network, Peurach notes that its managing organization, the SFA Foundation, has balanced being an advocate for disadvantaged students with a focus on equitable outcomes, with being an advocate in representing its own interests and securing additional funding.[16]

In 2004, researchers at Johns Hopkins University, including Slavin, received funding from the DoED to launch the Center for Data Driven Reform in Education (CDDRE). While SFA often is targeted at schools, CDDRE works at both the district and school levels. Much of the focus in CDDRE is on achievement data, both summative high-stakes tests and formative measures from the classroom, as well as data on solution implementation. CDDRE leadership training involves instructional walkthroughs, developing a culture of achievement, and supporting collegial learning teams.[17] In 2011, SFA competed in the DoED Investing in Innovation (i3) program to expand and continue its work. The process of rating involves a review that weighs several factors, including the merits of the program and any evidence supporting its effectiveness.[18] SFA's proposal for $50 million in additional funding received the highest rating of any of those awarded that year.

Data Wise

Few publications involving educational data have had the impact of the book *Data Wise: A Step-by-Step Guide to Using Assessment Results to Improve Teaching and Learning*, which came out of work at Harvard University in collaboration with the Boston Public Schools and with financial support from the Spencer Foundation. *Data Wise* was first published in 2005, but the project began in 2001, at the dawn of the educational data movement. The original book went into a second printing in 2006 (and reached its fifth printing in 2008). In 2007 there was a follow-up, *Data Wise in Action: Stories of Schools Using Data to Improve Teaching and Learning*, and a DVD with case studies of teachers using the *Data Wise* framework. Summer workshops also began to be held in 2007 in Cambridge, MA, where about 100 practitioners come each year in school teams to learn the framework and how to apply it to their practice.

Data Wise focuses on schools as sites of data use. *Data Wise* does not refer to the program as a PLC, but the book emphasizes teachers working in teams and using a range of information to solve instructional problems. The *Data Wise* process recommends that team members start with one data source and try to understand it deeply before using multiple data sources to triangulate. These data sources, however, are almost all test-based, and *Data Wise* constructs the connection to instructional practices as fairly direct. The *Data Wise* approach has three steps that are performed cyclically, as shown in Table 6.1.[19]

The process of acting then loops back to the inquiry activities as results from what has been attempted are reviewed along with other data to look anew at whether what was attempted, worked or not. The final activity then leads back to activity 3 with new data. As with other approaches based on student performance, *Data Wise* shows how standardized test scores can be aligned to individual learning areas such as *number sense* or *statistics and probability*. By looking deeply into the data to see where student performance may be breaking down, school improvement teams can identify likely problem areas and plan action accordingly. At the same time, *Data Wise* extends the understanding of how schools can use data by developing team-based approaches that include teachers and coaches, rather than the data being used primarily by school leadership. The program shows how to enlist support and buy-in from teachers, to draw upon their understanding of the students and student circumstances, and to enlist their help in developing specific actions that can be tracked. It promotes using data as part of a shift in thinking from what is wrong with students or the system to what the educators can do, saying, "To improve the quality of teaching in a school, leaders must push the conversation about the learning problem past the level of what students are and aren't doing to look at what teachers are or aren't doing."[20] Unlike SFA, *Data Wise* does not have a deep record of studies that document its success, and its continued support is not tied to large federal grants, but rather to workshops and publishing.

SCHOOL LEADERS AS PROFESSIONAL MANAGERS

During the years following the enactment of NCLB, several programs emerged to develop the management skills of school leaders. This training was developed not as an alternative to instructional leadership, but to augment it with an emphasis on performance management analogous to the kinds of techniques used in businesses and other highly successful organizations. Many of these programs are consistent with the school leadership vision promoted by the Wallace Foundation (endowed by the publishers of *Readers Digest*), which has invested in research into school and district leadership. In 2012 the Wallace Foundation issued a report stating that effective school leaders should focus on five core areas:

1. Shaping a vision of academic success for all students,
2. Creating a climate hospitable to education,

TABLE 6.1. Data Wise Steps

Prepare:	Inquire:	Act:
1. Organize for Collaborative Work	3. Create a Data Overview	6. Develop an Action Plan
2. Build Assessment Literacy	4. Dig into Student Data	7. Plan to Assess Progress
	5. Examine Instruction	8. Act and Assess

3. Cultivating leadership in others (which could include PLCs),
4. Improving instruction, and
5. Managing people, data, and processes to foster school improvement.[21]

In 2000, an organization titled New Leaders for New Schools was founded in New York City to help train new school leaders for urban settings. It is like Education Pioneers and other programs that bring in those from outside of education into education careers and it parallels organizations like TFA that bypass traditional certification routes. Similar to Edmonds, New Leaders has an almost evangelical approach to universal student success.[22] Not surprisingly, it places a strong emphasis on data and has developed a program that deconstructs the task of leading schools into different dimensions and areas called the Urban Excellence Framework, which "focuses on five categories of school practices. Among them are two primary drivers of student achievement: rigorous, goal and data-driven learning and teaching and achievement and belief-based school-wide culture."[23] These are supported by three other practices: staff aligned to the school's vision, operations and systems, and personal leadership.

In 2005 another school leadership program was launched by the National Center for Education and the Economy with support from both the Broad and Gates foundations called the National Institute for School Leadership. Unlike New Leaders for New Schools, this program trains existing school principals in concepts and techniques required to be school leaders. Like KEYS, it drew upon research and was designed with the support of leading academics. Some of them came from education, with expertise in standards-based instruction, literacy, math, and science. Others came from outside of education—from programs that focused on leadership, organizational studies, ethics, and strategic thinking. By 2011, it had provided training to over 10,000 principals in 14 states. While not quite an MBA for principals, it does provide perspectives on different fields and does teach them how to use data for school improvement. It also includes specific training on pedagogy involved with different subjects so that principals will be better prepared to lead instructionally. In addition, an MBA program for school leaders recently was developed at Jones Graduate School of Business of Rice University titled the Rice Educational Entrepreneurship Program (REEP). REEP was funded in large part by the Houston Endowment (began by businessman Jesse Jones and his wife in 1937) and offers three different educational leadership programs: an MBA, a Business Fellowship, and a Summer Institute for School Leaders.

SPECIAL EDUCATION:
THREE LEGACY APPROACHES FOR STUDENT DIFFERENCE

Largely separate from research into data use in general, the literature on formative assessments, the MET study, and most of educational research is *special education.* Special education became a field as the result of several decades of legislation, policy, and regulation. It covers a range of student differences and involves specific types of educator jobs and services that almost always are discussed outside of mainstream education. The professional research communities and literature are almost always separate. Under NCLB, special education was a difficult topic for school leaders. On the one hand, the special education subgroup provided important visibility to the community of those with special needs. On the other, that subgroup was often a source of many schools' failure to make adequate yearly progress. Special education also has been a leader in information use. Attention to data for special education began decades before NCLB. It is from this area that the first data use literature emerged in 2004, when the *Journal of Education for Students Placed At Risk* published some of the first research articles on this topic.

Special education is a broad category. It includes many students who are English language learners, as well as those with physical and emotional difficulties. The range of students that receive special education services is extensive. Some are physically and physiologically normal but have mild learning or emotional challenges. Some have extreme physical and cognitive impediments. Special education is also more prevalent in schools with higher poverty. Students of color and those with language challenges are more likely than others to be assigned to special education. Special education is also an evolving field. At one time it was largely segregated. Now, more and more students are mainstreamed and more are able to take the same kinds of assessments as their peers. At the same time, some special education conditions, such as autism and behavioral disorders, seem to be increasing.[24]

While for many special education is a side story to mainstream education issues, it actually aligns with a focus on individual attention and personalization that many educators now attend to. As Chapter 7 will discuss, there are some surface similarities between special education, personalization, and what has occurred in noneducation sectors. In retail, for example, many organizations use technology to customize their offerings and show customers those things first that they are most likely to buy and send suggestions for products they might be interested in. Finance, news, and health care all have similar patterns of personalization and individualization.[25] Education is different from most other fields in that special education is a legally regulated activity. Whereas companies often can decide which categories of potential customers to focus on, public schools cannot. They are required by law to teach a broad spectrum of students. Special education is a diverse field also in terms of its data, as the three examples below illustrate.

Individual Education Programs (IEPs)

One of the most important information tools for students receiving special education services is the Individual Education Program (IEP) document. IEPs are plans developed for specific students and contain ten parts as required by the federal Individuals with Disabilities Education Act (IDEA):

1. Levels of academic achievement and functional performance,
2. Areas of strength,
3. Areas of need,
4. Impact of the disability,
5. Annual goals and objectives,
6. Reporting on the child's progress,
7. Offered services,
8. Participation in general education,
9. Assessment, and
10. Transition plan.

Students with IEPs have larger folders and more records about them, so they are different from other students even when the disability is minor. The IEP documents are now fully digital in most districts and IEP databases, and they are becoming resources for analyzing patterns of student needs and services, although they have significant data quality issues. The quality issues stem from several reasons. One major issue is that the diagnosis of conditions leading to IEP disability classification may not be regulated, so there can be differences in who gets what types of classifications. Also, many decisions about how to support and teach students with IEPs are negotiated, so that the way specific children are supposed to be taught, which will be encoded on their IEP documents, is subject to which people were involved in the decision and what they agreed was best. In addition, the actual instruction of children may or may not follow the IEP plan. Finally, the record keeping for IEP documents may be subject to clerical errors and inconsistencies.[26]

Curriculum Based Measurement

Another data practice that has become a staple in parts of special education is Curriculum Based Measurement (CBM). CBM occasionally is called Curriculum Based Assessment, although the latter term has a wider meaning. The name makes CBM seem similar to curriculum-embedded formative assessment or possibly even interim assessments (discussed below). However, this is not exactly how it has been used. CBM is primarily for elementary school reading and math to evaluate basic skills and track special education students' performance to their IEP goals. CBM is, then, a very narrow kind of formative assessment, usually involving very brief response tasks and given inside the special education context to individual students, in contrast to formative or interim assessments, which usually are given to a whole class.

Response to Intervention

Response to Intervention (RTI) is another educational data practice related to norms of performance based on data analysis. While it is not specifically for special education, RTI is one way that students can be classified as having a learning disability, which will lead to their having an IEP.[27] RTI began in the 1970s as a way of screening students who might need certain interventions, usually in early literacy and more recently in math. RTI's data-driven diagnostic process has multiple levels or tiers that often begin at a school level. At the first tier, large groups of students are given the same tests to help identify those who are struggling. Students who do not perform well on a first-level intervention are moved to a second level, and so on, through three or four levels where each intervention is based on what research has shown works with different students.

INTERIM ASSESSMENTS

One of the changes that came to the field following the enactment of NCLB was a new data species and a new kind of test that figures into many different school-level practices: the *interim assessment*. As the name implies, interim assessments sit between annual summative assessments and more frequent formative ones in the classroom. They usually are implemented for a district and aligned with district standards. While almost unheard-of before NCLB, they are now fairly commonplace and there is the beginning of a literature that discusses them.[28] From a distance, the interim assessment seems to bridge the gap between these historically disconnected areas of accountability and instruction. However, there are important questions about interim assessments to be answered. While teachers can use them and many do, interim assessments are also useful for looking across *different classrooms*, so that they fit into instructional leadership processes led by principals and PLCs, as well as supporting teacher work.

Interim assessments are a focus for many data-reporting vendors and parts of district data warehouses. They are included as part of the Race to the Top assessment programs, discussed in Chapter 3. In 2010 the *Study of Education Data Systems and Decision Making* reported these connections:

> Schools in districts involved in implementing a major system of districtwide interim assessments were the most likely to show an increase in data use from year to year, and also provided the most striking examples of changes in teacher data use practices, such as the institution of collaboration around the review of assessment results to derive implications for instruction.[29]

The reason for these connections seems to be as straightforward as the availability of information resources that can be used across classrooms and toward meeting end-of-year targets. Since accountability policy made end-of-year performance consequential for school leaders, it follows that schools interested in their end-of-year results would utilize information that helps track progress toward it.

However, despite a straightforward logic for interim assessments, this part of the data movement raises some important questions. In 2009, Lorrie Shepard, a national expert on assessments and past president of the American Educational Research Association, the National Council on Measurement in Education, and the National Academy of Education, questioned whether a need for them had been established, noting:

> Interim assessments could sometimes be a good thing, but they are brand new and wholly unexamined. As recently as 2001, a significant National Research Council report, *Knowing What Students Know* (Pellegrino, Chudowsky, & Glaser, 2001), addressed coherence between large-scale and classroom assessments but did not even recognize intermediate, interim assessments. Therefore, some amount of skepticism and search for evidence is warranted.[30]

Shepard further discussed some of the practical issues with administering periodic assessments, including developing meaningful tests that relate to specific parts of the curriculum taught at different points in an instructional year, as opposed to the simpler process of using tests that parallel the end-of-year learning targets but raise problems when they try to test targets the teachers have not yet taught. While developing reliable and high-quality assessments is complicated under most circumstances, parsing out the content in a way that adequately reflects what teachers will be teaching at different points in time can be more difficult, especially if different teachers take different routes to the same end-of-year instructional goals. It is a technical challenge that most item-bank vendors and district test developers may not have the resources to adequately address.

Within the issue of interim assessments we can see some of the big issues and questions of the educational data movement itself. Interim assessments are straightforward from an engineering and management science perspective. They are also an idea that has little support in the orthodoxy of educational research and are not referenced at all in the seminal assessment compendium—*Knowing What Students Know*—to which Shepard refers. There are nontrivial technical and measurement issues, and little is known about how practitioners are able to use these new assessment forms. Does this mean interim assessments are not useful in the ways intended and/or possibly other ways? Is it that interim assessments are like other innovations, including the personal computer and mouse, that did not fit with the prevailing theories and practices of their time when first introduced but later made significant sociotechnical space for themselves? Is it possible that the ways that interim assessments become valuable in practice will differ based on the part of the curriculum and the nature of circumstances the school is responding to? These questions await new kinds of research.

INSIGHTS FROM PRACTICE

Just as there is a scarcity of detailed research into how teachers use data, there are few investigations of school-level data use processes. There are two lines of research that help view what might be occurring in practice around different kinds of artifacts. These two lines of research combine in-depth study of schools with some study of data and other forms of evidence being used for instructional leadership. One features principals and the other, PLCs. Interim assessments do have some relationship to these processes, although they are only one of many forms of evidence used and their singular value is unclear.

One line of research that includes interim assessments and school teams comes from University of Wisconsin professor Richard Halverson, whose early career research included a program called Data Driven Instructional Systems. Halverson, a former teacher, technology coordinator, and school administrator, was, during his doctoral studies, part of the Distributed

Leadership Study at Northwestern University that shed light on the bubble kids. Halverson started to look at the ways that data systems could be used at the school level with a focus on school leaders. He found that test data, along with other information, can be brought together in a cycle that includes data acquisition, data reflection, program alignment and integration, instructional design, formative feedback, and test preparation. This cycle is designed to make the link between accountability and instruction in what he titled *school formative feedback systems*.[31]

Halverson's approach is similar to *Data Wise* in that it is iterative and leads to data being part of staff discussions. His research also looks at both social and technical artifacts, including how these different data forms intersect with the problems that some practitioners in schools are focusing on. He has described how school leaders can invent data collection processes, in one case around interim math assessment, and how these leaders also create the scheduling opportunities for staff to come together to review different forms of data, including: community survey data, guidance and behavior information, schedules and budgetary data, teacher observation, student demographics, and curriculum details and IEPs.[32]

Deep research into teacher collaboration has been the focus of Stanford University researcher Joan Talbert for many years. Talbert has discussed the tension in the types of activities that often comes into play between top-down mandates that tend to cause teachers to respond in ways that show "ritual compliance," but don't get at the real issues of teacher abilities and areas they know are weak, and teacher-dominated communities that may veer away from accountability. Talbert worked with New York City (NYC) schools and their development of PLCs. Her research focuses on groups of teachers who can be empowered to make the instructional changes needed in their classrooms. Talbert reported on a PLC program at the NYC schools that began in 2006. New York City is an important district in the educational data movement and has received tens of millions of dollars in foundation funding. Not only is it one of the super-large systems with a diverse student population, including many with social and economic disadvantages, but it also has been one of the first districts to try various approaches involving data. New York's Achievement Reporting Information System (ARIS) was one of the largest district data efforts ever undertaken. The PLC program Talbert studied went through several iterations, including being led by principals and then later with more teacher leadership. At the time she published her research, the NYC system was pursuing a "professional rather than bureaucratic approach," in which communities tend to focus more on creating opportunities for teachers to open up their instruction to their peers. This type of PLC often is led by a facilitator or master teacher who will strive to help teachers be honest about what they know and don't know, and what they are doing well and not well. Sometimes these communities are built around the successful Japanese program called *Lesson Study* where video records of lessons are discussed by the group. The inclusion of data helps to keep the focus on student learning rather than just teaching.[33]

Talbert reported that many schools had made the switch to a data culture so that using data in PLC processes was a natural extension. Rather than subgroups—the fixed categories of students used in NCLB for all schools regardless of their particular makeup—Talbert discussed how each school had a "sphere of success," that is, those students that it served well. The goal in these PLC efforts was to bring more and more students into that sphere. Teams worked with data and identified specific areas or groups of students where the school was not successful and then used the data to help develop a plan to address those areas. The results from NYC were encouraging enough for Talbert to offer them as an "existence proof" that these types of communities could work, they could use data, and they could shift the focus from instruction to student learning. She did, however, highlight challenges with the data systems and the importance of data specialists, as well as variability in school culture. She, like Halverson, also reported a range of evidence that was used in the PLCs, including test scores, examples of student work, student assignments, transcripts of classroom talk, and video records of classrooms.

While the work of Halverson and Talbert is a small sample from a growing literature related to educational data use, it is important as examples of insights from practice. Contrasting the evidence types that these different researchers presented, as shown in Figure 6.1, allows us to see how different instructional leadership efforts *might* value different kinds of evidence. Talbert's PLC was more focused on the kind of work students do in class, and Halverson's principal-led school team used information related to classrooms and teaching, including teacher observations as well as student demographics, finance, calendars, IEPs, and other information that cross individual classrooms and departments. Test scores are common in this very small example space, not necessarily as the most accurate or even the most valuable information, but perhaps as a common organizational language.

SCHOOLS:
A CRITICAL, COMPLICATED, AND CHANGING UNIT OF ANALYSIS

The work of Halverson and Talbert is illustrative of the kinds of information school leadership teams might use as they look at improving instruction. In a climate where simple solutions are sought, there can be a temptation to look at these few programs as exemplars and models for developing solu-

FIGURE 6.1. Contrast in Evidence Types from Principal- and Teacher-Led Initiatives

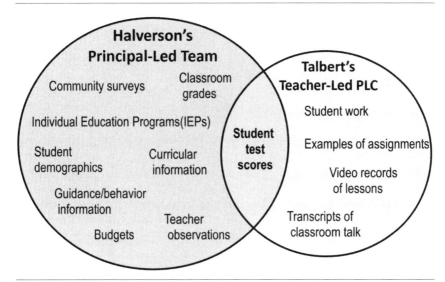

tions for other schools. However, they represent a very small sample of the over 120,000 schools in the United States. This is a broad organizational landscape with significant variation in circumstances and programs. While schools can be stable organizations, they also can evolve. Schools that are considered failing can be subjected to turnaround processes where new leaders and often new staff take over and try to lead the school into a different level of performance. Charter schools can replace public schools. Schools can go through changes because their populations shift through family mobility and changes in district boundaries. While other fields—hospitals, bank branches, retail stores—encounter changing organizations, the type of changes that can occur with schools seem to be in a different class. While not all schools are going through dramatic changes and many experience long periods of stability, schools that are adjusting their management, staff, and programmatic milieu are not unusual. They are common. And yet, in most research, especially research involving schools and data, the school is treated as a static entity that the programs and data will have an effect on. There can be implications for how changes that schools are experiencing can impact the capacity to use data and the types of data that are most helpful for them. Understanding the changes that schools experience and how different kinds evidence fit into these school-level practices may be one of the greatest challenges of this movement.

Under NCLB, there was a heavy reliance on test scores, and for many schools the response was counterproductive as some leaders focused narrowly in an effort to stave off sanctions. Is it fair to ask how new organizational technology—bringing together assessment with other forms of information related to accountability policy—might impact schools? Will new data approaches appeal to practitioners' needs to game the system or focus on short-term strategies? As some parts of the country implement value-added models for teacher evaluations, and soon perhaps for principals, will we see changes coming in terms of school cultures, with teachers and principals looking out more for their own jobs as measured in their individual evaluations and being less inclined to be team players? Will we see cultures develop where practitioners become tied to their school data systems in the same way that many corporate departments become structured by their computer systems, or will the variation and change common in schools act to make it difficult for standardized forms of information to be used effectively by many school teams? The research on evidence use at this level is in the earliest stages and in many ways still searching for appropriate research frameworks and methods.

7

Improving and Reimagining the Technical Core

The traditional structure of schools has long been criticized. The ideas for new approaches to schooling have rarely been new. The data movement, however, does introduce some interesting possibilities for educational design. This chapter reviews some new technologies and emergent models that show how greater productivity in the technical core and different educational designs are possible with the support of information technology. While the improvements in productivity involve familiar activities, the new designs and new models are still unproven on a large scale and with rigorous research. In these new areas, we see even more diversity in what counts as data or could be useful information for practitioners in the future.

REVIEWING THE CLASSICAL MODEL OF TEACHING

The classical model of teaching centers discussed in Chapter 5 on the role of the teacher as manager of the classroom, conveyer and evaluator of knowledge. In this model, teachers direct everything that happens for all the students inside a classroom. Once the door is closed, teachers usually decide in what order the information will be taught, which students will sit or work together, and how to gauge and measure student understanding. The classical model of teaching is part of a traditional school design where all of the staff are arranged in a way that supports teachers' autonomy. Schools that have specialists—usually reading, math, and special education—use those specialists to augment the traditional classroom teachers.

Decades of research and the evaluation of teachers are showing that teaching according to the classical model is often complex. As teacher evaluations, and large studies like the Measures of Effective Teaching discussed in Chapter 5, show, it is a job few do very well at any given time. When researchers study what expert teachers do, they see a rich performance of organizing student activity, questioning, supporting, explaining, presenting, assessing, and providing feedback, all of which occurs inside classrooms. Randi Weingarten, President of the American Federation of Teachers, said:

> Teaching, I don't care who [which kinds of students] it is, teaching is incredibly hard—you are managing. . . . When you are teaching, you are managing, whether it is 20, 30, or 40; or if you are a high school teacher 150 to 200 kids at a time . . . you really have to manage kids and engage them . . . particularly if you want to go deep.[1]

The term *managing* can have a number of meanings. It can mean classroom management: the most basic of teacher jobs. It also can mean more advanced management of instructional processes, particularly, as Weingarten says, "if you want to go deep." Teachers also work outside the classroom in planning and developing materials and at times collaborating. This work is also complex and managerial.[2] What is surprising, given that they are surrounded by people in their jobs, is that many teachers work largely alone. Both inside and outside the classroom, they are solo practitioners because the classical model structures their job in this way. Principals as instructional leaders and professional learning communities, which were discussed in Chapter 6, are largely supplements to individual teaching rather than a fully continuous, collaborative team structure. The cultures that leaders in a school develop are often cultures of solo practitioners cooperating rather than regular collaboration on the needs of specific students. In most cases, teachers teach individually and work with one another and their leaders as an exception. This is teaching in the classical model and it can be good, or excellent, in some cases, and less good in others. For some students, a given teacher may be an ideal match, but not for others. The classical model is so entrenched in our culture that many see this as the only way that adults and children can be organized to support learning.

Whether in elementary or secondary schools, with the same group for an entire day or with different groups in periods, teaching in the classical model requires the application of complex knowledge in performance. To teach almost any subject, for example, high school biology or middle school literacy, a teacher needs to know not just the subject matter content in terms of the science or how to write, but also how to teach it to students learning it for the first time. This extra knowledge, called *pedagogical content knowledge* or *knowledge for teaching*, includes understanding the different ways students make sense of the material and ways to help guide the learning of different kinds of students.[3] Teaching, then, requires that that knowledge be put into action with a class that can include 20 to 40 young people at a time, each bringing various conditions and backgrounds into the process. The performance is critical and it requires that teachers have the ability to engage and interact, usually on their feet and walking around, day after day. Teaching also requires communication with parents, along with a host of other administrative tasks. But it is the actual performance, or enactment of lessons, that is the critical element of the classical model of teaching. And it is very hard to do well over long periods of time. The day-in, day-out performance demands are greater when students come from difficult situations and require even more support from the teacher. The performance demands, even for those that have excelled at it, is likely a factor in attrition of new teachers and a fading in performance of many teachers who have been successful.

Teaching performance skills are multidimensional. The different ways teachers can be good and weak vary. Some may know the material and understand kids, but not explain well. Some may work better with small groups than large ones, and with some types of students than others. Good teachers gauge how the students comprehend and then adjust and move forward. Some begin with natural abilities, and many require experience and training to become good. Many of the challenges in developing a rich teaching workforce involve the fact that many teachers are good at some things and not always others.

One of the greatest challenges of the classical model is personalization of learning. The classical model is designed for large-group instruction, and personalization of learning occurs in one of two primary ways: outside the classroom for special education students and as small-group activity managed by the teacher within the classroom. The special education context usually addresses a specific need, such as language or behavior, rather than academic interests, and group instruction is not usually individual in nature, but allows some measure of customization within a classroom. There are other ways that students can get additional help: pull-out programs where students leave the normal classroom in elementary schools, and in later grades when students can select classes that are appropriate to their academic interests and level. One of the criticisms of the classical model has been that because individual students do not always get instruction related to their specific interests and talents, as a result they disengage with education, although little research actually has documented the extent to which this is a problem.

THE HISTORICAL AND ORGANIZATIONALLY MODULAR CLASSICAL MODEL

While teaching in the classical model is hard, historically it has had many advantages. It can demand little coordination. The relationships between teachers and classrooms are stable and predictable. New teachers can be inserted into an existing school with a minimum of adjustment or managerial involvement. Because teachers have been able to control their classrooms in an organizational sense, each classroom is often like a black box to those on the outside. Teachers usually have the freedom to shape and control what goes on inside it. They can develop and adapt curricula as they choose, make individual and often substantive contributions to the lives of students, and have a big voice in evaluating how well students do and how they are perceived in the school through the grades teachers issue. Ultimately teachers in the classical model decide whether to make instruction a simple presentation of facts or engage with opportunities for student participation. The former is easier for the teacher, but not always good for all students. The latter can require more work from teachers to do well, but is better for students.

The classic model has been dominant for so long that it has permeated the culture of those who prepare teachers, those who manage teachers in school systems, and those who measure teachers, parents, and teachers themselves. Under the classical model, a teacher, at a minimum, will manage the classroom environment, that is, ensure students stay in their seats, follow the rules, and do not interrupt. Classroom management is a prerequisite for everything else a teacher does under this instructional approach. Managing learning, however, is a greater challenge. This could be what Weingarten means at the end of her quote when she says, "if you want to go deep" and ensure all or even most students are *really learning*. To do this, teachers may need to create novel ways to engage. They may need to adapt their style and approach while monitoring how well students comprehend big ideas. This kind of teaching is risky because it requires teachers to improvise, and new strategies may not always work. It is what some call *adventurous teaching*.[4] It is often harder for outsiders to recognize and understand, so teachers who try to go deep may be taking chances when they are evaluated.

For many teachers, the introduction of high-stakes testing brought about some difficult changes. For teachers working in an NCLB-tested subject, there was the requirement of preparing students to take tests that might have had little relationship to what had been occurring in the classroom before. Many teachers of other subjects saw resources and the culture of their schools shift toward the tested subjects. NCLB brought for many teachers a culture of fear. It also introduced alternative ways of viewing the classroom through data. While flawed in many ways, the tests that came with NCLB brought new lenses into the black box of instruction in this classical model. At the same time, these tests provided little value for teachers to use in their work.[5] The greater visibility and accountability came at the cost of a greater workload and often fewer tools and resources to use in classrooms.[6]

Now alternative forms of information about students are proliferating so that others in the school building will have the ability to see, albeit imperfectly, into classrooms and make inferences about what is going on inside those black boxes. These information streams can be used to collaborate and discuss different students. This can lead to a decentering of instructional responsibility and with it a fundamental change in the authority structure of teachers.

At the same time that information about students helps to open up the black box of the classical model classroom, policies of data use can make the classical structure stronger. For example, teacher evaluation programs that focus on the performance of individual teachers, rather than on whole schools, actually could serve to reinforce individuality and strengthen the walls that divide classrooms rather them open them up.

INFORMATION-DRIVEN PERSONALIZATION

One of the issues to emerge in policy discourse and from funders as the educational data movement was taking hold involved *personalized learning*. Education has seen pendulum swings around standardization versus personalization for decades, but what is new is the idea of using data and information to drive individual attention to student needs. While other fields are routinely using datasets about specific customers, and others similar to those customers, to present more relevant options and services, the classical model in education is still largely focused on providing the same options to students irrespective of what information about those students might suggest.[7] Other fields have used data about individuals to help segment and divide a large market into smaller groups to which services can be targeted. Of course, students within a classroom and teachers within a school are already part of a small group. It is possible, however, that students and teachers are parts of larger groups by having similarities with others in different locations and that data can provide some opportunities to see what types of approaches and tools will work well with those students and teachers.

Personalization *does* occur in education today. However, the decisions about tailoring to specific students are largely the responsibility of teachers and school staff. Large-scale, information-driven personalization is a concept, a dream, at this point in education. The data do not yet exist or are not yet sharable across a wide expanse for this to be possible. Further, the classical model of teaching, and the structure of schools built around it, is not designed around using large amounts of information to personalize learning. Personalization is largely left up to a handful of professionals—classroom teachers and specialists—who may or may not perform this in the optimal way. Many teachers and indeed many schools find their practice constrained by the cycle of test preparation and response. However, the potential for a flexible and dynamic educational process appears to exist, and there are some tools and early programs suggesting that it is at least possible for the technical core to be altered for more individual attention.

While there have been pressures in many schools to meet individual needs, the shift toward VAMs and other growth models being used to evaluate teachers may help to drive more emphasis on individual student growth. In focusing on growth, it becomes necessary to orient policies toward students (and teachers) from where they are in any developmental sequence and how they can progress through some interactions with curriculum, teachers, and programs. These teacher evaluations are occurring for many reasons. They also represent part of a fundamental reorientation in the field, especially as it becomes clear that the large majority of teachers are in the middle of the distribution—their performance is neither great nor awful—and so there are likely needs for targeted professional development to grow teacher skills. Rather than attempting to move uniform groups of students through a standard curriculum and treating teachers as interchangeable, which the data show they are not, there is a pendulum swing toward individual needs and skills.

Information-driven digital personalization involves leveraging sometimes large datasets to make personalization the norm rather than the exception. It is a reform strategy aimed squarely at the classical model. While this potential of using data about students and teachers in different localities could apply to all students and teachers, special education may be an area where it could be especially powerful, since those students are distributed across wide areas with great variation in conditions. In many cases, the combination of conditions for a specific special education student is not found in others within the same school system, so that large-scale databases that could identify parallel situations could be leveraged to learn about how to personalize support for that student and others with similar circumstances.

In some ways, digitally personalized learning is analogous to interim assessments, discussed in Chapter 6. From one perspective and set of logics it makes sense, but there are significant gaps in research that demonstrate the actual need for personalization and how many students would benefit from it. There is a theory that lack of individual attention and personalization may be a cause for lower productivity and engagement. At the same time, there are sociocultural theories that learning occurs in groups; those theories may complicate a highly personalized approach to schooling. Nevertheless, personalization is a new strategy of reform—a gambit many funders are convinced is a winning strategy—and the resources are being applied to see whether it can be successful.

ABUNDANT DIGITAL TOOLS AND
BOOSTING CLASSROOM PRODUCTIVITY

There is now a new wave of technologies that are becoming available to be integrated into classroom work. After years of expectations, classroom teachers are now presented with an abundance of digital tools that range from classroom devices to resources that are easy to find on the Internet and use with students. This abundance has been fueled by the decreasing cost of electronics and the same forces of digital publishing that have impacted the ways books are now purchased and read. These technologies fall into several broad categories, although there is often overlap between them. Below are three broad and non-mutually exclusive areas for consideration: open educational resources, new data generators, and dashboards and analytic platforms.

Open Educational Resources (OERs)

One of the most powerful technical forces involves free open educational resources (OERs) as well as products with low cost points. These can include instructional presentations, quizzes, videos, assessment items, journals, and other types of texts that can be used in schools. Textbook publishers increasingly are providing integrated suites that may contain a similar wealth of tools as OERs. As more schools gain technologies, from digital whiteboards to universal computing devices, educators will have the platforms they need to easily use these resources with students. The real power behind these new digital resources is not only the way they present information and allow customization, but their *economic value*. Because digital media live not in physical things, but in electronic sources, publishing and sharing them often can be done with few additional costs.[8] There is similarly a low cost for sharing across classrooms, and in many cases the same media can be used with different devices. For example, one teacher can get a digital asset from the Internet, email it to a colleague who integrates it with a lesson they created themselves, and then share it on a laptop or project it on a digital whiteboard with ease. Likewise, in many cases materials from one media can be put into another easily so a teacher can take a digital resource, use it in the classroom, and then put part of it in a test with little effort.

There have been great expectations that these OERs will help revolutionize schooling, and the DoED has promoted several initiatives to increase the federal contributions to this area and encourage teachers and innovators to create even more digital content. In 2011, as a way to both study how new technologies work in practice and provide support for research and for schools, the administration, with congressional funding, launched a new national research center called *Digital Promise*.[9] According to Arne Duncan in the announcement of the initial funding of the center:

> With technology, teachers and parents can deeply engage students in learning. They can personalize instruction. And they help solve the inequities in our communities and in our schools by providing all children with access to world-class educational resources—anytime, anywhere.[10]

As the amount of online information increases, it becomes more important to help people find it in an organized way. Teachers, parents, and students searching online could be overwhelmed by the millions of potential educational resources that come in different depths and quality. In 2011, the DoED Office of Education Technology developed a program called the *Learning Registry* to help connect educators with resources. A related project to make educational material easier to find was started a little earlier; it is called the Learning Resources Metadata Initiative (LRMI) and has similar goals, but more corporate support and more direct involvement from foundations. In 2011, a project emerged, with funding from the Council of Chief State School Officers (CCSSO), the Bill and Melinda Gates Foundation, and the Carnegie Corporation of New York, called the Shared Learning Collaboration (SLC), based on the Common Core State Standards (discussed in Chapter 3), to create an environment where developing and sharing open tools is practical. This project, later converted into a not-for-profit named inBloom, also uses the LRMI and Learning Registry components in its architecture. The intended and likely result of these efforts is that the process of locating digital materials will become both faster and easier, and teachers will then have to spend less time sorting through things they don't need and have more time to integrate those they do need into instruction.[11]

While increasingly available, these tools come in many different instructional depths and connection to learning research. Some are based on deep learning activities that engage students in investigations or problem solving. One such research-based deep program is the Web-based Inquiry Science Environment (WISE). WISE allows students and teachers to build an integrated experience: engaging as scientists, pursuing questions, making their thinking explicit and open to discussion, and with substantive assessments.[12] WISE began in 1998 with funding from the National Science Foundation and now is used in thousands of classrooms worldwide. WISE generates research findings, drawing on a range of data sources, and has helped launch several additional projects, including those that have rich assessments and data-reporting options.

Others are more loose collections produced by teachers or parents or startups. One notable startup is the Khan Academy, which began in 2006 when Salman Khan, a former hedge fund manager, developed short lectures in his house and posted them on the Internet where they were accessible for free. Before long Khan attracted attention and soon funding. The Gates Foundation invested several million dollars and Google donated $2 million for translation. By the end of 2011, the Khan Academy had over 2,700 lessons and more than 93 million lesson views. Today, the Khan Academy also features data tools to allow teachers and educators to see how their classes are performing in specific areas, and has developed new elements including "challenges" and "badges" to indicate competency. The Khan Academy staff had grown to include developers, managers, and several academic deans. It also has staff that can help schools with the process of integrating material and data products into classrooms.

New Data Generators

Many of these new tools, both OERs and those available from commercial publishers, also bring the ability to *generate data*. Some of the data they can provide will come from traditional assessments when the resources are tests or parts of tests. Some of the data will be new forms of digital information, including *activity trace*s that log different events and tasks that students engage in and their sequences, *metadata* about the characteristics of the resources, and *paradata* about the circumstances when they were used. Just as the Internet has led to new types of data about who is using what, where, and when, the learning tools that teachers may integrate into the technical core also will be able to provide new sources of data. People have referred to these data as *big data* because of the size of the digital collections that can be produced.[13] Some of these data will be owned or controlled by those that provide search engines and those that sell products, but they nevertheless will allow new insights into activity in what surely will be a rapidly developing segment of education. Some of the data may be made available to teachers to use in evaluating student work and their grouping of students.

One important way that digital tools will help with data about students is in new forms of assessments that are embedded within them. Many of the new digital learning environments—games, simulations, and other immersive activities—that allow students to experience more authentic learning are being built with assessment components included. These embedded assessments can measure both cognitive and noncognitive skills. At Harvard University, Professor Chris Dede has been developing what his team calls *virtual performance assessments* where students are assessed in terms of what they can do as well as what they know. Dede's research involves a simulated ecosystem that students use to conduct science experiments, collect data, and explain their thinking. The virtual environment allows them to experience science in ways that would be impractical without technology. Dede's data show not only the students' performance on tasks, but also the paths they take through the digital world, leading to insights on their behaviors and challenges.[14] University of California at Berkeley professor Marcia Linn's research merges assessment, instruction, and opportunities to learn complex science inquiry through the use of technology. The students (and teachers) are provided with continuous feedback on their performance as they learn.[15] Florida State University professor Valerie Shute has taken the idea of embedding assessments further with what she calls *stealth assessments* that psychometrically measure student abilities, but do so through tasks that do not appear to the students to be assessments.[16] DiCerbo and Behrens, with the Cisco Networking Academy, developed a massive global data collection program that combines game and simulation activities with traditional tests based on Evidence Centered Design. They are extending this work into what they call *hidden assessments* where the student is not always presented with artificial tasks, but where the flow of action can provide the evidentiary basis for inferences that test items have done in the past. These are just a few examples of new approaches to assessment that will provide more data to teachers beyond basic math and literacy characteristic of the NCLB era.

Dashboards and Learning Analytics

Along with new technology to support instruction and assessment, there are also data visualization tools—dashboards—designed specifically for classroom or small–group–level analysis. Some are assessment-focused and some, like a new startup called Kickboard for Teachers, which is used by many charter schools, include behavioral and well as achievement data.[17] In some cases, the reports and dashboards are generic in terms of subject area and come from products that data warehouse vendors provide. In some cases, they cover specific curricular areas such as the early literacy and math tools from Wireless Generation that allow teachers to record data on handheld devices that connect with their central data stores. Many SLDS implementations also have dashboards and visual displays, although the information often is limited to annual summative data rather than data from within classrooms. In some cases, the dashboards are built by district offices.

Because creating dynamic visual displays is fairly straightforward using technologies that have been used in businesses and other fields for some time, just about any technology that collects data about student work can also have visual tools and reports available for educators to use. In these reports, student data can be represented according to performance categories like those encoded in NCLB (e.g., proficient through below basic) as well as their progress toward performance goals over time in new ways that practitioners can use. As long as there are digital data, they can be represented visually. While there are some studies showing the increased availability of these tools, there are few studies that explore the extent to which they actually are used and actually are useful, and for which types of teachers/ situations. There is potential in these technologies to support greater use of digital formative assessment by providing teachers with integrated sets of tools to both collect data on student learning and integrate those data into personalization and planning activities.

Related to the growth of tools for visualizing student data, are tools for analysis of student learning. This is a new area and it is not clear to what extent teachers or others in the school or school system will be able to use these technologies and what patterns they may show across different settings. However, it is a rapidly growing space. As online tools are used, they will generate volumes of cost-effective data about preferences, patterns of use, and learning pathways. Much of the power in these types of analytics involves linking different sources of information. Since the field of education still has only sporadic interoperability of administrative data systems, most data warehouses that could be used for fine-grained analytics are likely to be local. However, large online environments such as those discussed above have no such restrictions and conceivably could capture data on students nationwide and worldwide if they were used. As with dashboards, the step from automatically collected digital data and having a dataset for analysis can be short.

DISRUPTIVE INNOVATION
AND LEARNING ORGANIZATION OBJECTS

The discussion in this chapter until now has been focused on new technologies and how they can be used within traditional, classical teaching models. Much as other technologies have improved individual worker productivity in other fields, these tools have the potential to boost the effectiveness of classroom teachers by giving them resources that are easy to use for presentation, assessing students, and visualizing progress. Now the conversation shifts beyond making the classical model of teaching more productive to *reshaping the fundamental nature of school organization and classroom practices*. As Chapter 2 discussed, information technology has been used both to make existing jobs more efficient and to reshape the ways that jobs are performed and which types of positions are necessary. As education develops more basic data capacity and those familiar with business and management consulting have a greater voice in education policy, it could be expected that the reshaping of educational processes would become promoted and possible.

While there are many voices advocating new models for education, one of the most prominent is Harvard Business School professor Clayton Christensen, who pioneered the popular business theory of *disruptive innovation.* Disruptive innovation as a field is deeply related to sociotechnical revolutions. Disruptive innovation researchers look at broad social changes from the perspective of key technologies that are catalysts for the change. These disruptive innovations not only provide a competitive edge for some commercial sectors, but they also help reshape industries.[18] In 2008, Christensen published a bestseller titled *Disrupting Class: How Disruptive Innovation Will Change the Way the World Learns.*[19] He proposed that digital resources will lead to fundamental changes in the way schools are operated, allow greater personalization of learning, and create paths to lower the cost of education. Christensen proposed that the economics of digital tools would allow the reshaping of education through the blending of traditional and technology-rich distance and self-study methods.

Blended Learning

Even before Christensen's book, blended learning had occurred in education. According to Indiana University professor Curt Bonk, the practice began in the 1920s with supervised correspondence courses.[20] Using this principle with younger children is more recent, however. It is one thing for adult students, even professionals continuing their education, to integrate different resources into an educational path they control. It is another for an elementary or middle school student to learn the same way. Blended learning is more than teachers using these tools in their classrooms or students using these tools at home for homework. In a sense, blended learning is not totally new since all classroom practice is an amalgam of different approaches. As Karen Cator, director of the Office of Educational Technology, said:

> So, blended learning is a funny term, because classrooms have always been blended. They're a blend of individual work, and group work, and teacher-directed work, and reading books, and all sorts of other interactions. Now we're just adding another element to that—a whole digital environment.[21]

What *is* new is that there is now a broad array of digital tools that can be included into the classroom environment with the potential to support some of the difficult management work of teaching, including planning, presenting, and assessing. So even the formulas for classroom management can be different when blended tools are used, as students, individually or in groups, can be given assignments to do with digital tools in ways paper textbooks did not allow.

Blended learning is becoming a term for the systematic incorporation of OERs and other digital resources into school design so that portions of the instructional workload can be shifted from teachers to the technology. Blended learning is itself a broad category as there are many different ways of arranging the work of school staff. As the first decade of this century was ending, blended learning with K–12 students was being tried in a few public and many charter school systems, often with the support of the same foundations that supported the data movement. What seemed at first to be a mere matter of combining technological materials into traditional classrooms has now grown to include using these tools to support rearranging classroom practices. In 2011, an organization founded to study Christensen's ideas in education, called the Innosight Institute, produced a classification of K–12 blended learning approaches that identified four main variations:

1. *Rotation,* in which students move between instructor and technology-driven sessions,
2. *Flex,* in which content and instruction are delivered primarily online and students work on individual programs,
3. *Self-blend,* in which students take one or more courses online to supplement their standard curriculum, and
4. *Enriched virtual,* in which students divide their time between traditional face-to-face learning and online courses.[22]

Each of these approaches combines brick-and-mortar traditional schooling with digital resources in different ways. The rotation model, where students move between teacher-led and technology-rich settings, has the most variations, including the station rotation, lab rotation, flipped classrooms, and individual rotations. The flipped classroom model has been promoted by the Khan Academy and others as a way of transforming learning. In a flipped classroom, presentation and lecture are done by the students on their own using technology, and the teacher acts as a tutor, essentially reversing or flipping the teacher's primary role from presenter to coach. This classification system has gone through several iterations and likely will join many other ways to classify this quickly developing part of the educational world.

The School of One and Rocketship

A high-profile example of blended learning is the School of One, a public school program serving approximately 3,000 middle school students in New York City. It was developed by the New York City Department of Education with major philanthropic support in 2009, with a goal to expand the approach to many more schools in the city.[23] The School of One's design responds to the condition that many urban schools face where students come in with extreme differences in language and academic preparation. Some are fluent readers with strong achievement records, and some are recent immigrants still adjusting to the culture. The school provides students with access to computers and software within an enriched virtual structure that decouples traditional classroom organization to put more students in the driver's seat. At the center of the School of One program is a complex "learning algorithm" that looks at what is next on each student's learning path to produce daily digital playlists and teacher/student schedules. The algorithm (built by Wireless Generation and Microsoft) includes standards and assessment as well as different approaches to learning. Initial research by the New York City Department of Education and an external evaluator showed promise, but it is too soon to tell how effective the program is in producing learning gains and how cost-effective it is compared with other educational options.[24] In 2010, the School of One received a DoED Investment in Innovation (i3) Fund grant worth almost $5 million that will enable the program to build its technology platform, expand, and undergo "a rigorous evaluation."[25]

While the School of One operates within a public school system, many of the innovations in school structure have come from charter schools. One notable example is Rocketship Education, founded in 2006 by former technology executive John Danner and TFA corps member Preston Smith. After selling his successful Internet marketing firm, Danner, trained originally as an engineer, returned to school to earn a master's in education from Vanderbilt University. He then worked with charter schools, including leading a KIPP school, before launching Rocketship in San Jose, CA, at the invitation of a local parish priest.

Like the School of One, Rocketship serves a disadvantaged population, with 90% qualifying for free lunch and 75% classified as English language learners. The *Rocketship Blended Model* is rotation-based, with students moving between a main classroom where literacy and social studies are taught, a math and science classroom, and a large media lab where aides rather than teachers support their individualized practice. It is hard to compare Rocketship with other school models in one dimension or another. The Rocketship approach needs to be thought of as part of a holistic program that also includes committed teachers and high parental involvement. The program uses younger teachers who likely would have lower salaries in other systems, but Rocketship has a higher pay scale and expects a greater time commitment of its teachers. It also has academic deans who work specifically with the teachers on instruction. The campus I visited did not have a library/media center or a central gymnasium/all-purpose room, but did have a large playground and student garden. It did not use traditional textbooks and instead had large files of curricular materials that were reproduced as needed. Rocketship developed a scheduler algorithm similar to the one used at the School of One with funding from both the Gates and Broad Foundations and in 2011 was awarded a $1.8 million grant from the DoED to support its expansion into more states.

These are two examples of blended learning in the K–12 space that are grounded in traditional campuses and classroom settings. There are many more approaches being tried online and in charter schools, with foundation funding. If the growth of the charter sector is any precedent, K–12 blended learning experimentation also will see rapid growth in the coming years.

Learning Organization Objects

With blended models like Rocketship and the School of One comes a new kind of data artifact that I call *learning organization objects*. In addition to assessments, demographic data, metadata and paradata, and all the other forms of data in use in education today and coming through new tools, is this new category that blended learning programs need in order to organize different sociotechnical components to make a modified school structure possible. They can come under different names—the School of One and Rocketship use the term *learning algorithm*. The SLC, described earlier, uses a learning map, and the Khan Academy has similar kinds of objects that organize the content and assessments it makes available. Regardless of the name, these objects all serve a similar purpose: organizing information about student goals and progress. This growing category of technologies—the learning organization objects—will become essential for scheduling of activities and visualization of results.[26] These objects are not necessary in a school organized around the classical model. In the classical model, each teacher's classroom defines what is learned within it, and each teacher maintains fundamental responsibility for assigning and coordinating the activities of their students. Where specialists are involved, the teachers work with them to coordinate what students do. In these new blended learning models, however, there is no longer that single point of responsibility for the students, who can be learning across settings as part of their regular school day. This leads to a need to coordinate and organize that instructional work, and the learning organization objects serve that role.

These artifacts are analogous to parts in the State Longitudinal Data Systems (SLDS) that connect different kinds of information at a larger scale. The SLDS programs are not in themselves so much data systems as *integration systems* that are intended to connect other forms of data. These newer organization objects have a similar purpose at the student level, tracking cognitive steps and recording student activity. These objects also can represent a shift in organizational control. Rather than the teacher being the manager, the management of instruction becomes at least partly regulated through these learning organization objects. These objects have corollary information structures in businesses that structure processes such as call centers and production lines with automation and information tools. However, unlike businesses, which often can clearly define their processes, educational approaches can vary from setting to setting and often from one part of the curriculum to the next. And teachers often need to vary their approach to respond to particular student circumstances in order to teach well, so tight prescription and regulation in learning organization objects could well be counter to good instruction. Moreover, it cannot be stated strongly enough that the research base that could inform best practices in many curricular areas is either light or nonexistent, so there may not yet be adequate theory to support the design of these objects in many part of the curriculum.

THE FAMILIAR QUESTIONS OF SUCCESS AND SCALE

This chapter has covered some new ideas and technologies and their potential to make traditional classroom instruction more efficient and personalized. These innovations also have the potential to support new designs for schools and classrooms in which the classical model of instruction is altered, students can be more in control of their own education and more engaged, and assessment is less intrusive. While there is much new affecting the technical core of K–12 education, new technology to transform education is not an entirely new story. Across many decades, different innovations have been presented as having the potential to reshape education. Some of the technologies that promised to revolutionize learning include film and video, personal computers, interactive websites, collaboration technologies, and immersive games. For the most part, these innovations and technologies have failed to live up to the hype. There is also a history of over-promising and under-delivering in alternative school designs. One of the more prominent and relevant examples was a movement to promote what was called "open education" or "schools without walls," which began in Britain in the late 1960s and was rapidly adopted in the United States shortly thereafter. The open education movement revolved around a different conception of the teacher: less a knowledge transmitter and more a tutor. It placed an emphasis on student-directed learning, collaboration among teachers and students, and individualization of learning—many of the ideas encoded in the new blended models for education.[27] As with many reasonable education reform ideas that have some indications of possible success, the open education movement ultimately failed to take hold and transform education as we know it. Some have cited the way it was implemented, the expectations of parents and other stakeholders for more traditional education, and the advent of the back-to-basics movement and standards-based reform as reasons for its failure.[28]

Over years and through countless new innovations, the classical model of teaching has held its ground. Not only do classrooms often look the same as they have for decades, but they often behave the same. What is it about these new technologies and approaches that is worth a deeper look?

One new aspect of today's mix of technology and alternative blended designs is that there are *both social and technical* components covering a broader range of the parts of the technical core than many previous attempts have. Most of the technologies put forward in the past as transformative were single technologies. And when these technologies were used, the classical, social structure of the classroom, the teacher's role in the school, was unchanged. Also, the earlier "new" school designs did not include technologies that would help coordinate and manage the new school processes. Interestingly, Success for All, discussed in Chapter 6, combined a set of learning tools, data tools, and organizational principles, and it is still thriving. Whether the impact of this program is beneficial for different kinds of circumstances is a matter separate from the fact that the comprehensive programmatic approach, with a combination of social and technical components, is able to survive where disconnected elements often have failed. We can speculate that an integrated design that combines tools and organizational structure can lead to better results. And there are now a range of tools that could work together to support many new school designs. The examples of successful blended models such as Rocketship can be seen as proofs of concepts where integrated technology plays a role in disrupting the classical model of teaching.

While there is much promise in these new tools, there are also reasons to be cautious in terms of expectations for what they can deliver. As real as these possibilities are, so are the challenges that the field of K–12 education faces in achieving them. Many of these challenges will come from the deep cultural investment in the classical model. From teacher preparation through teacher evaluation, the vast majority of the educational world is organized around this traditional classical approach. This traditional approach does have organizational and market advantages in its modularity. It also has advantages for teachers, for whom teaching is complicated, but this model gives them much individual control. Also, because these technologies and approaches are so new and have not yet been rigorously evaluated, there are important questions about whether and in what situations new designs and tools will represent an improvement on the classical model. It may be that after some substantive experimentation and study, the classical model will be found to be more effective and efficient than alternatives for many school systems. Or it could be that the classical model slowly yields to more flexible technology-rich and information-driven approaches. These questions await new methods of study.

ENDURING CHALLENGES
AND FUTURE DIRECTIONS

While the educational data movement has moved at a brisk pace with new programs and developments occurring in succession throughout the first decade of this century, the path has not been easy. Across different levels of the educational enterprise, in the peripheral components and the technical core, we see a complicated story. While data advocates project dramatic benefits from using data, the evidence is not universal or conclusive. While there are some who resist the use of data and approaches that have been labeled "business reforms," few alternatives have been presented. Through understanding the roots of the educational data movement and how it is impacting different educational players and stakeholders, it is possible to see how this sociotechnical revolution can be a connector of previously disparate programs of research and development and different points of view. For all of the challenges this movement raises, it seems unlikely that policymakers will turn the clock back on pressing educators to collect and use information in their work. There are few examples of human fields that have rejected the use of formal information, even when it is imperfect, once it became available. The question, it seems, is not so much whether education will continue down the path toward greater reliance on information tools, but how. These final two chapters address this as they look at how the next steps in the data movement might unfold.

The first chapter in this part shows that the field of education has specific challenges manifested in its data. These are ways that education can claim to be special. While technology in many cases can help with these challenges, the solutions are not easy or close at hand. They will take years to provide, as the problems are rooted in the social, cognitive, and political nature of American education. While many of the business examples used in this book come from large corporations that span regions and social sectors, I do not believe any are as complex as education. Chapter 8 touches on some reasons why, by exploring data quality and reliability issues. Chapter 9, the final chapter in this book, addresses how we can look at this new era: what concepts may be helpful in understanding the educational world with data, and how those wishing to work within it can take some concrete steps toward a better-designed information future.

The earlier parts of this book featured some tensions in the political landscape of education. Some of the proponents of the educational data movement have been associated with a range of reform organizations that often have been at odds with traditional educators, their unions, and colleges of education. While the details of the educational data movement show nuance and how difficult it can be to draw clear lines in terms of which groups support what, the tensions are nevertheless still present in this movement. While the data movement can be a connector, it is unlikely to remove some of the strongly held beliefs and competing interests. This final part does not harmonize all of these issues or paint a sanguine portrait of education's future in the data world. Rather, the terrain of education, with greater data availability and use, will still be contested. Whether all interests will be equally empowered by the data that are made available is an important, and very much an open, question. What the conclusion of this book may provide is some common understandings and conceptual tools to help those who wish to work across boundaries in the next developmental stage of this transition.

8

Looking at Data:
The Big Challenges
That Are Part of Education

In February 2012, the New York City schools released value-added scores for more than 12,000 teachers, ending a years-long struggle between unions and officials over the collection and use of teacher evaluation data. New York State had been a winner in the Race to the Top (RttT) competition, getting $700 million in federal funds with the assurance of linking teacher and student data for teacher evaluation. As had been happening in many parts of the country, this work in New York had been difficult and filled with political tensions over how to consider value-added model (VAM) scores for teachers along with other types of measures. A year and a half earlier, the *Los Angeles Times* had released its own rankings of teachers in a similarly controversial move that also was bitterly contested. Teachers unions were outraged. U.S. Secretary of Education Arne Duncan called the release of the information necessary, saying "Silence is not an option."[1] In New York the situation was also tense. Bill Gates, whose foundation spent large amounts of money and influence promoting data collection, wrote an Op-Ed for *The New York Times* the day before the release arguing against publishing the rankings. Gates pointed out, as the MET study his foundation funded had found, that value-added scores are just one imperfect measure of teacher effectiveness. He argued that the shame from bad scores was no way to help teachers and that these measures did not contain enough detail to actually help teachers improve.[2]

Contrary to what the teachers union had said were assurances they would not release the scores, the New York City Department of Education handed members of the media disks with raw data about teachers, and *The New York Times* promptly published the results. One teacher, listed with the lowest score, was reported to work with immigrant students who often had limited English proficiency.[3] Armed with the public data, the media descended on this teacher's home, calling her the "worst teacher in the city" and questioning her employment by the school. By all accounts, similar to other teachers who have been identified as poor performers through VAMs, this teacher was well respected and considered competent by her colleagues.

It is widely acknowledged by all involved with VAMs that the scores are often unstable. A VAM measure can vary in some cases from what statisticians believe could be the real underlying value by 30–50%.[4] What is less discussed, but widely acknowledged by many familiar with them, is that VAM scores can be based on data with errors and quality issues that are difficult to resolve, including the records of student to teacher assignments, which seemed a simple policy matter a few years earlier.[5] What critics and some researchers report is that teachers could be given ratings on courses they did not teach. Students could be attributed to teachers who never saw them. School and class rosters often are unverified and in many cases are wrong. The issues are not limited to New York, as many district data systems have similar inaccuracies. We may wonder how this can be. Certainly districts have been collecting data like this for decades. Surely by now they must have figured out how to have reliable information so as to be able to evaluate teachers. Actually, data quality remains one of the biggest challenges of this era. For many of the 12,000 teachers in New York in 2012 and a similar number in Los Angeles in 2010, their names were published for all to see with scores that in some cases could have been based on questionable data.

As the data movement in education builds and evolves, many of those working within it have come to realize that educational data are different from data in other fields such as those discussed in Chapter 2. There are more challenges in the way the data appear that often seem particular to education. Just as the business foundations of this movement are important for appreciating this transition, so are the challenges to educational data critical to understanding what is unique or special about this field. Some of these challenges stem from the multileveled social nature of education, and some are made greater by the way educational institutions are arranged and managed in America. These issues are more pronounced, perhaps, in the technical core. However, the issues that affect educational data in the technical core will reverberate throughout the system, as the example of teacher evaluation scores shows. These are some of the reasons the Data Quality Campaign (DQC) is still around years after its initial project was scheduled to end. Some of these quality problems can be thought of as weaknesses in the technology for data collection. However, there are other, social factors involved.

This chapter will explore some of the ways that educational data can be weak or fallible, which ends up impacting the uses for the data, including evaluating teachers. This discussion entails understanding data quality and consistency—not usually exciting topics that capture the imagination, such as equity, teacher effectiveness, college and career readiness, allocation of resources, or return on investment. However, these troublesome data-quality issues are an essential part of the educational data movement story. These seemingly technical issues become important considerations for what is practical and what is reasonable for policy. They cast a shadow over efforts to bring data-oriented management tools into education.

CANARIES, CHEATING, AND CAMPBELL'S LAW

In the early days of coal mining, one way to detect a buildup of lethal methane gas was to bring a live canary into the mine. A dead bird was an early warning to miners to evacuate. Now the phrase "a canary in a coal mine" has become part of our vernacular. It indicates impending danger. For the educational data movement, a canary in the coal mine began to emerge with reports of widespread cheating on high-stakes tests. From 2010 on, it became routine for high-profile districts that had shown solid test score improvements, including Baltimore, Washington, DC, Boston, Philadelphia, and notoriously Atlanta, to be accused of widespread cheating.[6] Usually the cheating involved helping students answer questions or teachers erasing students' wrong answers and filling in the right ones. Many believe that even more cheating actually took place than was reported, because to clearly identify these practices an in-depth investigation would be required, which few school systems funded. Because a finding of cheating would be an embarrassment, cheating investigations rarely receive much local support. Atlanta was an especially significant example because a multi-year and costly investigation conducted by the Georgia Bureau of Investigation concluded that almost 180 teachers and principals participated in widespread systemic cheating.[7] It was a dramatic turnaround for Atlanta. In 2009, the leader of the Atlanta Public Schools had been hailed as a successful reformer, winning Superintendent of the Year for her ability to use data and raise student achievement.[8]

What these scandals made clear is that educational data can be subject to direct manipulation and that practitioners will, in certain circumstances, collude to mislead. Different people interpret this differently. Some question educators' integrity, saying they are more focused on their own jobs than on the children, and that they will work together to willingly mislead those trying to help education. Others take the view that educators were put in an untenable position by the accountability system and reacted in an unfortunate, but understandable, way. What is more important than determining the extent of cheating is recognizing it as a clear sign that much of educational data cannot always be taken at face value. It isn't just test scores that can be manipulated. Class rosters, schedules, and many other essential data require human intervention, opening the door for errors and misrepresentation.

We can think of cheating in a larger sense that also includes cases where teachers game the system: coach students and teach specifically to the types of questions on tests. These practices undermine what the tests are intended to do, which is sample from student knowledge to support inferences about what they are learning. We can see both cheating and coaching as being related to a problem that any social system might have. Even if scores are not changed, when teachers teach to the test or focus instruction on some students, such as the bubble kids discussed in Chapter 5, the purpose of the indicator is corrupted. This is known as *Campbell's Law*, after American psychologist Donald Campbell, who observed in 1976:

> The more any [one] quantitative social indicator is used for social decision-making, the more subject it will be to corruption pressures and the more apt it will be to distort and corrupt the social processes it is intended to monitor.[9]

Campbell's Law also can be applied to newer forms of social indicators, for example, teacher or principal effectiveness ratings. While these new data forms exist for important reasons, they invite new questions. What actions might educators take to exclude some students from being counted? How might they manipulate scores to show "growth" within their own classrooms? How might consequential value-added evaluations of teachers encourage them to focus on taking care of their own students' test scores rather than approaching teaching as a collective school process?

Other fields may have similar ways in which indicators affect social behavior. But the issue looms large in education because the very nature of the technical core of education is social. In medicine, which often has been used as a close analogy, there is little evidence that the act of measuring vital signs (temperature, blood pressure, heart rate, etc.) causes physiological changes. The fact that so much of educational data is manually entered, including student class attendance, civil rights compliance information, and data to track federal program expenses, makes the problem of false or unreliable information a general problem. Without the kind of automated collection that many other fields routinely use to retrieve operational data, education has opportunities for human error and deliberate misreporting.

CHALLENGES WITH MEASUREMENT AND KNOWING WHAT STUDENTS KNOW

From an information science point of view, educational measurements are the first link in chains of data that end up being used over and over again. We can think of the student test score as analogous to a deposit in banking, a blood pressure reading in health care, or a purchase of products in retail.

These source data form the foundation of larger information architectures. If the foundation is weak, it will ripple through the rest of the system and introduce other errors and excessive data noise. Once recorded, student test scores (at least the high-stakes ones) do not get thrown away. They end up being saved in data warehouses and longitudinal data systems where the data can be combined, summarized, and used for many different analyses. Other fields often can collect consistent source data directly from instruments connected to machines so that reliable data end up in data warehouses to be used with analytics and problem solving. In education, the data warehouses and longitudinal data systems are fed by streams of information that include significant imprecision and little diagnostic detail.

At every level of the educational enterprise discussed in this book, student assessments have played a dominant, although not exclusive, role. But they do have issues. Although, at times, the scores from educational tests can be quite accurate and reliable, in many cases they are not. They are often imprecise and represent only fragments of information. The information that is collected may be the most practical, but not always the most useful. These problems are not limited to data use in VAMs, but rather are fundamental to the nature of educational assessments. Few measurements in the history of modern civilization have been the object of more study and efforts to refine them than educational assessments. They can vary across different types of students and within the same student from test to test. They can be inexact, coarse and limited for diagnostic purposes, and often intrusive on practice. The result is that they usually cover parts of the curriculum and support narrow analyses. Each of these issues is discussed in more detail below.

Imprecision

The challenges with getting accurate scores, while not unique to education, are beyond what most other fields deal with because there is so much variation in the cognition to be measured across many grades and subjects, and because cognition is only part of the issue with the social process of learning.[10] The issue is not specific to the tests, although most people blame testing for it. One of the reasons for the significant costs of implementing state testing, which routinely reach tens of millions of dollars per state per year, is the development work to increase the reliability of tests.[11] Educational measurement under any circumstances entails fundamental challenges. Across many fields that measure, imprecision—known as *measurement error*—is common. A 2011 report from the National Research Council on the use of tests for providing performance incentives for educators stated:

[Large-scale tests] are neither perfect nor comprehensive measures. . . . Test scores will typically differ from one occasion to another even when there has been no change in a test taker's proficiency because of chance differences in the interaction of the test questions, the test taker, and the testing context. Researchers think of these fluctuations as measurement error and so treat test results as estimates of test takers' "true scores" and not as "the truth" in an absolute sense.[12]

The large-scale tests that are the backbone of accountability policies and at the center of State Longitudinal Data Systems implementations contain numerous measurement errors and variation. The term *measurement error*, however, can be misleading. It allows educational test scores to appear similar to other types of measurements where devices introduce some noise and variation. It tends to make variation seem a minor technical matter, yet much of this error is not technical, but social. It has to do with real students and their interactions within social activities. For example, in mixed number arithmetic with fractions (e.g., 2 ¼ + ½), students are more likely to get the right answers on some test items if teachers teach one set of strategies for solving these problems than if they teach another set of pedagogically sound strategies.[13] This is a specific, researched example of how the tests can be sensitive to particular teaching approaches that often vary by teacher. Using the medical analogy, if a physician used a thermometer or blood pressure meter on a person several times in a row, the readings likely would be slightly different. This is a normal kind of fluctuation that occurs with the tools used to take the measurements. If those medical readings were like educational assessments, they at times might seem to be the result of devices in frequent need of calibration.

Diagnostic Challenges

The vast majority of conventional educational tests lack diagnostic detail. Part of this has to do with their traditional psychometric design. Psychometrics involves the theories and approaches of psychological measurement used to gauge knowledge, abilities, attitudes, and traits. Some could argue it is one of the most advanced educational sciences. The psychometric measurement forms the backbone of all high-stakes tests used in the United States. Many of the interim assessments that occur throughout the year and other available types of tests also are designed using psychometric principles. Whether they use multiple-choice or more open responses, psychometric test items are designed to map students onto a predetermined range or scale of ability. This is, however, a fundamental limitation in mapping learning onto cognitive scales. When knowledge does not translate easily onto a sequence of levels, but rather is more cognitively complex and varied, then traditional psychometric techniques can break down. One reason so many tests seem artificial to educators is that the types of questions used in them are ones that easily fit a psychometric scale rather than those that measure the complex multidimensional skills and abilities that relate to student learning, such as asking questions or explaining their thinking.

In 2001, at the dawn of the NCLB era, the National Research Council, a division of the National Academy of Sciences, issued a seminal report called *Knowing What Students Know: The Science and Design of Educational Assessment*. This report brought together leaders in the field of educational measurement who reviewed what was known at that time about assessment and said:

> Traditional tests do not focus on many aspects of cognition that research indicates are important, and they are not structured to capture critical differences in students' levels of understanding. For example, important aspects of learning not adequately tapped by current assessments include students' organization of knowledge, problem representations, use of strategies, self-monitoring skills, and individual contributions to group problem solving.[14]

The authors organized the assessment process into three distinct parts: cognition, observation, and interpretation, which form what they called the *assessment triangle*. The assessment triangle is a way to explain that to give students an assessment, there should be an underlying cognitive model. The cognitive model is used to structure both the assessment tasks for the students and how the students' responses should be interpreted. Even though leaders in the field were able to describe an ambitious promise of rich cognitive assessment in 2001, the reality is that most of the assessments developed for NCLB and used today are heavy in traditional multiple-choice items with limited diagnostic potential.[15] Importantly, there are significant diagnostic challenges to measuring these cognitive states. Prevailing theory strongly indicates that learning is a social as well as a cognitive process and that learning occurs in many ways and settings inside and outside of school, factors that are extremely difficult to measure with narrow and imperfect psychometric measurements.[16]

Practical Challenges to Educational Measurement

Educational measurement as a research activity often is focused on important technical details that will increase cognitive measurement breadth and accuracy. Educational measurement in practice, however, occurs within constraints. It involves trade-offs just as other management systems do. In addition to being less reliable than measurements from other fields, educational measurements need to fit tight budgetary and time windows in their administration. This also makes them tend toward the artificial and away from what should be occurring naturally in learning.

One of the most important trade-offs involves the types of tasks that students are given in assessments. Traditionally, these tasks involve responding to limited stimuli: selecting an answer, or providing a short response. Longer-response test items do occur, but they are less common. While it is convenient to criticize the multiple-choice test format used in many high-stakes tests and to contrast it with the type of work students do, or that we want them to be doing, in class as they develop deep skills and competencies, the multiple choice item format is efficient and cost-effective to score compared with other methods available today. The multiple-choice tests are often more reliable at the same cost than alternatives. More authentic, constructed response items traditionally have required human raters, which drives up costs and drives down reliability.

Before NCLB, many states and many textbook publishers had developed richer forms of assessments using authentic tasks (performance assessments) or collections of student work (portfolio assessments). These more authentic forms did have greater connection to the kinds of issues that teachers were dealing with. They were also extremely expensive to administer and had greater error than traditional items. A 2005 history of the use of educational tests, by professors Edward Haertel from Stanford and Joan Herman from UCLA, explained why states moved away from these ways of measuring students:

> Disillusionment with high costs, low reliability, and poor student performance on these examinations, coupled with the dramatic increase in amount of testing required under NCLB, have brought a shift back to heavy reliance on multiple-choice tests; the promise and potential of performance assessment remain unfulfilled.[17]

Another practical challenge comes from the fact that educational assessments are often intrusive in the classroom. To collect measures that gauge instructional effectiveness usually requires interrupting the natural flow of instruction. Many other fields are able to collect core process information automatically. In manufacturing, a shop floor device can provide a steady stream of data about its own operation without affecting that operation. Credit card companies get records of all account transactions automatically because purchase technology provides them without affecting the process. Health care is a little different. At one time, almost all health indicators required someone to physically visit the patient to collect the data, which were then recorded on paper. Even then, however, the act of measuring, for example, blood pressure had little impact on the flow of blood. Today, thanks to technology, many important health indicators, such as blood pressure and temperature, also are increasingly automated. In contrast, educational measurement still typically requires the instructional flow of a class to be interrupted.

The formative assessment movement, discussed in Chapter 5, has great potential to provide data points, but formative assessments historically have not been digital and typically have not been of a quality that can be used for robust statistics. They often are not based on psychometrics and are not easily aligned with other assessments, although this area also could see growth in the coming years. While there is promise in new forms of assessment technologies, including natural language processing and games and simulations, discussed in Chapter 7, many are still in the research stage. Few have reached the level of quality that they can be widely used for high-stakes purposes.

Fragmented Data

Compared with other fields that have used information successfully for transformation, educational data can be extremely spotty. Because of the practical costs of developing and administering tests, the information collected today from most educational assessments is fragmentary. Rather than a detailed record of instruction and cognition or a view of the spectrum of what students need to learn, educational datasets are largely measures of small bits of knowledge in those areas that are easiest to test.[18] This is different from other fields, which often can gain data easily across the spectrum of their activities. In banking, each and every financial transaction for an account is recorded. In retail, virtually every shipment and every sale are recorded. Health care, again, is a little different in that it is largely diagnostic, whereas education has some diagnostic as well as ongoing monitoring uses for information. Walmart can predict with a high degree of accuracy all of the items that are in a warehouse, in their trucks, and in stores, and those that have just been purchased. At best, educational tests represent only a scattering of points in the educational process. The backbone of educational testing occurs in a handful of subjects and grades. It would be as if a grocery store chain were functioning with data about produce and dairy products, but not meat, frozen food, or canned goods. Further, the tests used for accountability, the ones that feed into the SLDSs, are designed to be administered all at once to all students irrespective of where the students are in the learning process, so that they are increasingly at odds with personalization.

LEARNING TARGETS

Another critical component of an educational infrastructure is the definition of learning targets, also known as learning objectives, goals, standards, or benchmarks. Learning targets and their complexity is another area particular to education. These targets, which define what should be taught, are naturally related to assessments. Learning targets helped usher in the standards-based reform movement that began in the 1980s.[19] The logic was simple: Explicit student learning goals would result in better performance. This was another simple promise that has proven difficult to fulfill. Many states implemented their own standards that in some cases were not rigorous and generally were different from the way other states did it.

One of the challenges today in comparing the results of different groups of students in different parts of the country is that different states have developed unique sets of standards that do not align well. As a result, comparing test results from one state to another has been problematic. State-by-state comparisons can be done using the National Assessment of Educational Progress (NAEP) test. But the NAEP tests are limited because not all students take them. Also, NAEP comparisons are based on the NAEP test structure/goals rather than on state learning goals, which should be the common reference point for both instruction and assessment. The Common Core, discussed in Chapter 3, holds much promise as do the Next Generation Science Standards, also in development. And the new assessments aligned to these standards also hold promise. However, these standards cover only part of the curriculum and they are all unproven in widespread practice. As good as these standards are and as much research as they are based on, they still suffer from some of the same challenges as any other learning standards do in terms of clearly specifying what it means to learn something. Like assessment, specifying learning targets is an inexact process that results in specifications that may work better with one community, for example, assessment developers, than another community, such as teachers.

If we were to look for an analogous type of information object in other fields, the master lists for products that are used to link retail and manufacturing data or the master subject lists used by libraries might be close. Educational learning goals, however, are much more complex. They can be used to design test items, to organize results, and to align professional development. But they are unique information objects. They can be short declarative statements or expositions with examples. They have rarely been studied in detail and yet are critical for allowing information about student learning to be effectively collected and shared.[20] They are an important part of the learning organization objects that blended learning models, discussed in Chapter 7, depend upon. And where those other fields often convened standard-setting bodies to help develop their common reference lists, in education the decentralized nature of educational governance has provided little mechanism for such a common collaboration. The challenges with learning targets are compounded when they are organized into collections of standards systems. These collections typically group individual targets and in some cases organize them into curricular sequences or progressions. This organization can be influenced by research in some parts of the curriculum, such as math or physics, where there are clear cognitive dependencies. In other areas, for example, social studies and parts of science, there can be a wide variation in practice and fragmentation of the research base so that it is difficult to know clearly which curricular approaches are best.

TWO CONDITIONS FOR INFORMATION USE: DATA CONSISTENCY AND COMPARABILITY

The progress that other fields have made in using information technology for organizational improvement (discussed in Chapter 2) often has been based on data that were consistent and comparable. Organizations that used software suites to integrate different parts of their operations were able to do so because the information was consistent enough to replace interpersonal communication. When those organizations started to use data warehouses to aggregate data and later as a platforms for analytics, the data they used were often uniform so that they could easily be used in pattern analysis algorithms. In contrast, educational data are often rife with inconsistencies stemming from the unique and context-sensitive ways schools are organized and staffed. Much of this is fundamental to the multilayered social nature of schooling, with individual and organizational conditions that vary by location.

Variation has always been an important topic in the development of any organizational information technology. The professionals who design such systems spend significant effort determining what things are similar enough to be classified in the same way and how to handle information that describes how one item or organization or role differs from another. The process of building these systems—whether for human resources, accounting, shipping, sales, or health care—essentially involves reducing complex things into simple categories. This reduction is a prerequisite for interchange of information. In many fields, the reduction to simplified categories involves little loss of information. For example, electronics manufacturers and book publishers both sell products through Amazon. They are different types of organizations, but might be reduced into the same category of "vendor" in Amazon's technology. My neighbor and I are both customers of Amazon and we might be reduced into the same category of "customer" even though he buys kitchen appliances and I buy kids' toys. However, Amazon is able to track us with the similar data categories, including shipping addresses and purchasing preferences. In other fields, the real-world entities—people, organizations, and products—are more complex than the simplified categories developed to track information about them. Yet those differences usually are not consequential for how the organization does business. In education, the differences between the things that are compared are usually extremely important to the operation of education. Different teachers, for example, are different in ways that matter to school organization and how they are assigned.

As data accumulate in data warehouses for analysis, the classifications used to record them lead to a homogenization of information. Differences between schools and districts often will be reduced into simple codes, or more likely will not even be reflected. When the data subsequently are used for analysis, the differences can become stealth data-quality issues. The entities in the data warehouses, for example, schools, look comparable, but there can be programmatic differences that are hidden. It is common for people to recognize that students are individuals and that treating them all in the same way is problematic, yet teachers, classrooms, schools, school systems, and states all often have distinctive characteristics as well. In fact, the types of reporting required by funders and the technical ways that educational data structures are organized often reflect simplistic homogeneous views of educational systems, although in practice there are substantial differences.

This can be a problem for research as well as for meaningful analysis. Across many fields—medicine, geology, geography, and now education—databases are becoming more central to research. Many people and organizations, including the DoED and many of the reformers promoting the data agenda for education, look to the potential of datasets that will accumulate in coming years to open up new possibilities for research. And while many insights likely will come from these new collections that districts and states are building, there also may be analytic "phantoms" hidden within them that make schools and professionals look the same in analysis when they are, in fact, substantively different.

LINKING UP IS HARD TO DO:
THE CRITICAL TEACHER–STUDENT DATA LINK

In sociotechnical revolutions, there are often technical details that play a large role in how the movement unfolds. Frequently, these details are well understood by only some technologists. For example, the key to the printing press was the movable type that allowed fast reuse of a given press. It was a simple electromagnetic innovation that allowed the telephone to become practical and quickly ended the telegraph age. The Open Systems Interconnect communications protocol that allows information to be exchanged among different devices is a modern example. This standard is used to connect computers, cell phones, and tablets, and made the Internet practical. The kind of dynamic relationships that retailers like Amazon and Walmart have with suppliers is made possible through Electronic Data Interchange standards that allow them to transmit orders and payments instantaneously. In fact, many great sociotechnical possibilities, such as video phones, actually were predicted years before they happened, but needed certain key technical problems to be solved before they could realize their potential. In the educational data movement, one of the key technical challenges that needs to be met in order to allow greater analysis across educational systems is the ability to link previously separate information. One of the most important links in education is from teachers to students. Some have called this the Teacher–Student Data Link (TSDL). Linking these teacher and student records was a cornerstone of the RttT program and one of the driving issues for the DQC, especially in its early years.

The TSDL is an important problem that many districts and states have worked to solve during the past decade. And it is one that many are finding it extremely difficult to fully resolve because it involves much more than matching two database records. It entails sometimes complex relationships between educators and students, and accounting for the variation that occurs in real practice. At the state level, it requires reconciling different approaches that different districts take, which for some states can result in hundreds of variations. Beyond having a robust technical architecture, this association calls for a chain of actions and information to ensure the right data are properly connected and dealing with issues of data consistency, comparability, and quality, as discussed above.

The driving force behind the TSDL becoming a big issue is that it is required for the VAMs used in teacher evaluations. When this became a policy consideration and tied to federal money, states and districts needed to find a way to address it. Recognizing that many districts and states were unprepared for this, the Gates Foundation launched a TSDL project managed by the Boston-based Center for Education, Leadership and Technology.[21] This project began in 2010, working with 15 districts in five states.[22] The DQC was a partner in the project to support dissemination of results. What this project showed is just how hard a TSDL is to implement in practice. First, a teacher of record needs to be indentified for the students. Sometimes, there is more than one teacher responsible for the instruction of a single pupil and subject combination. This is complicated by technical dependencies, which include having reliable unique student and teacher identifiers, up-to-date course and schedule information in the school data system, and accurately maintained class rosters. Before the TSDL requirement, class rosters and course listings had little importance, so in many cases districts and schools had not taken these areas seriously. The situation becomes harder when trying to account for other aspects of practice where the connections between teachers and students vary, including team teaching and mobility, special education, and online/distance courses. Each of these areas presents different issues that have to be contended with in order to have a reliable TSDL and then meaningful VAM scores. With team teaching and mobility, there can be two or more teachers for a given student in a given year. When there is more than one teacher or when teachers leave, how is the contribution to learning to be measured by annual tests? Do all teachers have an equal weight or influence on learning, or can the learning be assigned to the students in percentages? When students move in mid-term, a similar situation occurs; in addition, their progress is likely disrupted, presenting new instructional challenges for teachers who need to incorporate them into a class in the middle of a year. Both of these complex realities are often more prevalent in high-poverty areas.

Special education presents similar challenges. In some cases, the students are educated only by special educators, but more than one, as each can support a different area for the student. In the majority of cases, special education students are included in mainstream classes some or most of the time. The circumstances with "mainstreamed" special education kids vary since each has his or her own Individual Education Program (IEP). In some cases, the student moves between a regular and a special education classroom. In some cases, the special educator moves with the student. A robust TSDL would need to account for many of these situations. Since special education teachers are limited resources, different schools may handle these arrangements differently in order to ensure that the students with special needs get the most support from the resources available in the particular school. Assigning values to these different teachers is both a policy and a practical decision. It could be a simple matter to identify the different educators who help a student with special needs. It is quite another to try to assign weights to those contributions for a high-stakes teacher evaluation.

There is a potential danger in these challenges that policymakers will attempt to make practice fit a simplified view in their technology. The use of a TSDL for a VAM may require that school districts make specific choices regarding how to implement the linkage between teachers and students:

whether to give only one teacher credit for a student's learning or to share it among all those who have been involved with the child. If educators decide to assign students to classes to make the models more reliable, or to assign educators to students in ways that make their TSDL cleaner, they also may be shortchanging their ability to make reasonable decisions about how to best educate their students given the resources they have.

While there are benefits in terms of accountability and reporting from these linkages, some of the most promising technological innovations may make achieving these benefits more difficult. Distance education introduces new challenges since the instructional responsibility can be shifted outside of the school system. This is one of the fastest-growing areas in education today and yet for a TSDL program it can bring new headaches. When a student takes a single online class in secondary school, the district would need to account for the student's learning and attribute it to some individual. With distance education the online teacher is likely not an employee of the school system; therefore, assigning a value to his or her contribution is difficult. As education moves toward more blended models, in which teachers can have parts of courses taught through distance options (some even without teachers), the issues of attributing student learning to different teachers and then calculating contributions in a meaningful way become more and more complicated.

The TSDL is one specific challenge in educational data. The VAM is a high-profile use for it. It is also an example of the general challenges with linking data across diverse practices. From the perspective of a database design, the linking of teacher and student records seems trivial. But in order for this link to be realized and usable for its intended aims, a host of policy and practical issues need to be addressed, including how districts and schools maintain records, how mobility and collaborative teaching are managed, and the technologies that are used to maintain this information. To make this matter a little more complex, each jurisdiction that manages these types of data—state, district, and in some cases schools—can approach the decisions differently, and harmonizing the approaches different jurisdictions take is not trivial.

We also can think of the TSDL as an example of a general type of challenge that education will face as we try to make data connections to support more types of analyses about people and institutions. Many other linkages may run into difficulties similar to those the TSDL did. For example, the definitions of courses, which are essential for comparing results, can vary across districts and even schools. The rub here is that linking provides greater visibility into education at a systemic scale, but that visibility can be cloudy.

SEARCHING FOR BALANCE
IN THE EDUCATIONAL DECISION SCIENCES

We are in a new era of American education. Most of the chapters in this book have looked at the forward momentum toward a data-rich future. This chapter has covered reasons that progress may be slow, messy, and difficult. These reasons revolve around the social and cognitive nature of education, the ways that educational information often requires people to provide it directly or through their actions, the difficulties in measuring student knowledge and learning, the challenges in specifying what learning means, the fact that many parts of the educational world can seem comparable through the data systems when they are not, and the very real practical challenges with linking up some educational data required for deep analysis. The issues discussed in this chapter are will not go away easily, nor are they immovable barriers to progress. They are, however, significant and deeply rooted. Recognizing them may lead to a new kind of understanding of the particular aspects of education that impact data use. The fundamental and well-known challenges surrounding measuring student learning beg the question why policymakers and reformers bent on holding teachers accountable would use any system based on assessments with these inherent limitations. Educational test scores, even without tampering, are often only rough approximations. In reality, for all their flaws, they are still some of the best ways available to measure outcomes of classes in a systematic way. Alternative methods have suffered from even bigger problems! This, however, is part of the challenge of educational data: that the best that is available is often not optimal for the goals we have for it.

If we think about the underlying conditions that lead to problems that are prevalent in educational data, we also can see that the debates over the release of VAM scores to the public, for example, can be an indication of a new type of discussion that is occurring about evidence in this field. We may be seeing a new type of decision science emerging and a new kind of validity discussion involving *usefulness* versus *accuracy*. For which purposes can data, even imperfect data, be used? The DQC often gives the message that data should be used as a flashlight rather than a hammer. If data are a light, when is a dim light (weak data) better than none at all? Is navigating using flawed data better than navigating by intuition and custom? Educators and others in the field recognize the tensions around bottom-up versus top-down reform, around centralized versus decentralized control, and so on. Now, there is a new type of tension around data: how good is good enough to be used and for which purposes? The debates about VAMs exemplify this. Those opposed to VAMs focus on the unreliability of the data. The proponents counter that the data are often good enough to make informed decisions, especially when other forms of information can be used to triangulate. Beneath both is this shift in perspective on evidence and implications for the evidence movement, as was discussed in Chapter 1.

As a new kind of decision science, the educational version will be partly political science. Unlike most businesses, the educational world involves issues and contests about data that have little to do with the data themselves, and much to do with the social and political nature of education. The data aren't just about objects and processes. They are about specific groups of kids and adults. The data aren't just about how to approach a task in a different way, but often relate to the very fabric of expectations for what it means to teach and what it means to be a learner. Rather than being dry and hard facts, educational data are often at the boundaries of important issues that likely will affect efforts to collect, interpret, and use the information. The stories at the beginning of the chapter show that as organizations attempt to gain advantage in their sometimes decades-old struggles over the role of labor and free enterprise in education, data likely will continue to be a tool they use. The decision sciences for education will need to find some way of including these issues that often are only partly technical and in many ways social.

9

Toward an Integrated Design Science

This book has shown how the educational data movement is part of a historical sociotechnical transition. Although its roots began in the later part of the 20th century, the educational data movement became more prominent at the beginning of the 21st century, with legislation, philanthropies, and elected officials playing catalytic roles. This movement has now affected different levels of the complex American educational system, individually and simultaneously. At the beginning of this movement, it seemed for many that "data" and "testing" were synonymous. However, over time we see evidence that assessments are one of many categories of information that are being used in practices across multiple levels and time scales. For each type of assessment—including high-stakes and summative, interim in schools, formative in classrooms, and those embedded within learning technologies—an information ecology is evolving around it. We also see, around these diverse data, complex practices that often are not well understood.

Big promises have been made about data in education. Many of them remain unfulfilled. In many statements that can be made to summarize this movement, there needs to be the following qualification: While we see promise in one aspect, the reality falls short and the future will be challenging. The State Longitudinal Data Systems (SLDS) program has made progress in providing increased data capacity across the states, but these systems often are not compatible so that sharing data across them is difficult. Over the past decade, many districts have been building data warehouses that bring together different sources of information about students, teachers, and programs. Still, many of those infrastructures are plagued by technical difficulties and slow adoptions. There are reports of data being used to highlight the quality of teachers and teacher education programs, but many of these uses have been controversial and at times plagued with questions about reliability and fairness. And although there have been reports of data being integrated into programs of instructional leadership and professional learning communities, there is little evidence these practices are widespread, and teaching is still largely an isolated activity. One statement that needs no such qualification, however, is that the educational data movement is continuing. Bit by bit, fueled by the support of elected leaders, major foundations, new social and technical developments that provide more data and/or contribute to their use, and its own inevitability, the educational data movement marches on. This chapter introduces some ways to view the educational world through the lens of the data movement and how educators and others interested in advancing data use can approach this new world.

FIVE SOCIAL SECTORS TO WATCH
THROUGH THE DATA MOVEMENT

Sociotechnical revolutions reshape landscapes of actors and sectors. Through these revolutions, certain interests, groups, and fields emerge as more important than they were before; others, less so. Telephone operators, illustrators, photographers, inventory specialists, and middle managers are all examples of professions changed by technology. Sometimes, new vocations and combinations of interests emerge as a result of the new ways of working that technology helps make possible. The educational data movement seems similar. Through it we can see familiar actors and new actors arranged in sometimes novel ways: in merging roles and raising questions about traditional conceptual boundaries and definitions. There are five categories that this book has shown are either changing, emerging, or important to reconsider through this revolution. I have not included *data scientists* in this list. While there is reason to expect new professionals with expertise in educational data will be emerging, I believe this new breed of specialist likely will emerge in several sectors rather than being a discrete movement in itself. I do discuss this kind of work near the end of this chapter, but recognize that much about the technical professionals working with educational data remains unknown.

Front-Line Practitioners: Traditional and Reform

Few areas are as important to consider as practitioners. We can think of practitioners in broad categories as including both traditional educators and educators in reform organizations. Traditional practitioners include teachers, principals, and others who work in schools; their unions; and advocacy organizations largely trained in colleges of education and through practical experience. Reformers include practitioners from alternative preparation programs such as Teach for America (TFA) and in charter school networks such as the Knowledge Is Power Program (KIPP), along with networks of organizations that support and advocate for them. These practitioners and others who do not teach but are associated with these organizations have been called "corporate reformers" by their critics.[1] Both groups of practitioners—traditional and reform—have been impacted by the data movement, but in different ways.

In the data movement, traditional practitioner communities have seen themselves become the object of study and evaluation. Colleges of education, the places where practitioners traditionally get their training and where much educational research is conducted, have seen questions arise about their role. Just as the data movement has focused a lens on teacher productivity, it also has focused a lens on these institutions and allowed researchers to ask questions about their effectiveness. These are the same places where some of the most important foundational work in how to support students was done, including the effective schools movement, formative assessments, and special education. Studies such as those discussed in Chapter 3 are now using available data to compare and rank these institutions based on their graduates' performance. New studies by researchers Edith Gummer and Ellen Mandinach and at the National Center for Teacher Quality have shown that teachers who have been trained in these institutions are rarely prepared to work with data and that data literacy is rarely part of any teacher preparation curricula.[2]

The story is almost the opposite in the reform sector that has flourished within the data movement, helped shape the movement, and has reasons to gain from greater use of data. This sector enjoys strong support from both foundation funders and the federal government. Charters and alternative preparation programs are deeply committed to using data. Many of the examples of innovation involving data have come from this community. In a sign of the ascendancy of the reform sector and the role of data in it, in 2011, KIPP, along with other charter programs in New York, started a new graduate school of education. After a 2-year pilot at New York's Hunter College called *Teacher U*, with the backing of leading foundations, the *Relay Graduate School of Education* was chartered in New York State—the first new education school chartered in 90 years. The name Relay is inspired by one of the fathers of the educational VAM movement, William Sanders, who found that having three great teachers in a row (a relay) could significantly boost a student's chances of success.[3] Relay serves the teacher preparation and continuing education needs of the charter systems in New York and neighboring states. Like KIPP, Relay is balancing between the commitment to hard numbers and the realization that achievement is not the whole story, as Relay provost (and former TFA teacher) Brent Maddin said:

Data driven instruction, along with the work at KIPP around character, is infused into the heart and soul of our program. We think they're both very important and a hallmark of the program's second year. In order to graduate from the Relay Graduate School of Education, you need to convince us that you have led your students to one year's worth of growth in one year's time.[4]

The implications of these disparities are not clear. At a time when many important infrastructural components are still being built and will not be fully usable for some time, we may not know what the level of traditional practitioners' involvement in shaping parts of the data movement will mean or even whether this imbalance will continue. In coming years, in order for the data movement to impact and reshape education's technical core, more involvement from those with in-depth knowledge of the technical core will be required, and the vast majority of these people are associated with the traditional education communities. Without active involvement of traditional practitioners, we may see that many of the promises of the data movement are difficult to achieve. As the complexity of the practice landscape increases through the proliferation of reform educators, there will be new challenges to seeing education through traditional lenses and infrastructures largely designed in the NCLB era. At the same time, there will be new types of information collections to use as different reform organizations continue to build their own data programs. These new datasets will be able to be used to support different kinds of cross-system analyses. As the data movement continues to develop, more support for the reform sector can be expected, and while new schools such as Relay may not pop up everywhere, increasing partnerships between traditional and reform organizations can be anticipated.

The Vendors and Innovators

Much of the work to advance the educational data movement will come from vendors and innovators. Vendors, including the large firms that publish textbooks and tests, have not been discussed much in this book. They have always been present in the data movement and are active in developing tools and products to sell to educational systems. The fragmented nature of the American educational enterprise is in some ways a fertile ground for adept publishers who can target specific products to regions and are able to align test prep material with textbooks and integrated suites of products, including dashboards and other information tools discussed in Chapter 7. While some of the organizations in this category are names that have been established for decades, many of those emerging now are new. The educational product sector in many ways parallels other business sector expansions, including the kind of dynamic commercial growth that followed the development of the Internet. The growth of this sector, much as with other business technology sectors, has been fueled by venture philanthropy and capital funds. With names like the New School Venture Fund and Learn Capital, these organizations provide funding and resources to new entrants. The money for these firms comes from a variety of individual and institutional sources, including some of the same philanthropies that are investors in the data movement.

Not all innovation may come from the private sector. The U.S. space program was a catalyst in advances in materials, food storage, and communications. The Internet began as a project within the Defense Advanced Research Projects Agency (DARPA), as did the Global Positioning System (GPS). With the Obama administration came the Investing in Innovation (i3) program, which provided federal investment in educational ventures. There are other federal efforts promoting new ideas and new forms of research, including an idea for a research program modeled after DARPA in education.[5] If the experience in businesses and other fields is an example, this type of entrepreneurial activity likely will lead to both successful and unsuccessful companies, with the successful ones bringing new ideas and approaches. Just as there has been asymmetric participation between traditional and reform communities in the data movement overall, this sector has had much more participation from nontraditional educators and those with little or no experience in education.

The Funders: Federal, State, and Foundation

The organizations that fund the educational data movement can be seen as a broad group, including federal and state governments and some large foundations. While the roles of these three subgroups are different—governments are required to support education and have constitutionally designated areas of responsibility, and the foundations participate voluntarily—in the context of the data movement their work often has been aligned around similar types of viewpoints and initiatives. People and ideas have moved fluidly between foundations, their funded projects, and government offices. To understand the trajectory of the educational data movement, it is important to include the foundations in this view. This would mean that to understand the policy directions of this movement, it is important to understand the interests of elected and appointed government officials as well as of the philanthropies that provide funding for staff and studies that help shape policy. Rather than seeing the foundations as a foreign element in educational discussions, perhaps it will be productive to acknowledge their role and encourage the same kind of information exchange with researchers that policymakers have often attempted.

Also, as this book has shown, a single broad category of foundations or government does not describe the variation that exists across these groups. While in some cases a group of foundations invest together, in the data movement different areas of interest are also evident: The Broad Foundation focuses on bringing new talent into education to work in districts and government offices, the Gates Foundation leads in building infrastructures and market systems, and the Dell Foundation targets performance management and strategic initiatives. These foundations are joined by Spencer, MacArthur, and other philanthropies that have invested in education for much longer. Rather than a singular set of organizations with common leadership, these foundations can be seen as a community. Unlike governments, which are subject to political pressures and change, this community is independent and can be internally driven. Foundations can move more quickly and in significant ways, as the Measures of Effective Teaching (MET) research discussed in Chapter 5 showed. That project was larger than most federal research and likely would have taken much longer to accomplish using the procedures required for publicly funded projects. Its results helped shift policies toward a more balanced approach to teacher evaluations. Likewise, governments are widely differentiated. Some states are more committed to using data than others. At the federal level, there are many different programs in the Department of Education, the National Science Foundation, and other agencies that have different kinds of relationships to this broad movement.

The Information Providers

The data movement has cut across research and information communities. As a result, the ways that we see information about education and information about the data movement itself need to be re-evaluated. The availability of large datasets has helped change the nature of research in many sciences.[6] So too is education at the forefront of a new era in terms of how a knowledge base is built. There are now many information sources with many potential data-quality issues and new formats for researchers to consider. Just as the field of educational research has had deep and in some cases contentious discussions about what counts as high-quality evidence, new datasets have been emerging with new properties for understanding student learning and program effectiveness that will lead to new questions about evidence, rigor, and methods.

These changes have implications for who is involved in creating knowledge. While much of educational research has been conducted in colleges of education and research organizations that are staffed largely by their graduates, as this book has discussed, the educational data movement has challenged traditional educational research communities to frame it and keep up with its rapid developments. All the while, this movement has brought other organizations—many with reform connections and foundation support—into the business of providing research and information. One example is the Data Quality Campaign (DQC). While it is rare that educational researchers will study states directly, and much of the research that originates in colleges of education is regional, the DQC has conducted annual surveys and published the results of the educational data movement in state education agencies. Similarly, a number of organizations that often are thought of as advocacy groups, including the New Teacher Project and the National Center for Teacher Quality, have conducted studies that have had major impacts on the educational data movement, such as the *Widget Effect* report discussed in Chapter 4. Large teacher preparation programs and charter management organizations, including TFA and KIPP, are developing their own measures and accumulating datasets that they can use to produce information about their programs and to advance their causes. These organizations, and others discussed in Chapter 4, including the Strategic Data Project, also are providing important insights about education through data. In an era of big datasets, we will see organizations like the National Student Clearinghouse (NSC), which has records on millions of students and their postsecondary paths, becoming players in providing information and evidence. Instead of crafting unique studies, researchers can now go to the large datasets that governments and organizations like the NSC have, for example, the datasets produced by the MET study.

The innovators and vendors discussed earlier also will bring with them new forms of evidence and datasets that in many cases they own, leading to a more complex and difficult-to-validate knowledge base.

In researching the data movement itself and helping to build a knowledge base on how educational data are being used and in what ways this aspect of practice can be improved, it may be important for researchers to strengthen ties to fields beyond education. Some of the most important specialties in the educational data movement—analytics, decision sciences, information science, management and organizational science—are almost always located outside colleges of education. As the field matures, it is likely that cross-disciplinary research collaborations will form between educational researchers, with their rich domain and practical knowledge, and specialists in these adjoining fields.

Institutional Boundaries: From Compliance to Support

In the examples above, I discussed social areas that have and are changing in terms of membership and emphasis. Changes also are occurring at the boundaries of fields and institutions. As with other sociotechnical revolutions, these changes are related to technologies, in this case, large-scale information technologies that allow new relationships to develop.

An important set of relationships is that between the federal government and the states/districts. Because so much education funding comes through federal programs that require the collection of data, and the DoED is responsible for maintaining accurate data about the country's students, the federal government sits in the data movement as an actor on many levels. Many data systems that emerged at the beginning of the data movement were modeled directly after the template laid down in NCLB and special education regulations. The ways that each state did this, however, varied, and there were no common standards for student performance or for educational data. Just as classroom teachers historically have had tremendous independence and differed in how effectively they used that power, so have states historically and constitutionally had independence to develop divergent approaches. It falls, then, to the federal government to try to reconcile these state differences to meet its oversight and in some cases statutory information requirements. As federal education policy moves away from the rigid mandates that marked NCLB toward a more flexible model, using and evaluating local data systems becomes another way the federal government can exercise its fiduciary responsibilities. In fact, one of the ways many states were able to get waivers of NCLB requirements from the DoED was through development and implementation of data system components, including linking of teacher and student records. In speaking to a DQC event, Republican Representative Duncan Hunter commented on the need for a federal interest in educational data:

> How do you enforce standards and good education . . . [and] ensure that the job's getting done? The answer is data . . . for every stakeholder from the local level going to the highest level. So the Federal Government can compare apples to apples but more importantly so teachers can and parents can and every stakeholder in that municipality or school district can look and see very easily what's going on.[7]

The relationships between states and districts also are experiencing some changes. States collect important data from districts and pass them on to the federal government. They operate many different programs—licensure, workforce, early childhood, and so on—that historically have been separate in terms of funding and operation. The role of states grew with NCLB as they developed testing, accountability, and basic reporting systems for their districts. The SLDS program further strengthens the state role, giving states ownership of more data and the ability to be an information provider for their districts. These technologies then allow the states to also shift away from a mode of enforcing compliance to being information services providers. For example, the 2010 DQC State Data Leader, Bob Swiggum, Chief Information Officer at the Georgia Department of Education, describes his state's architecture that allows individual district information portals to connect directly to the state data systems—a process he calls tunneling—to see the data the state has on its children.[8] This is *a service* the state government provides. In many other states that have a high number of small rural districts, such as New York and Colorado, similar technical links to the state's data systems were established. While there is increased capacity in districts because of these links, there are limitations. As the SLDS system can act as a de facto standard and data hub within a given state, it also can restrict information flow and filter information not included in its design.

USING A MARKETPLACE FRAMEWORK TO THEORIZE THE DATA MOVEMENT

Researchers, scholars, and policymakers often have searched for an adequate way to describe the educational data movement, a process that encompasses many kinds of stakeholders and multiple uses for different kinds of information. Much of the promise of information in organizations, including educational organizations, involves crossing and redefining historical boundaries. One framework that has not been used to characterize this period, but aligns with many of the characteristics described in this book, is that of a *marketplace*. Some have theorized that education generally can be thought of as an ecological system.[9] A marketplace lens, while similar to an ecological frame in acknowledging complexity, addresses issues of perception, values, and choice that seem to be important factors in the educational data movement.

Much of the promise of educational data has still to be realized, especially in its use by practitioners. It is not that practitioners, specifically teachers, do not use data. Many do and there are cases where some use data extensively. However, by almost all accounts, direct and indirect, practitioner use of data is far less than expected. There are many simple responses to why educational data are underused. Most are woefully incomplete. One kind of view is technical: More data availability and data literacy are the answer. Another focuses socially on perceptions and belief systems. Neither strategy seems to advance our understanding. Many who discuss educational data choose to ignore the problems with the data or the problems of practice that call for data. The issues are *both social and technical*. The technical and social barriers to data use can be thought of individually or as a general condition. Individually, each case of data disconnects suggests the need for a technical bridge between systems and guidance to practitioners for using it. However, what is clear is that educational data involve discrete decisions that are distributed over a large scale. The distribution of many micro decisions across a broad sector is what occurs in marketplaces.

Experience with business suggests that changes in markets can be a byproduct of organizational information technology, as Ciborra's *Teams, Markets and Systems*, discussed at the end of Chapter 2, illustrates. Online retail provides an excellent example of market changes that are related to technology. Rather than being only a factor in the ways companies sell, web technology is also a factor how consumers buy. The shift in retail occurred across the entire marketplace, not only for sellers, but also for buyers. For marketplaces to work, both the buyers and sellers need to decide that this form of commerce, this way of exchanging, is in their interests. The sellers also participate in information-driven markets that exchange ordering and payment information with suppliers. These are other markets—or market areas—that also are related to the same technologies, but different from the retail dimensions. The provider networks of doctors, labs, and insurance companies, now commonplace in health care, are in large part possible because information can be shared among different groups of caregivers. In automotive sales, networks of dealers and wholesalers operate a behind-the-scenes information system to expand the inventory that dealers can sell. Similar markets exist for credit, telecommunications, and transportation. These examples show that the marketplace lens can be used with those close to the technical core and those further from it, as well as including the tools and infrastructures that matter so much in the area of information.

Commercial and Noncommercial Markets

A market view naturally also includes understanding commercial dimensions. There are many commercial interests in education. It is a hundreds-of-billions-of-dollars-a-year business. Looking at the history of other sociotechnical revolutions suggests that fortunes are made during such transitions, and the educational data movement has, in fact, coincided with significant venture capital investment targeted toward the education sector. However, it would be wrong to see the educational data movement as entirely commercial. Rather, it has commercial dimensions. Just as the age of print involved substantial commerce related to being able to print books and newspapers more easily and cheaply, it also involved an opening up of communication channels and many cultural transformations. More recently, the open-source software movement has been a form of marketplace and exchange. People from around the world freely develop software that others can use for free. Their reward may be monetary or in other ways. Yes, there is tremendous financial opportunity related to educational data. But this kind of marketplace is not purely commercial, just as education is not a purely noncommercial endeavor.

Markets may be predominantly commercial or of a mixed purpose. A marketplace framing supports thinking broadly about the educational land-scape with its many types of institutions, including state education depart-ments, districts, and schools. It helps focus on specific types of actions and actors. Marketplaces are where different types of individuals and organiza-tions connect over common interests. An interesting public sector example of cross-institutional collaboration is the 51-member American Association of Motor Vehicle Administrations (AAMVA), which allows members to share information about cars and drivers. AAMVA administers a computer network that states can subscribe to. It is a network of exchange that is a hybrid in terms of its commerciality. Its core functions are noncommer-cial, but for some it is a financial market. For example, police and motor vehicle organizations use this network to identify traffic offenders. At the same time, many entities that sell products from identification cards to data systems also participate in the AAMVA network for financial gain. Also, or-ganizations interested in organ transplants, including the U.S. Department of Health and Human Services, have worked with AAMVA because states often collect organ donation preferences of drivers when they get driver's licenses.

The Value Exchange

A marketplace view is a way to consider different kinds of actors and communities, including school principals, teachers, and specialists, since all of them could participate in an educational information marketplace. These are the actors who are, in fact, critical for its success. Not only should those school workers be included as marketplace actors, but parents and students also should.[10] A marketplace view is perhaps most helpful in considering the level of choice that practitioners at all levels can have. At every instance of information use, an exchange is made; value is perceived. That exchange, in many cases, may involve simply spending time in one way or with one set of tools versus another. People and organizations participate best in markets when they gain something of value from the exchanges within them. When practitioners find value in the data for their teaching or managing, they likely will repeat the exchange.

A marketplace view lets us look at the kinds of actors and interests in-volved. It lets us look at the value that different kinds of information have, for whom, and for which purposes. This marketplace lens shows NCLB and other policies as imbalanced in terms of what type of value was prioritized. For teachers, NCLB tests were not totally worthless but the value was small for improving instruction, especially because the information often came when the students were no longer learning the tested material. As discussed in Chapter 3, longitudinal data do provide new ways of seeing education and educational processes; however, the information in most SLDS programs seems far more useful for policy and administration consumers than for instruction. Similarly, although the teacher evaluation movement is geared toward providing value for policymakers and administrators, important value is realized by teachers in the feedback they receive from observations and possibly from surveys.[11] The data were not universally good or bad, or worthy or not, but had value for specific individuals and purposes.[12]

In the emerging educational information market, we can see specific marketplace actors. Understanding their roles and interests is important. From time to time, educational researchers have discussed the complex relationships between educational organizations and the networks of innovators and vendors, but those relationships have been rarely explored in depth.[13] Chapter 3 discussed the DQC and the NSC. The DQC is noncommercial in advocating on behalf of more attention to educational data and standards so that different organizations can share and reuse information. The NSC is a nonprofit that sustains itself on fees for connecting data between K–12 and postsecondary institutions. Both of these activities, although different in their nature, are working at the level of the marketplace.

Market Systems: Standards, Infrastructures, and Innovation

Markets for either information or tangible goods rarely develop in isolation. Whether physical or digital, they often depend on infrastructures and standards. For social networks built around new media (e.g., Facebook, Twitter), the technologies that make them successful include computers, tablets, and mobile and media devices—which can all upload content—as well as the Internet itself. It isn't that the digital devices or the network make these social networks possible, but rather they are combined as part of an infrastructure that makes information exchange low cost and high reward. All of these components—technology, social rules, and regulatory frameworks—can be thought of as a *market system*.[14] The marketplace is the area where the exchange occurs. A market system can include marketplaces as well as the infrastructures, both technical and social, that allow those exchange decisions to be guided, not by a central authority, but by the value(s) those exchanges hold for the participants. The market system is a complex system that can grow and evolve as circumstances change. The immaturity and inconsistent progress of the educational data movement can be seen in its limited and relatively undeveloped market system. Rather than an environment where information exchange across contexts is an easy process with high value and low costs, exchanging information today is often cumbersome and expensive. The initial definition of this market system was largely influenced by NCLB, which was a partial view of the interests in education. It compelled participation and levied a high tax on practitioners, with little reward or representation. Now, as the field looks to move beyond NCLB, new market system components for measuring of student growth and evaluating teachers are appearing with new choices and opportunities to do better, but there is still precious little in terms of what practitioners need and what holds value for them.

Many of the federal efforts discussed in Chapter 3 can be seen as efforts to build a market system, not only to meet federal information requirements, but also to spur innovation. When market systems have useful and accessible standards, innovation can be unleashed as the innovators are able to design new products to meet large markets supported by those standards. The Internet is an example of an area where new ideas have led to viable companies in a short amount of time because innovators could design solutions to work within common and public standards. HyperText Markup Language (HTML) was a major force in the growth of the Internet because it allowed so much to be done with it. The Worldwide Web had existed for many years as an academic data-sharing system. HTML and digital media standards for images, sound, and video allowed people to do new things that they valued, and "the web" exploded. The success of the iPhone and other smartphone platforms has been their compatibility with existing standards and their own accessible standards that innovators like those developing inexpensive applications and games can build to.

Looking at the educational data movement as a marketplace doesn't make it simple. It is a frame of reference, a perspective, on a complex area with many components and interests. It is a collection of tools and practices that makes exchanges possible. Markets are also dynamic entities. They begin, grow, and evolve. They are rarely exclusive activities, but rather are in competition with other ways of exchange. However, they are also objects that can be studied in whole or in parts. Rather than an outerworld that is beyond scientific study, as many areas external to formal education have been, the marketplace view invites new methods of investigation and new ways of description that are sorely needed.

EDUCATIONAL DATA NEED AN INTEGRATED DESIGN SCIENCE

The educational data movement needs an approach for designing and building an information market system. The market system is not something that either exists or does not. Rather, it exists in parts, as infrastructural capacity is built and value exchanges are possible. Since the same data can be used at so many levels, the approach should be one that can be applied systemically. While it would be wonderful if a single policy or technology could bring about fundamental shifts in education and the blossoming of the educational information market that would provide comparable value to all corners of this enterprise, that scenario is remote. Just as the age of print did not occur overnight and just as the Internet took many different developments—some social and some technical—over many years, the educational information market will take a while. These efforts, like the data movement itself, impact many types of professionals from administrators, to assessment and content specialists, to teachers. All of these different professionals are part of the future of the educational data movement. There are also many professionals closer to the technology. Whether these professionals are called data scientists or have more traditional titles, the work they do also will move the field forward by improving the infrastructure and developing innovations that add value to the work practitioners do.

This work is fundamentally multidisciplinary. Because the same data, the same digital artifacts, can operate at multiple levels and relate to different organizations, educational data need to be thought of across organizational settings. The same test score can be used by a teacher, a professional learning community (PLC), a school leader, and a district leader. It may not have the same value for each, but can be useful to different people in many ways. So too can surveys of students and parents. So can video records of teachers in action. And all of these types of information can be combined in different kinds of organizational actions and routines. These types of information can apply to specific subject areas and/or can span topics. They can be used in classical classroom arrangements and new models of education. They have applicability in elementary, secondary, and postsecondary contexts. For this reason, understanding and advancing the data movement calls for a transdisciplinary approach. It involves knowledge of technology and what is possible for different technologies to do. And it equally calls for knowledge of educational practices and how practices vary in response to different circumstances. It is an organizational science as well as one focused on individual productivity. Also, since both data tools and educational programs are designed things, the best way to approach this field is as a design science: an *integrated design science.*

The idea of a distinct category of work called design sciences can be traced to the work of social scientist and futurist Herbert Simon who was a pioneer in organizational thinking, artificial intelligence, and psychology. Where natural scientists—physicists, chemists, psychologists—seek to rationally understand the fundamental character of natural or social worlds, design scientists use rational means toward human and social goals such as designing bridges or homes. In his 1969 *The Sciences of the Artificial*, Simon highlights some of the attributes of these fields:

> Everyone designs who devises courses of action aimed at changing existing situations into preferred ones. The intellectual activity that produces material artifacts is no different fundamentally from the one that prescribes remedies for a sick patient or the one that devises a sales plan for a company or a social welfare policy for a state.[15]

Design scientists apply technologies and operate within constraints. Structural designers are limited by materials and the environment they are designing for. Those constraints may be technical, social, or political, and all have been shown to be factors in the educational data movement. Design science may involve principled experimentation and the development of models. Educators also work within material, financial, temporal, and human constraints. Teachers are often designers and innovators in their approach to classes, groups, and individual students. School leaders will design their arrangement of programs and staff. District leaders design schools, school enrollment approaches, professional development, and evaluation systems. They will experiment and try models to test ideas.

By framing this field as an integrated design science, I am suggesting that designs of educational approaches, and the information systems (including assessments) intended to support them, be considered together. The design of programs should take into account what metrics and evidence approaches will be used and the reliability of these information sources. An integrated design science would have states and districts jointly conceive of new programs and technologies that support them. This integration might entail bridging traditional educational research communities with others in adjoining fields of information science, organizational and management sciences, and reformers, who all bring important fresh perspectives to these problems of learning in different contexts. The design of information approaches should specifically account for what kinds of value they might provide for which types of educators.

One big difference between education and fields such as engineering or architecture is that many educational constraints are unclear and contingent. In physical designs, the constraints usually are based in natural laws. The limits in education seem based on multiple logics. What is the maximum number of students a teacher can handle? How fast can a subject be taught with retention? How long can any two 4th-grade students sit still and listen to a lecture? How accurate does a test score need to be to be able to be used in gauging whether students were taught well? All of these questions are difficult to answer with certainty. There is the history of what has worked in the past as a guide. But the history of education is often one of failure. In this way, education is not so different from many businesses whose potential and limits are often uncertain and open to development.

META-PRINCIPLES FOR EDUCATIONAL DESIGN SCIENCE

Because designing educational solutions is so broad and complex an area, I suggest the educational design sciences can be guided by general meta-principles, concepts that transcend educational levels to promote designs that will be robust enough to meet the very special characteristics of educational practice in its many variations. I propose five such principles:

1. Focus on systemic processes across boundaries;
2. Recognize and design for often opaque data;
3. Use robust information structures;
4. Model temporality; and
5. Design flexibility for social structures.

These together can be considered some guidelines for educational design scientists and others working with them. I will touch on each of these issues briefly below.

Focus on Systemic Processes Across Boundaries

The educational world is made up of many small communities, including those who focus on teaching and learning (who further cluster by subject and type of school), leadership, curriculum, special education, and so on, and extending to the measurement and evaluation specialists. While these communities help to make the vast area of education manageable in many ways, the separation can work at cross-purposes to systemic design. Connecting these different groups to the practice that occurs in schools is a great challenge of this time. A teacher does not focus only on cognitive classroom work but also needs to understand school structure, instructional materials, and how to work with special educators. Principals need to understand instruction as well as district functioning. In the daily life of real school systems, different academic areas fuse. In conceiving of how to develop information tools, educational design scientists should think broadly. They should focus on both curricular and systemic areas. For example, in conceiving a program for emerging literacy or middle school project-based science, they also should think systemically about the information the program will need, the information the program can produce, and how the information tools they design will work in classrooms, inform parents, be useful in PLCs, assist principals in their job of leading and evaluating teachers, provide feedback for district offices and curriculum designers, and provide a basis for analytics—all at the same time.

If we look at how information tools have been successful in businesses, it is often by bridging different groups and easing boundaries. This approach can work for the development of both small- and large-scale systems. A teacher could look at data he or she would collect in a new classroom approach and how they could be used within the school and district offices. Likewise, developing an early childhood education system that connects schools with social services and public health could be conceived of holistically. The same approach should work with national data standards and educational products because it focuses on both the technical artifacts and the ways they are adopted and adapted socially.

Recognize and Design for Opaque Data

Data often can be thought of as an indicator of reality, or a measure of truth. In educational circumstances, the data that are available are usually partial and messy, and obscure reality. Some have used metaphors that data are a signal or a light because they can trigger actions or illuminate an area previously dark.[16] While both metaphors are useful, an *opaque lens* may be a better characterization. What different forms of educational data show is rarely completely wrong, but they generally leave much information out so that interpretation and seeking supplemental forms of evidence are almost always important. This view of information as an opaque lens acknowledges the fallibility of any single piece of information, whether a test score, survey instrument, or observation by a trained professional. All of these types of information are variable and fallible in ways that need to be accounted for. The emergence of using multiple measures rather than looking for a single score in evaluations of teachers, and the development of a student character report card by KIPP, an organization that prides itself on academic achievement, are both examples of the ways that practitioners are not relying on single pieces of data, but rather using many forms in combination in order to have multiple lenses. This aspect returns us to the concept of validity, once imagined to be a formula for measuring precision, but now recognized as a much more complicated topic that often leads to an inquiry process where complementary evidence is valued.[17]

Use Robust Information Structures

Education is complex. It is one of the most complex settings for information to be used in because of its variation and response to social circumstances. Information engineering involves developing frameworks and structures to represent reality as simply as possible. Because of its inherent properties, education often calls for robust and flexible rather than narrow and rigid information structures. For example, many views of educational data, specifically those coded into most data systems, are hierarchical. We see this in reports and policies that show students nested in classrooms nested in schools and all the way up to districts and states. In reality, many of these relationships are more complex. Many are networks where several entities (individuals and organizations) are related to several other ones concurrently. The widely erratic VAMs of teacher effectiveness are an example of an area where oversimplification of information about how students and teachers are educationally connected revealed limitations of simple data models and evidence designs.

While this has been a high-profile factor with teacher evaluations based on test scores, the issue is broader. The arrangement of staff into neat formal departments, as in many human resources systems, makes perfect sense until one looks at particular schools and sees the many reasonable exceptions. There are similar issues involving the relationships between locations and schools. From a distance, these relationships seem to be straightforward until one sees the exceptions in practice. Many districts have defined regions that particular schools draw from, but also have provided many ways that students can attend other schools in their districts and some cases in neighboring districts, depending on their circumstances. Because the field of education involves both the use of people and institutions with significant variation, and designs of organizational structures in response to local circumstances, simplified data models almost always will lead to a loss of information. Trying to reduce the complexity of education into simple categories for the convenience of information management will present data problems that can come out in inconvenient ways later on.

Model Temporality

Time scales, traversals, and trajectories are important analytic elements.[18] In many areas where information is used, and this certainly has been the case in education, there has been a focus on specific disconnected timeframes. This may be because it is easier to manage many small pieces of information than to try to assemble them into longitudinal patterns. However, education is made up largely of people and institutions that are interacting while also on their own individual trajectories. For students and teachers, the trajectories are developmental. For institutions and schools, those trajectories often will be in response to changes in their conditions or external pressures. Student development occurs as they traverse these different settings. Students learn over lifespans as they develop trajectories toward certain types of future learning possibilities.[19] We can more easily design information tools to show small time-scale activity, but they rarely will show a comprehensive picture. Growth models for students and understanding how education works over long-time scales are really just the beginning of a new frontier in educational information science. There are attractive targets in the disconnected pieces of educational information. But it is the *complex trajectories* that students, teachers, and even schools experience where some of the most important insights are to be found.

Design Flexibility for Social Structures

Information systems—ways of classifying—often end up becoming part of social structures, part of the consciousness of those who use them. This is not specific to education, but to different ways that information tools are used, whether by choice or compulsion. These systems can include social media tools like Facebook that many use to connect with friends, family, and colleagues. Accountability schemes like NCLB, with its subgroups, adequate yearly progress, and designations for schools and teachers, are ways educational information systems have generated categories that have become cultural. Just as we refer to "friending" people, we also refer to schools as "failing" or students as "proficient." There is a power in these definitions as they can become shortcuts in group social processes. There is also a danger when people give them too much importance and validity.

In looking at the variation across classrooms, schools, and districts, it is important to consider how flexible these categories are and whether they support the kind of local adaptation that educators need. Rather than a uniform solution that is developed in the district for all schools, perhaps districts will provide sets of options that different school leaders can use as they address the local circumstances that they and their teams are facing. One school might focus on student overachievement and how to extend learning in some subjects into the later grades. Another might focus on absenteeism, social services, and presenting students with positive role models. In one school, a new leader may need to focus new staff on understanding their students, using basic information about home life and performance. In another, the students may be well known, but the teachers may need to focus on particular aspects of their teaching and collaboration. For one school, the principal may decide to lead some curricular teams and have other ones led by teachers across grades. In another school, there may be reasons to organize differently. In designing solutions for schools and districts, it is important to realize that one-size-fits-all systems likely will mean they don't fit many circumstances very well. This principle naturally and specifically applies to federal and state initiatives.

CROSSING BOUNDARIES A KEY FOR STUDENT SUCCESS

This book has gone from a discussion of a narrow focus on data-driven decisions through different complex settings at state, district, school, community, and classroom levels, to finally arrive at a conception of an information marketplace with new kinds of marketplace actors. This way of looking at the educational data movement is a reorientation. It doesn't change what has been learned and the questions that have been asked about the use of data in practice, but it helps ask different kinds of questions. While the changes in this movement seemed sudden for many, the roots had been developing for some time. Although no longer new, the movement is still expanding. Even though it is saddled with often poor quality and integration that hinder data's ability to transform, new and imperfect data also bring new opportunities to understand education and develop new approaches to solving long-standing problems. The solutions and transformation, however, will take some time.

While the technology is important, it is only one reactant for this conversion. Socially, the conditions for those technologies also need to be present. Even if smartphones had been invented in the 1960s, most people probably would not have been ready for them. Unlike today, email was not widespread and digital photography barely known when men landed on the moon in 1969.[20] More important, the culture was not as immediate as it is today, and people were more accustomed to getting information from newspapers in the morning and/or afternoon, and the news at 6 or 11 p.m., rather than the continuous communications cycles we have now and for which smartphones are both information consumers and producers. Similarly, today, many of the social and technical conditions for an educational information market system are not yet in place. But they are being developed.

There are important needs for information and foresight at this time, as infrastructures can prioritize some practices over others. In education, this could translate into prioritizing some communities and types of students over others. There is a role, then, for principled and impartial research that can help policymakers understand the potential and real impacts of using these new technologies. At the same time, traditional educational research approaches, while experienced in many established multileveled areas of educational data, may not be sufficient. Many researchers prefer to observe those things they study with a separation that conveys impartiality. While this has advantages, a marketplace view may cause researchers to rethink their approach. A marketplace is full of different interests and segments. Naturally, one of the most important communities or market segments that often has been absent from big decisions about educational data and infrastructures has been teachers and other practitioners. Researchers too are a segment. They have interests in deepening their understanding of practice and the conditions under which it is executed well and poorly. By adopting a marketplace view, researchers can see how the design of these infrastructures can support not only accountability, commercial interests, and practitioners, but research interests as well.

This educational world of today may become history in a short time. The educational infrastructures of tomorrow are being built today. And once a set of technologies, with standards, becomes established, it often can persist for a long time as an infrastructure. This transitional time is especially important because it is when the consequential decisions about the infrastructure are being made. While these markets will not last forever, as the Apple and Wintel platforms show, they can last for quite some time and cast a big influence over the work many do. The core technologies underlying the Internet are now almost 50 years old and still going strong. The work being done in national and state education departments is an example of what sociotechnical researchers Ribes and Finholt refer to as "the long now of technology infrastructure"[21] because its development balances present-day constraints with a vision for the future. Education today seems to be facing that long now of adding to infrastructures and building new ones that may need to last for a long time and imprint on educational practice for millions of teachers and students. Unfortunately, much of the foundational work in designing these technologies has been done with little involvement of those closest to students, and their absence has been evident. This is the end of one book about the educational data movement, but not the end of this chronicle. As the next chapter in this story begins, it is time for all involved who care about education to begin to cross boundaries and design solutions that will lead to student success.

Notes

Chapter 1

1.   One of the most important studies of sociotechnical revolutions was Eisenstein's (1982) study of the printing press.

2.   See Bijker (1995, p. 6).

3.   This approach owes much to the work of Latour (2005) and actor-network theory that takes a similar approach with his definition of actors (human) and actants (technologies) that both can shape meaning making.

4.   This law now is often referred to by its original title, the Elementary and Secondary Education Act, or ESEA (No Child Left Behind Act of 2001, 2002).

5.   See Duncan (2010).

6.   See Friedman (2005). Boudreau, Loch, Robey, and Straud (1998) provide another and more academic reference point.

7.   Shelton was referring to a white paper by Mourshed, Chijioke, and Barber (2010).

8.   See Shelton (2010b).

9.   The abbreviation DoED is used for U.S. Department of Education to avoid confusion with DOE, which stands for the Department of Energy.

10.   See Kane, Rockoff, and Staiger (2008).

11.   See Hamilton et al. (2007).

12.   For reviews of growth and value-added models in education, see Lissitz (2006) and Harris (2011).

13.   See Carey and Manwaring (2011).

14.   In the summer of 2010, a commission of leading scholars, including five former presidents of the American Educational Research Association, Diane Ravitch, and others, signed a report that was critical of VAMs for teacher evaluation (Baker et al., 2010). Shortly thereafter the Brookings Institute released a report by an equally prestigious group of authors led by Grover Whitehurst, the second Bush administration's director of the Institute of Education Sciences, in support of the use of VAMs.

15.   McGuinn (2012) provides a glimpse into the often untidy community of education reform organizations.

16.   Ravitch (2009, p. 200).

17.   See Jorgenson (2001).

18.   Similar outcomes-based management principles are also being applied beyond education in social services through similar data-reliant management practices as outlined in Morino (2011).

19. See Christensen (1997) and Carayannis and Coleman (2005).

20. See Frederiksen and Collins (1989).

21. See Moss, Girard, and Haniford (2006) for a comprehensive discussion.

22. See Frederiksen and Collins (1989).

23. See Mislevy, Steinberg, and Almond (1999).

24. The first use of this term seems to have been by Michael Feuer (2008). Feuer was principally involved in the Scientific Research in Education project (National Research Council, 2002) and later became president of the National Academy of Education.

25. See Slavin (2002).

26. See Coburn, Toure, and Yamashita (2009, p. 1116). In addition to framing the straightforward thesis of educational data use that was associated with its early days, the authors show how complex it is in real practice inside educational district offices.

27. See Wayman and Stringfield (2006).

28. See Diamond and Spillane (2004) for a discussion of the bubble kids, those targeted for remediation at the expense of others in the school.

29. Some have focused on teacher beliefs and how teachers believe, or do not believe, in the value of data for their practice (Coburn & Talbert, 2006; Ikemoto & Marsh, 2007; Ingram, Louis, & Schroeder, 2004).

30. See Hamilton et al. (2009, p. 7).

31. Spencer Foundation (2009).

32. See Boudett, City, and Murnane (2005), Coburn (2005b), Coburn and Talbert (2006), Knapp, Swinnerton, Copeland, and Monpas-Huber (2006), and Wayman and Stringfield (2006) for some discussions.

33. This is what is called "parallel play." Tate, King, and Anderson (2011).

Chapter 2

1. See Scott (1987) for his discussion of systems as rational, natural, and open. This work was influential in the development of the technical core approach to looking at organizations that has been used by subsequent educational scholars (see Elmore, 2004; Peterson, Murphy, & Hallinger, 1987; Spillane, Parise, & Sherer, 2011). Scott posits that schools have strong institutional control, but weak technical control. Many of the reforms that involve measurement and standards of performance for teachers could be viewed as strengthening technical control. Meyer and Rowan (1977) also discuss an important aspect of school systems in terms of their presentation of one structure for their stakeholders versus the structure they use in practice.

2. See Bennet (2011, emphasis added).

3. See Cuban (1986, 2003).

4. See Star and Griesemer (1989) for the initial definition and Bowker and Star (2000) for a more contemporary view. Moss, Girard, and Haniford (2006) take the next step in terms of relating this concept to educational testing systems.

5. Rogers's seminal work *Diffusion of Innovations* (1995) is considered one of the best resources, although the concept has been looked at by other scholars over the years. Rogers looked at how networks of highly respected individuals and

organizations could be responsible for helping others to see the benefits of adopting something new. Interestingly, one area Rogers discusses in his book is how educators adopted new approaches under centralized or decentralized district control.

6. See Ramiller, Swanson, and Wang (2008) and Wang (2010), where he discusses the relationship of these innovations to productivity, indicating that those firms that adopt early may do so for symbolic as well as practical reasons, but that many show increases in productivity after a period of time.

7. See McFarlan (1984) for discussion of competitive benefits of information technology.

8. See Hammer (1990, p. 107).

9. See Darling-Hammond et al. (2007).

10. See LaValle, Lesser, Shockley, and Kruschwitz (2010).

11. The Society of Learning Analytics Research (SOLAR) has received support from several foundations, including the Gates Foundation.

12. See Baker and Yacef (2009), Romero, Ventura, Pechenizkiy, and Baker (2010), and U.S. Department of Education (2013).

13. See DiCerbo and Behrens (2012).

14. The communities-of-practice framework has been applied both to large organizations by Wenger (1998) and also as a way of organizational learning and innovation by Brown and Duguid (1991).

15. A foundational review of knowledge management is presented in Alvani and Leidner's (2001) article that discusses different conceptions of knowledge, teams, and the roles that IT can play in supporting them.

16. See Skinner (1986), David (1990), and Roach (1990) for early discussions of the Productivity Paradox and Brynjolfsson (1993) for a later and influential discussion about limitations of this model. Brynjolfsson and Hitt (2000) also discuss the different roles of technology beyond productivity improvement.

17. See Ciborra (1993).

Chapter 3

1. See Ribes and Finholt (2009).

2. See National Science Foundation (2007, p. 37). See also Pea (1993) for a foundational view of the mixture of tools and practices in learning settings.

3. President's remarks on the launch of the Race to the Top grant program (Obama, 2009).

4. This is new policy territory for the federal government with little precedent in terms of authority. Hess and Kelly (2012) discuss issues around the federal role, but not in the area of technology standards.

5. See U.S. Department of Education, Office of Educational Technology (2004).

6. See usingdata.terc.edu. While initially funded by NSF, the program continues to support itself with workshop fees.

7. See U.S. Department of Education, National Center for Education Statistics (2003).

8. The creation of IES and its focus on funding statistical studies, using the randomized trial as the "gold standard" (National Research Council, 2002), was

controversial in educational research. Many believed that strengthening the rigor of educational research was needed, but that the way it was done was partial and exclusionary. See Moss (2005) for some discussions of the issue.

9. See Education Sciences Reform Act of 2002.

10. Information about these survey programs is available from the National Center for Educational Statistics (NCES) at http://nces.ed.gov/surveys/Survey-Groups.asp?group=1.

11. According to Carey and Manwaring (2011), when planning for NCLB, the administration would have preferred a growth model over the achievement cohort model that eventually was put into the law. However, at that time, few states had the technological capacity for anything else.

12. See http://oregondataproject.org/.

13. See Lissitz (2006) for an introduction to some of these issues.

14. A few years earlier, Standard & Poor's had attempted a large national education data project that would rate schools nationally in the same way S&P rated other fields. The project is reported to have involved tens of millions of dollars in foundation funding and was managed by the Council of Chief State School Officers. There are few traces of it today, but those involved learned that many districts and states were unprepared to provide high-quality information about their schools.

15. Material provided by the DQC and available on the organization's website: www.dataqualitycampaign.org.

16. Many people interviewed for this book gave credit to researcher Chrys Dougherty for leading the development of core ideas about longitudinal educational data. NCEA is one of many ties between the current national data efforts and the states that were early leaders in data systems, including then-Governor Bush's Texas.

17. DQC staff indicated that there had been discussions about how to include vendors in the work that the DQC does. Historically, however, there is little evidence that the DQC has been a vendor-led organization, and I did not find evidence in their projects or board members that indicated connections to vendors.

18. See Data Quality Campaign (2009).

19. See Guidera (2009).

20. See Domenech and Torres (2010).

21. See Domenech and Torres (2010).

22. See Noell and Gansle (2009) and Noell and Gleason (2011) for additional details. Noell's work has been criticized for not being published in peer-reviewed journals. It is an important criticism, but it is important to note that Noell is not an education professor and so education journals might not have as much value for his career, and the subject area might have low value in his home discipline of psychology.

23. See Koedel, Parsons, Podgursky, and Ehlert (2012) and Goldhaber and Liddle (2012).

24. See announcement for the Open Data Initiative (http://www.whitehouse.gov/innovationfellows/opendata).

25. See U.S. Department of Education (2011).

26. See Weiss (2012). Original comments edited in consultation with the speaker.

27.   See Buckley (2012). Original comments edited in consultation with the speaker.

28.   There has been a National Education Data Model and a Common Education Data Standards effort, as well as a National Instructional Materials Accessibility Standard used only for accessibility.

29.   A Federal student-record database is prohibited by two statutes: (1) The Education Sciences Reform Act of 2002 and (2) The Higher Education Opportunity Act of 2008.

30.   The Michael and Susan Dell Foundation states it has shared a close relationship with the CEDS project and is represented in the CEDS K–12 stakeholder group.

31.   The relationship between the unions and the DQC, like the relationships the unions have to the data movement, is complex. The AFT hosted the DQC's first national meeting on linking teacher and student data in 2007, and NEA co-authored a publication with the DQC. Despite these instances, little other observable work could be found even after requests to all organizations for information about collaborations.

Chapter 4

1.   See Streifer, 2001.

2.   See Creighton (2001).

3.   See Moody and Dede (2008) for a discussion of this system that looks at three different theories of action for using data.

4.   This is discussed in Childress, Doyle, and Thomas (2009).

5.   See Marsh et al. (2005).

6.   See Coburn and Talbert (2006) and Coburn, Honig, and Stein (2009). Other researchers, including Falk and Drayton (2004) and Ingram, Louis, and Schroeder (2004), also have studied how the cultural aspects of educators and district staff impact their approach to information use.

7.   See Coburn and Talbert (2006, p. 488).

8.   See Dembosky, Pane, Barney, and Christina (2006).

9.   An important review of different kinds of research is Mandinach and Honey's (2008) volume.

10.   See Bowers (2010) for some discussion of the emerging literature on district effectiveness.

11.   Wayman, Conoly, Gasko, and Stringfield (2008) discuss special education inquiry in central offices that leads to school-level action, and Datnow, Park, and Wohlstetter (2007), whose study was funded by the New Schools Venture Fund and the Gates Foundation, looked at school-based management specifically. Also see Supovitz (2006).

12.   See Moss and Piety (2007, p. 3).

13.   See U.S. Department of Education, Office of Postsecondary Education (2011, p. 91).

14.   Coburn and Turner (2011, p. 200).

15.   See Mathews (2001).

16.   Broad Foundation (2001).

17. Drawn from Broad Foundation public information and not independently verified.

18. Provided by Erica Lepping of the Broad Foundation.

19. See Kalogrides, Loeb, and Béteille (2011).

20. Project conducted by Dr. Chris Matthews, Executive Director of Counseling, Psychological, & Social Work Services; Korynn Schooley, Strategic Data Fellow; and Niveen Vosler, Program Evaluation Analyst.

21. Developed by Donna Mitchell, Deputy Officer, Teacher Leader Effectiveness Unit, and SDP Fellow.

22. This project was conducted by Thomas Tomberlin, Senior Analyst for Human Capital Strategies and SDP Fellow.

23. Education Resource Strategies website: http://erstrategies.org/about/.

24. See Miles and Frank (2008). Miles holds a Doctor of Education degree from Harvard and is also the daughter of Willis Hawley, Professor Emeritus at the University of Maryland and a leading author in the area of teacher development and policy.

25. See Weisberg, Sexton, Mulhern, and Keeling (2009). The New Teacher Project, a reform organization, was founded by Michelle Rhee and has been funded by many leading foundations, including the Gates Foundation.

26. See Marzano (1992).

27. See Danielson and McGreal (2000).

28. Anna Gregory, personal communication, July 13, 2012.

29. See Headden (2011).

30. Anna Gregory, personal communication, July 13, 2012.

31. See Kamras (2010).

32. Personal communication and based on a prior and longer quote in a public forum.

33. See critique of the value-added calculations by Columbia University Professor Aaron Pallas (Pallas, 2010) at http://voices.washingtonpost.com/answer-sheet/dc-schools/were-some-dc-teacher-dismissal.html.

34. This is a claim that often is made about IMPACT, but there is little concrete evidence to show that this disparity was due to anything other than teachers of different abilities working in different parts of the city.

35. See Turque (2012).

36. Figures provided by Anna Gregory, Chief of Staff for the Office of Human Capital. Bonuses offered do not precisely equate to those taken. Since taking the bonus lessens a teacher's future protection from termination, some teachers declined to accept the bonuses. A comprehensive, but brief, evaluation of IMPACT was released in 2011 by the bipartisan think tank EdSector (see Headden, 2011).

37. See Turque (2011).

38. See Winerip (2011).

39. See Winerip (2012).

40. See The New Teacher Project (2012).

Part III

1. See Halverson (2010a).

2. Some important examples of research related to data that does span dis-

tricts and schools include Coburn and Talbert (2006), U.S. Department of Education (2008, 2009), Supovitz (2006), Wayman et al. (2008), and Young (2006).

Chapter 5

1.	Several studies reported this, including Coburn (2005b) and Ikemoto and Marsh (2007), who give examples of practitioners repeating the data-driven slogans of their districts while not showing much evidence of integration into practice. Elmore (2004) and Nichols and Berliner (2007) also provide important critiques of the NCLB era and its effect on schooling. See also Spillane, Halverson, and Diamond (2001).

2.	See Valli et al. (2008, p. 25).

3.	See Nichols and Berliner (2007).

4.	See Confrey and Makar (2005).

5.	See U.S. Department of Education (2009, p. viii).

6.	See U.S. Department of Education (2010, p. 83).

7.	Wayman et al. (2012) discuss some of the barriers to teacher use.

8.	Time scales is a very important concept that originated in terms of organizational systems with the linguist and sociocultural theorist Lemke (2000), who described relationships between ecosocial levels and frequency of meaning-making activity. Others, including Hickey and Anderson (2007), Crawford, Schlager, Penuel et al. (2008), and Pellegrino (2011), have further elaborated Lemke's models in relation to assessment.

9.	Black and Wiliam (1998). Also see Pellegrino (2011) for a review.

10.	See Bill and Melinda Gates Foundation (2012).

11.	Annie Lewis (2011) spoke at the University of Michigan's seminar on teacher education.

12.	See *New York Times* article by Tough (2011) for an introduction to the development of this metric.

13.	See Mathews (2009).

14.	See Duckworth and Seligman (2005) for a technical discussion of the character measures used in this report card. Angela Duckworth was a graduate student at the University of Pennsylvania working on the character studies that Levin was involved in. She also had worked in charter schools prior to returning to the university, where she earned her Ph.D. in psychology and joined the faculty.

15.	Siedlecki (2012) provides a short discussion of some of the policy challenges raised by entering into high-stakes teacher evaluation without a consensus on what the profession should involve.

16.	See Pianta and Hamre (2009) for an overview of CLASS.

17.	The real cost was reported to be close to $50 million from additional projects according to David Parker, personal communication, April 25, 2012.

18.	See Bill and Melinda Gates Foundation (2010).

19.	See Kane, Rockoff, and Staiger (2008).

20.	The Charlotte-Mecklenburg Schools were the winner of the Broad Prize in 2011, which the New York City Department of Education won in 2008.

21.	See Bill and Melinda Gates Foundation (2013, p. 10)

22.	See Bill and Melinda Gates Foundation (2010, 2012).

23. I spoke with several MET teachers informally who reported they appreciated the feedback in much the same way as the DCPS teachers reported benefiting from feedback under IMPACT.

24. See Goldhaber and Hansen (2010).

25. See McClellan, Atkinson, and Danielson (2012).

26. A seminal discussion of classrooms from the perspective of students is *Life in Classrooms* by Philip Jackson (1968). Cohen (2011) wrote an important reflection on teaching and its relationship to practice that investigates the central elements of the teaching profession. When Hiebert, Gallimore, and Stigler wrote their classic, "A Knowledge Base for the Teaching Profession: What Would It Look Like and How Can We Get One?" in 2002, just as the NCLB era was beginning to unfold, there was already a much stronger knowledge base about teaching than had existed 20 or 30 years earlier. It was much richer in some parts than others, but in a few cases, especially in mathematics, it was quite detailed.

Chapter 6

1. The study of distributed leadership was led by Spillane and his students. See Spillane, Halverson, and Diamond (2001) and Spillane (2005).

2. See Coleman et al. (1966).

3. See Borman and Dowling (2010) and Konstantopoulos and Borman (2011) for discussion of the computational limitations in the Coleman study and some adjustments that they made as a result.

4. The new models involve multileveled statistics, of which one of the most popular is Hierarchical Linear Modeling, as discussed in Lee and Bryk (1989), Raudenbush and Bryk (2002), and many others.

5. See Lee and Bryk (1989), Raudenbush and Willms (1995), Raudenbush and Bryk (2002), and Borman and Dowling (2010).

6. See Edmonds (1979).

7. See Edmonds (1982) and Brookover et al. (1982) for some discussions of instructional leadership; Hallinger and Heck (1996) for a review of the early research; and Marzano, Frontier, and Livingston (2011) for samples of more current views.

8. Earl and Fullan (2003) and Knapp, Copeland, and Swinnerton (2007) present early discussions of data and school leaders.

9. See Pajak (1993) for a discussion of clinical supervision.

10. See DuFour and Eaker (1998) for an early discussion of PLCs and Halverson (2003) for discussion of how school leaders can support them though their designs.

11. Jacques Nacson, KEYS designer and facilitator, in a personal communication, May 9, 2011.

12. See Hawley and Rollie (2002).

13. See Slavin et al. (1996).

14. See Success for All: http://www.successforall.org/Early-Childhood/Professional-Development/GREATER-Coaching-Model/.

15. As described by Peurach (2011), these reports include findings from a meta-analysis of comprehensive school reform by Borman et al. (2003).

16. See Peurach (2011).
17. Retrieved from the CDDRE website: http://www.cddre.org.
18. The effectiveness of the program was reported from a large randomized control study in Carlson, Borman, and Robinson (2011) and Slavin et al. (2011).
19. Boudett, City, and Murnane (2005) and Boudett and Steele (2007).
20. See Boudett, City, and Murnane (2005, p. 100).
21. See Wallace Foundation (2012).
22. Jonathan Schnur, co-founder, was a senior education staffer in the Clinton administration, worked for Al Gore's office, and served on the Obama administration transition team.
23. See http://www.newleaders.org/wp-content/uploads/2011/08/UEF-Concept-Maps1.pdf.
24. See Leonard et al. (2010) for some discussion of the complexities of the apparent growth in autism.
25. See Peters and Saidin (2000) for a discussion of customized services and Collins and Halverson (2009) for a discussion of customization in public education.
26. See Carran, Tsantis, Castellani, and Baglin (2010) for a discussion of some data quality issues with IEPs.
27. This ability to use RTI as a step in the IEP process is new with IDEA 2004.
28. See Goertz, Oláh, and Riggan (2009) and Perie, Marion, and Gong (2009).
29. See U.S. Department of Education (2010, p. 62).
30. See Shepard (2009, p. 35).
31. See Halverson (2010b).
32. See *The New Instructional Leadership* (Halverson & Thomas, 2007) for how the different school teams varied in their approaches.
33. For more information on Lesson Study, see Fernandez, Cannon, and Chokshi (2003) and Lewis, Perry, and Murata (2006).

Chapter 7

1. See Weingarten (2011).
2. See Lampert (2003) for an introduction to the theory of and research on teaching complexity.
3. See Shulman (1987) and Kennedy (2002).
4. See Cohen (1989) and Wilson, Miller, and Yerkes (1993).
5. The research is inconclusive in this area. Many teachers report that they do not like standardized tests. A recent large survey of 10,000 teachers funded by the Gates Foundation showed teachers found standardized tests to have some limited value for their work. See Bill and Melinda Gates Foundation (2012).
6. See MetLife Foundation (2012).
7. See Peters and Saidin (2000).
8. See Shapiro and Varian (1998) for a discussion of digital economics.
9. See www.digitialpromise.org for more details.
10. See Duncan (2011).
11. The SLC is being piloted in several states and has launched a program with high-powered organizations from education and business providing support; see www.slcedu.org. For more information on inBloom, see www.inbloom.org.

12. See Slotta and Linn (2009).

13. See Manyika et al. (2011) for a discussion of big data potential. DiCerbo and Behrens (2012) have described this area of analytics as the Digital Ocean because of both the volume of data and the challenges with analysis.

14. See Dede (2011).

15. See Linn and Chiu (2011) and Linn et al. (2012).

16. See Shute et al. (2011).

17. See www.kickboardforteachers.com.

18. See Christensen (1997) for an initial discussion and Christensen, Baumann, Ruggles, and Sadtler (2006) and Markides (2006) for more contemporary views. Also, Carayannis, Gonzalez, and Wetter (2003) present a discussion from the perspective of the learning involved with these innovations.

19. See Christensen, Horn, and Johnson (2008).

20. See Bonk, Graham, Cross, and Moore (2006) and Osguthorpe and Graham (2003) for some historical discussions of blended learning in a corporate and higher education space.

21. Cator (2012). Comments were condensed and clarified in consultation with the author.

22. See Staker and Horn (2012) and Horn and Staker (2011).

23. Funders include the Bill and Melinda Gates, Eli and Edythe Broad, Michael and Susan Dell, and Wallace foundations; the Carnegie Corporation of New York; Cisco Systems; the New Schools Venture Fund; Robin Hood (a foundation started by New York's wealthy to help New York's poor); Education Collaboration Fund, a donor-advised fund of J. P. Morgan Private Bank; and J. P. Morgan Chase & Co. Global Philanthropy.

24. See New York City Department of Education (2010).

25. The Investing in Innovation (i3) grant program is managed by the Office of Innovation led by James Shelton, former management consultant and Gates Foundation Program Officer.

26. The possibility for this type of architecture was discussed in Piety and Palincsar (2006).

27. See Barth (1974) and Walberg and Thomas (1972) for an introductory discussion and Brown and Adler (2008) for a more contemporary discussion.

28. See Cuban (1993, 2004) as well as Giaconia and Hedges (1982).

Chapter 8

1. See Santos and Gebeloff (2012, p. A1) and Lovett (2010).

2. See Gates (2012).

3. See Darling-Hammond (2012).

4. This means a teacher ranked at the 50th percentile actually could be at the 80th or 20th percentile, although more likely to be closer to the 50th.

5. The research is light in this area, in part because there is no research genre for data quality in education and few studies are funded to specifically look at data quality. Important work in this area comes from reports out of the University of Wisconsin's Value Added Research Center. See Watson, Thorn, Ponisciak, and Boehm (2011) and Kraemer, Worth, and Meyer (2010).

6.   In 2012 several news stories emerged from New York and other metropolitan areas about the scorecards for teachers or schools. See Winetrip (2012) and Turque (2012) for examples. According to Andres Alonso, CEO of the Baltimore City Schools, the system responded with measures to control test cheating and found that scores in many schools declined just after indicating the problem was pervasive. These declines did not, however, erase most of the gains made in the city, indicating that real progress had been made. Alonso, personal communication, May 16, 2012.

7.   See CNN Wire Staff (2011) and Toppo, Gillum, and Bello (2011).

8.   Laura Diamond's (2009) article details the achievements of the Atlanta Public Schools, including support from foundations for instituting reforms.

9.   See Campbell (1976, p. 35).

10.   There are actually many researchers and theorists who believe that the first theoretical frame for education, including assessments, should be social rather than cognitive. This is a huge debate in education. See Anderson, Greeno, Reder, and Simon (2000) for some introduction.

11.   The actual costs of testing are difficult to accurately estimate. See Solmon and Fagnano (1990) and Phelps (2000).

12.   See National Research Council (2011). Tom Kane, the researcher responsible for managing the MET project, was part of the panel that produced this report.

13.   See Mislevy (1996) for some discussion.

14.   See Pellegrino, Chudowsky, and Glaser (2001).

15.   New work on diagnostic assessment by Rupp, Templin, and Henson (2010) and others, including Shute et al. (2011), involving embedding assessment inside of technologies, is providing new options.

16.   The social and sociocultural nature of learning has a strong research base that is beyond the scope of this book. The National Research Council (1999) compendium *How People Learn* provides an important introduction.

17.   See Haertel and Herman (2005, p. 28).

18.   See Mislevy, Behrens, DiCerbo, and Levy (2012).

19.   See O'Day and Smith (1993) for one of the classical arguments for standards-based reform.

20.   See Blank, Porter, and Smithson (2001) for an important discussion and Davis and Krajcik (2005) and Krajcik, McNeill, and Reiser (2007) for discussions that look at the language and structure of standards.

21.   See Battelle for Kids (2009) and Data Quality Campaign (2010a) for an overview discussion. Details also provided by Nancy Wilson, personal communication, February 26, 2012.

22.   See http://tsdl.org/ProjectDescription.aspx for details on the project.

Chapter 9

1. McGuinn (2012) discusses the role of these organizations and their collaboration as well as differences in their membership.

2.   See Mandinach and Gummer (in press) and National Center for Teaching Quality (2012).

3.   See Sanders and Rivers (1996).

4. Statement to seminar at University of Michigan, November 11, 2011, and condensed with permission.

5. Some have called this new research initiative DARPA-ED.

6. See Bowker (2006).

7. See Hunter (2011).

8. The process is described in a Data Quality Campaign (2010b) video, http://www.youtube.com/watch?v=uaZk57oNLkA.

9. The literature characterizing education in ecological terms includes Firestone (1989), Weaver-Hightower (2008), and Lemke and Sabelli (2008).

10. The issue of using data directly with students has been discussed by the Dell Foundation in its case study on Charlotte-Mecklenburg Schools (http://blog.msdf.org/wp-content/uploads/2012/01/MSDF_CMS_Hi.pdf).

11. Teachers' response to survey data has not been reported on as often as observation feedback has.

12. Under NCLB, each state could define its own test schedule so that some states did not have data available for teachers until the next academic year, while some did provide results during the same year.

13. See Coburn (2005a), Cohen (1995), Honig (2004), and Burch (2006) for some examples. Rowan's (2002) discussion of fads and innovations also touches on this area, as he references the organizations often involved in the fads.

14. See Lindblom (2002) for a discussion of traditional markets and market systems.

15. See Simon (1996, p. 111).

16. I believe this metaphor began with Aimee Guidera and the Data Quality Campaign.

17. Messick (1989) and Moss, Girard, and Haniford (2006) provide important introductions.

18. Lemke's (2000, 2002) work is important in seeing how meaning-making can cross ecosocial levels and become associated with different types of symbolic (e.g., quantitative and qualitative) systems.

19. See Bransford and Shwartz (1999) and their discussion of preparation for future learning rather than transfer of skills.

20. Digital imaging became practical with the development of the charge-coupled device in 1969, and email, which had existed in specialized forms, became practical on a wide scale with the invention of the Telex network.

21. See Ribes and Finholt (2009).

References

Alvani, M., & Leidner, D. (2001). Review: Knowledge management and knowledge management systems: Conceptual foundations and research issues. *MIS Quarterly, 25*(1), 107–136.

Anderson, J. R., Greeno, J. G., Reder, L. M., & Simon, H. A. (2000). Perspectives on learning, thinking, and activity. *Educational Researcher, 29*(4), 11–13.

Baker, E., Barton, P., Darling-Hammond, L., Haertel, E., Ladd, H., Linn, R., . . . Shephard, L. (2010). *Problems with the use of student test scores to evaluate teachers* (EPI Briefing Paper No. 278). Washington, DC: Economic Policy Institute.

Baker, R., & Yacef, K. (2009). The state of educational data mining in 2009: A review and future visions. *Journal of Educational Data Mining, 1*(1), 3–17.

Barth, R. S. (1974). *Open education and the American school.* New York: Schocken Books.

Battelle for Kids. (2009). The importance of accurately linking instruction to students to determine teacher effectiveness. Retrieved from http://portal.battelleforkids.org/BFK/images/Link_whitepagesApril2010web.pdf

Behrens, J. T. (2000). Exploratory Data Analysis. In A. E. Kazdin (Ed.), *Encyclopedia of psychology.* New York: Oxford University Press.

Behrens, J. T., Mislevy, R. J., DiCerbo, K. E., & Levy, R. (2012). Evidence centered design for learning and assessment in the digital world. In M. Mayrath, J. Clarke-Midura, & D. H. Robinson (Eds.). *Technology-based assessments for 21st Century skills: Theoretical and practical implications from modern research* (pp. 13–54). Charlotte, NC: Information Age Publishing

Bennet, M. (2011, October 5). *Strengthening the feedback loop: Using data to support the college- and career-ready agenda.* Keynote address presented at national meeting of College Summit and the Data Quality Campaign, Washington, DC. Retrieved from http://www.capitolconnection.net/capcon/dataqualitycampaign/100511/DQ-C100511launch.htm

Bijker, W. E. (1995). *Of bicycles, bakelites, and bulbs: Toward a theory of sociotechnical change.* Cambridge, MA: MIT Press.

Bill and Melinda Gates Foundation. (2010). *Working with teachers to develop fair and reliable measures of effective teaching.* Retrieved from http://www.metproject.org/downloads/met-framing-paper.pdf

Bill and Melinda Gates Foundation. (2012). *Gathering feedback for teaching: Combining high-quality observations with student surveys and achievement gains.* Retrieved from http://www.metproject.org/downloads/MET_Gathering_Feedback_Research_Paper.pdf

Bill and Melinda Gates Foundation. (2013). *Ensuring fair and reliable measures of effective teaching culminating findings from the MET project's three-year study.* Retrieved from http://www.metproject.org/downloads/MET_Ensuring_Fair_and_Reliable_Measures_Practitioner_Brief.pdf

Black, P.J., & Wiliam, D. (1998). *Inside the black box: raising standards through classroom assessment.* London: King's College London School of Education.

Blank, R. K., Porter, A., & Smithson, J. (2001). *New tools for analyzing teaching, curriculum and standards in mathematics and science.* Report from Survey of Enacted Curriculum Project (National Science Foundation REC98-03080). Washington, DC: Council of Chief State School Officers. Retrieved from http://seconline.wceruw.org/Reference/SECnewToolsreport.pdf

Bonk, C. J., Graham, C. R., Cross, J., & Moore, M. G. (2006). *The handbook of blended learning: Global perspectives, local designs.* San Francisco: Pfeiffer.

Borman, G., & Dowling, M. (2010). Schools and inequality: A multilevel analysis of Coleman's equality of educational opportunity data. *Teachers College Record, 112*(5), 1201–1246.

Borman, G. D., Hewes, G. M., Overman, L. T., & Brown, S. (2003). Comprehensive school reform and achievement: A meta-analysis. *Review of Educational Research, 73*(2), 125–230.

Boudett, K., City, E., & Murnane, J. (Eds.). (2005). *Data wise: A step-by-step guide to using assessment results to improve teaching and learning.* Cambridge, MA: Harvard University Press.

Boudett, K., & Steele, J. (2007). *Data wise in action: Stories of schools using data to improve teaching and learning.* Cambridge, MA: Harvard Education Press.

Boudreau, M. C., Loch, K. D., Robey, D., & Straud, D. (1998). Going global: Using information technology to advance the competitiveness of the virtual transnational organization. *The Academy of Management Executive, 12*(4), 120–128.

Bowers, A. J. (2010). Toward addressing the issues of site selection in district effectiveness research: A two-level hierarchical linear growth model. *Educational Administration Quarterly, 46*(3), 395–425.

Bowker, G. (2006). *Memory practices in the sciences.* Cambridge, MA: MIT Press.

Bowker, G., & Star, S. L. (2000). *Sorting things out: Classification and its consequences.* Cambridge, MA: MIT Press.

Bransford, J. D., & Schwartz, D. L. (1999). Rethinking transfer: A simple proposal with multiple implications. *Review of research in education, 24*, 61–100.

Broad Foundation. (2001, November 16). Announcing the Broad Center for Superintendents [Press release]. Retrieved from http://broadeducation.org/news/137.html

Brookover, W., Beamer, L., Efthim, H., Hathaway, D., Lezotte, L., Miller, S., & Tornatzky, L. (1982). *Creating effective schools.* Holmes Beach, FL: Learning Publications.

Brown, E. (2012, November 8). Study chides D.C. teacher turnover. *Washington Post.* Retrieved January 11, 2013, from http://articles.washingtonpost.com/2012-11-08/local/35506333_1_controversial-teacher-evaluation-system-teacher-turnover-highly-effective-teachers .

Brown, J., & Duguid, P. (1991). Organizational learning and communities-of-practice: Toward a unified view of working, learning, and innovation. *Organizational Science, 2*(1), 40–58.

Brown, J. S., & Adler, R. P. (2008). Open education, the long tail, and learning 2.0. *Educause Review, 43*(1), 16–20.

Brynjolfsson, E. (1993). The productivity paradox of information technology. *Communications of the ACM, 36*(12), 66–77.

Brynjolfsson, E., & Hitt, L. (2000). Beyond computation: Information technology, organizational transformation and business performance. *The Journal of Economic Perspectives, 14*(4), 23–48.

Buckley, J. (2012, April 14). *The development of P–20 common education data standards (CEDS) to advance education research.* Paper presented at the annual meeting of the American Educational Research Association, Vancouver, British Columbia, Canada. Retrieved from http://www.aera.net/tabid/12972/Default.aspx

Burch, P. (2006). The new educational privatization: Educational contracting and high stakes accountability. *Teachers College Record, 108*(12), 2582–2610.

Callahan, R. E. (1964). *Education and the cult of efficiency: A study of the social forces that have shaped the administration of the public schools.* Chicago: University of Chicago Press.

Campbell, D. T. (1976). *Assessing the impact of planned social change.* Public Affairs Center, Dartmouth College, Hanover, NH.

Carayannis, E., & Coleman, J. (2005). Creative system design methodologies: The case of complex technical systems. *Technovation, 25*(8), 831–840.

Carayannis, E. G., Gonzalez, E., & Wetter, J. (2003). The nature and dynamics of discontinuous and disruptive innovations from a learning and knowledge management perspective. In L. V. Shavinina (Ed.), *International handbook on innovation* (pp. 116–138). Elsevier Press.

Carey, K., & Manwaring, R. (2011). *Growth models and accountability: A recipe for remaking ESEA.* Education Sector, Washington, DC.

Carlson, D., Borman, G., & Robinson, M. (2011). A multistate district-level cluster randomized trial of the impact of data-driven reform on reading and mathematics achievement. *Educational Evaluation and Policy Analysis, 33*(3), 215–229.

Carran, D., Tsantis, L., Castellani, J., & Baglin, C. (2010, Fall). *Data mining electronically linked part C-part B data sets to identify usage patterns and predict need.* New Horizons for Learning, School of Education, Johns Hopkins University, Baltimore, MD.

Cator, K. (2012, September 4). *Data analytics and web dashboards in the classroom.* Comments presented at Brookings Institution event, Washington, DC.

Childress, S. M., Doyle, D., & Thomas, D. (2009). *Leading for equity: The pursuit of excellence in Montgomery County public schools.* Cambridge, MA: Harvard Education Press.

Christensen, C. M. (1997). *The innovator's dilemma: When new technologies cause great firms to fail.* Cambridge, MA: Harvard Business Press.

Christensen, C. M., Baumann, H., Ruggles, R., & Sadtler, T. M. (2006). Disruptive innovation for social change. *Harvard Business Review, 84*(12), 94.

Christensen, C., Horn, M., & Johnson, C. (2008). *Disrupting class: How disruptive innovation will change the way the world learns.* New York: McGraw-Hill.

Ciborra, C. (1993). *Teams, markets and systems: Business innovation and information technology.* Cambridge, UK: Cambridge University Press.

CNN Wire Staff. (2011, July 5). *Dozens of Atlanta educators falsified tests, state report confirms*. Atlanta, GA: CNN.

Coburn, C. (2005a). The role of non-system actors in the relationship between policy and practice: The case of reading instruction in California. *Educational Evaluation & Policy Analysis, 27*(1), 23–52.

Coburn, C. (2005b). Shaping teacher sensemaking: School leaders and the enactment of reading policy. *Educational Policy, 19*(3), 476–509.

Coburn, C. E., Honig, M. I., & Stein, M. K. (2009). What is the evidence on districts' use of evidence? In J. Bransford, L. Gomez, D. Lam, & N. Vye (Eds.), *Research and practice: Towards a reconciliation* (67–87). Cambridge, MA: Harvard Education Press.

Coburn, C., & Talbert, J. (2006). Conceptions of evidence use in school districts: Mapping the terrain. *American Journal of Education, 112*(4), 467–495.

Coburn, C., Toure, J., & Yamashita, M. (2009). Evidence, interpretation, and persuasion: Instructional decision making at the district central office. *Teachers College Record, 111*(4), 1115–1161.

Coburn, C. E., & Turner, E. O. (2011). Research on data use: A framework and analysis. *Measurement: Interdisciplinary Research and Perspectives, 9*(4), 173–206.

Cohen, D. K. (1989). *Teaching practice: Plus ça change*. In P. W. Jackson (Ed.), *Contributing to educational change: Perspectives on research and practice* (pp. 27–89). Berkeley, CA: McCutchan.

Cohen, D. K. (1995). What is the system in systemic reform? *Educational Researcher, 24*(9), 11–31.

Cohen, D. K. (2011). *Teaching and its predicaments*. Cambridge, MA: Harvard University Press.

Coleman, J. S., Campbell, E. Q., Hobson, C. J., McPartland, J., Mood, A. M., Weinfeld, F. D., & York, R. L. (1966). *Equality of educational opportunity*. Washington, DC: U.S. Department of Health, Education, & Welfare, Office of Education.

Collins, A., & Halverson, R. (2009). *Rethinking education in the age of technology: The digital revolution and the schools*. New York: Teachers College Press.

Confrey, J., & Makar, K. (2005). Critiquing and improving the use of data from high-stakes tests with the aid of dynamic statistics software. In C. Dede, J. Honan, & L. Peters (Eds.), *Scaling up success: Lessons from technology-based educational improvement* (pp. 198–226). San Francisco: Jossey-Bass.

Crawford, V. M., Schlager, M., Penuel, W. R., & Toyama, Y. (2008). Supporting the art of teaching in a data-rich, high performance learning environment. In E.B. Mandinach & M. Honey (Eds.), *Data-driven school improvement: Linking data and learning* (pp. 109–129). New York, NY: Teachers College Press.

Creighton, T. (2001, April). Data analysis in administrators' hands: An oxymoron? *The School Administrator*. Retrieved from http://www.aasa.org/publications/saarticledetail.cfm?ItemNumber=3757&snItemNumber=950a+nNumber=1995

Cuban, L. (1986). *Teachers and machines: The classroom use of technology since 1920*. New York: Teachers College Press.

Cuban, L. (1993). *How teachers taught: Constancy and change in American classrooms, 1890–1990*. New York: Teachers College Press.

Cuban, L. (2003). *Oversold and underused: Computers in the classroom*. Cambridge, MA: Harvard University Press.

Cuban, L. (2004). The open classroom: Were schools without walls just another fad? *Education Next, 4*(2), 4.

Danielson, C., & McGreal, T. L. (2000). *Teacher evaluation to enhance professional practice.* Alexandria, VA: Association for Supervision and Curriculum Development.

Darling-Hammond, L. (2012, March 14). Value-added evaluation hurts teaching. *Education Week.* Retrieved from http://www.edweek.org/ew/articles/2012/03/05/24darlin ghammond_ep.h31.html

Darling-Hammond, L., LaPointe, M., Meyerson, D., Orr. M., & Cohen, C. (2007). *Preparing school leaders for a changing world: Lessons from exemplary leadership development programs.* Stanford, CA: Stanford University, Stanford Educational Leadership.

Data Quality Campaign. (2009). *Leveraging the power of data to improve education* [Press release]. Retrieved from http://www.dataqualitycampaign.org/resources/details/419

Data Quality Campaign. (2010a). *Effectively linking teachers and students: The key to improving teacher quality.* Retrieved from http://www.tsdl.org/resources/site1/general/White%20Papers/DQC_TSDL_7-27.pdf

Data Quality Campaign. (2010b). *Georgia's collaborative journey: Linking and sharing data: Why it's important.* Retrieved from http://www.dataqualitycampaign.org/files/GA's%20Alliance%20of%20Ed%20Agency%20Heads%20DQC%209%20 18%2010.pdf

Datnow, A., Park, V., & Wohlstetter, P. (2007). *Achieving with data: How high-performing school systems use data to improve instruction for elementary students.* Los Angeles: University of Southern California, Rossier School of Education, Center on Educational Governance.

David, P. (1990). The dynamo and the computer: An historical perspective on the modern productivity paradox. *The American Economic Review, 80*(2), pp. 355–361.

Davis, E. A., & Krajcik, J. S. (2005). Designing educative curriculum materials to promote teacher learning. *Educational Researcher, 34*(3), 3–14.

Dede, C. (2011). Emerging technologies, ubiquitous learning, and educational transformation. In C. D. Kloos, D. Gillet, R. M. C, Garcia, F. Wild, & M. Wolpers. *Towards ubiquitous learning (Proceedings of the 6th European Conference on Technology-Enhanced Learning),* (pp 1–8). New York, NY: Springer.

Dembosky, J. W., Pane, J. F., Barney, H., & Christina, R. (2006). *Data driven decision-making in southwestern Pennsylvania school districts Santa Monica, CA*: RAND Corporation.

Diamond, J., & Spillane, J. (2004). High-stakes accountability in urban elementary schools: Challenging or reproducing inequality? *Teachers College Record, 106*(6), 1145–1176.

Diamond, L. (2009, February 22). Atlanta public schools head-of-the-class reformer. *Atlanta Journal Constitution.*

DiCerbo, K. E., & Behrens, J. T. (2012). Implications of the digital ocean on current and future assessment. In R. Lissitz & H. Jiao (Eds.), *Computers and their impact on state assessment: Recent history and predictions for the future* (pp. 273–306). Charlotte, NC: Information Age Publishing.

Domenech, D., & Torres, R (interviewees). (2010). *AASA and NSC—tracking student performance* [Video]. Arlington, VA: American Association of School Administrators.

Duckworth, A., & Seligman, M. (2005). Self-discipline outdoes IQ in predicting academic performance of adolescents. *Psychological Science, 16*(12), 939–944.

DuFour, R., & Eaker, R. (1998). *Professional learning communities at work: Best practices for enhancing student achievement.* (Available from National Educational Service, 1252 Loesch Road, Bloomington, IN 47404-9107).

Duncan, A. (2011, September 16). *The digital promise* [Remarks by Secretary Duncan at the launch of Digital Promise]. Retrieved from http://www.ed.gov/news/speeches/digital-promise

Duncan, A. (2010, November 27). *The new normal: Doing more with less* [Remarks by Secretary Duncan at the American Enterprise Institute] Retrieved from http://www.ed.gov/news/speeches/new-normal-doing-more-less-secretary-arne-duncans-remarks-american-enterprise-institut

Earl, L., & Fullan, M. (2003). Using data in leadership for learning. *Cambridge Journal of Education, 33*(3), 383–394.

Edmonds, R. (1979). Effective schools for the urban poor. *Educational Leadership, 37*(1), 15–24.

Edmonds, R. (1982). Programs of school improvement: An overview. *Educational Leadership, 40*(3), 4–11.

Education Sciences Reform Act of 2002 (Pub. L. No. 107-279). Retrieved from http://www.ed.gov/legislation/EdSciencesRef/

Eisenstein, E. (1982). *The printing press as an agent of change.* New York, NY: Cambridge University Press.

Elmore, R. (2004). *School reform from the inside out: Policy, practice, and performance.* Cambridge, MA: Harvard Education Press.

Falk, J., & Drayton, B. (2004). State testing and inquiry based science: Are they complementary or competing reforms? *Journal of Educational Change, 5*(4), 344–387.

Fernandez, C., Cannon, J., & Chokshi, S. (2003). A US–Japan lesson study collaboration reveals critical lenses for examining practice. *Teaching and Teacher Education, 19*(2), 171–185.

Feuer, M. (2008, December). *Building an evidence base: Lessons learned from systematic reviews.* Opening comments at the Conference on Education Research: Moving Evidence on What Works into Practice Washington, DC. Retrieved from http://ies.ed.gov/ncee/wwc/multimedia/20081212evidenceintopractice/wwc_121208_transcript.pdf

Firestone, W. (1989). Educational policy as an ecology of games. *Educational Researcher, 18*(7), 18–24.

Frederiksen, J., & Collins, A. (1989). A systems approach to educational testing. *Educational Researcher, 18*(9), 27–32.

Friedman, T. L. (2005). *The world is flat: A brief history of the twenty-first century.* New York: Farrar Straus Giroux.

Gates, B. (2012, February 22). For teachers, shame is no solution. *The New York Times.* Retrieved from http://www.nytimes.com/2012/02/23/opinion/for-teachers-shame-is-no-solution.html

Giaconia, R. M., & Hedges, L. V. (1982). Identifying features of effective open education. *Review of Educational Research, 52*(4), 579–602.

Goertz, M. E., Oláh, L. N., & Riggan, M. (2009). *From testing to teaching: The use of interim assessments in classroom instruction.* Philadelphia, PA: Consortium for Policy Research in Education.

Goldhaber, D., & Hansen, M. (2010). *Is it just a bad class? Assessing the stability of measured teacher performance.* Seattle, WA: Center on Reinventing Public Education.

Goldhaber, D., & Liddle, S. (2012, January). *The gateway to the profession: Assessing teacher preparation programs based on student achievement* (CALDER Working Paper No. 65). Retrieved from http://www.cedr.us/papers/working/CEDR%20 WP%202011-2%20Teacher%20Training%20(9-26).pdf

Guidera, A. (2009, March 12). *Speech at launch of Data Quality Campaign releases action guide for state and federal policy makers* [Press release].

Haertel, E., & Herman, J. L. (2005). A historical perspective on validity arguments for accountability testing. In E. Haertel & J. L. Herman (Eds.), *Uses and misuses of data for educational accountability and improvement* (pp. 1–34). Malden, NJ: Blackwell.

Hallinger, P., & Heck, R. H. (1996). Reassessing the principal's role in school effectiveness: A review of empirical research, 1980–1995. *Educational Administration Quarterly, 32*(1), 5–44.

Halverson, R. (2003). Systems of practice: How leaders use artifacts to create professional community in schools. *Education Policy Analysis Archives, 11*(37) . Retrieved from http://epaa.asu.edu/epaa/v11n37

Halverson, R. (2010a, April). *Methods for accessing and assessing how school leaders improve teaching and learning.* Paper presented at the annual meeting of the American Educational Research Association. Denver, CO.

Halverson, R. (2010b). School formative feedback systems. *Peabody Journal of Education, 85*(2), 130–146.

Halverson, R., & Thomas, C. N. (2007). *New instructional leadership.* WCER Working Paper No. 2007-1. Retrieved from http://sss.wida.us/publications/workingPapers/ Working_Paper_No_2007_01.pdf

Hamilton, L., Halverson, R., Jackson, S., Mandinach, E., Supovitz, J., & Wayman, J. (2009). *Using student achievement data to support instructional decision making* (No. NCEE 2009-4067). Washington, DC: U.S. Department of Education, Institute of Education Sciences, National Center for Education Evaluation and Regional Assistance.

Hamilton, L. S., Stecher, B. M., Marsh, J. A., McCombs, J. S., Robyn, A., Russell, J. L., Naftel, S., & Barney, H. (2007). *Implementing standards-based accountability under No Child Left Behind: Responses of superintendents, principals, and teachers in three states.* Santa Monica, CA: RAND Corporation.

Hammer, M. M. (1990, July–August). Reengineering work: Don't automate, obliterate. *Harvard Business Review,* 104–112.

Harris, D. N. (2011). *Value-added measures in education.* Cambridge, MA: Harvard Education Press.

Hawley, W. D., & Rollie, D. L. (2002). *The keys to effective schools: Educational reform as continuous improvement.* Sage Oaks, CA: Corwin Press.

Headden, S. (2011). *Inside IMPACT: D.C.'s model teacher evaluation system* [Education Sector Report]. Retrieved from http://www.eric.ed.gov/ERICWebPortal/ detail?accno=ED521326

Hess, F. M., & Kelly, A. P. (Eds.). (2012). *Carrots, sticks, and the bully pulpit: Lessons from a half-century of federal efforts to improve America's schools.* Cambridge, MA: Harvard Education Press.

Hickey, D. T., & Anderson, K. T. (2007). Chapter 11 situative approaches to student assessment: Contextualizing evidence to transform practice. *Yearbook of the National Society for the Study of Education, 106*(1), 264–287.

Hiebert, J., Gallimore, R., & Stigler, J. W. (2002). A knowledge base for the teaching profession: What would it look like and how can we get one? *Educational Researcher, 31*(5), 3–15. doi:10.3102/0013189X031005003

Honig, M. I. (2004). The new middle management: Intermediary organizations in education policy implementation. *Educational Evaluation and Policy Analysis, 26*(1), 65–87.

Horn, M., & Staker, H. (2011). *The rise of K–12 blended learning.* San Mateo, CA: Innosight Institute. Retrieved from http://www.innosightinstitute.org/innosight/wp-content/uploads/2011/05/The-Rise-of-K-12-Blended-Learning.pdf

Hunter, D. (2011, October 5). *Strengthening the feedback loop: Using data to support the college- and career-ready agenda.* Address presented at national meeting of College Summit and the Data Quality Campaign, Washington, DC. Retrieved from http://www.capitolconnection.net/capcon/dataqualitycampaign/100511/DQ-C100511launch.htm

Ikemoto, G., & Marsh, J. (2007). Cutting through the "data-driven" mantra: Different conceptions of data-driven decision making. In P. Moss (Ed.), *Evidence and decision making: Yearbook of the National Society for the Study of Education* (Vol. 106, issue 1, pp. 105–131). Chicago: National Society for the Study of Education.

Ingram, D., Louis, K. S., & Schroeder, R. (2004). Accountability policies and teacher decision making: Barriers to the use of data to improve practice. *Teachers College Record, 106*(6), 1258–1287.

Jackson, P. W. (1968). *Life in classrooms.* New York: Teachers College Press.

Jorgenson, D. (2001). Information technology and the U.S. economy. *The American Economic Review, 91*(1), 1–32.

Kalogrides, D., Loeb, S., & Béteille, T. (2011). *Power play? Teacher characteristics and class assignments.* CALDER Working Paper 59. Retrieved from http://www.urban.org/url.cfm?ID=1001530

Kamras, J. (2010, July 23). DCPS parent chat on IMPACT [Video file]. Retrieved from http://www.youtube.com/watch?v=pvTA8RYDPUw

Kane, T., Rockoff, J., & Staiger, D. (2008). What does certification tell us about teacher effectiveness? Evidence from New York City. *Economics of Education Review, 27*(6), 615–631.

Kennedy, M. M. (2002). Knowledge and teaching. *Teachers and Teaching: Theory and Practice, 8*(3), 355–370.

Knapp, M., Copland, M., & Swinnerton, J. (2007). Data-informed leadership: Insights from current research, theory, and practice. In P. Moss (Ed.), *National Society for the Study of Education yearbook: Part 1. Evidence and decision making* (pp.74–104). Chicago: NSSE. Distributed by University of Chicago Press.

Knapp, M. S., Swinnerton, J., Copland, M. A., & Monpas-Huber, J. (2006). *Data-informed leadership in education.* New York, NY: Wallace Foundation.

Koedel, C., Parsons, E., Podgursky, M., & Ehlert, M. (2012, July). *Teacher preparation programs and teacher quality: Are there real differences across programs?* (CALDER Working Paper No. 75). http://economics.missouri.edu/working-papers/2012/WP1204_koedel_et_al.pdf

Konstantopoulos, S., & Borman, G. (2011). Family background and school effects on student achievement: A multilevel analysis of the Coleman data. *Teachers College Record, 113*(1), 97–132.

Kraemer, S., Worth, R., & Meyer, R. (2010). *Classroom assignment practices in urban school districts using teacher level value-added systems.* Value Added Research Center, University of Wisconsin, Madison. Retrieved from http://varc.wceruw.org/pubs/AEFP_2011/Kraemer%20et%20al-AFEP%2711-FINAL.pdf

Krajcik, J., McNeill, K. L., & Reiser, B. J. (2007). Learning-goals-driven design model: Developing curriculum materials that align with national standards and incorporate project-based pedagogy. *Science Education, 92*(1), 1–32.

Lampert, M. (2003). *Teaching problems and the problems of teaching.* New Haven, CT: Yale University Press.

Latour, B. (2005). *Reassembling the social: An introduction to actor-network theory.* New York: Oxford.

LaValle, S., Lesser, E., Shockley, R., Hopkins, M., & Kruschwitz, N. (2010, December 21). Big data, analytics and the path from insights to value. *MIT Sloan Management Review, 52*(2).

Lee, V., & Bryk, A. (1989). A multilevel model of the social distribution of high school achievement. *Sociology of Education, 62*(2), 172–192.

Lemke, J. (2000). Across the scales of time: Artifacts, activities, and meanings in ecosocial systems. *Mind, Culture, Activity, 7*(4), 273–290.

Lemke, J. (2002). Travels in hypermodality. *Visual Communication, 1*(3), 299–325.

Lemke, J., & Sabelli, N. (2008). Complex systems and educational change: Towards a new research agenda. *Educational Philosophy and Theory, 40*(1), 118–129.

Leonard, H., Dixon, G., Whitehouse, A., Bourke, J., Aiberti, K., Nassar, N. . . . Glasson, E. J. (2010). Unpacking the complex nature of the autism epidemic. *Research in Autism Spectrum Disorders, 4*(4), 548–554.

Lewis, A. (2011). *Four key questions in developing teacher preparation programs* [TeachingWorks seminar series at the University of Michigan's School of Education]. Retrieved from http://www.teachingworks.org/training/seminar-series/event/detail/teach-for-america

Lewis, C., Perry, R., & Murata, A. (2006). How should research contribute to instructional improvement? The case of lesson study. *Educational Researcher, 35*(3), 3–14.

Lindblom, C. E. (2002). *The market system: What it is, how it works, and what to make of it.* New Haven, CT: Yale University Press.

Linn, M. C., & Chiu, J. L. (2011, Winter). Combining learning and assessment to improve science education. *Research and Practice in Assessment, 5,* 5–14.

Linn, M., Liu, L., Gerard, L., Kirkpatrick, D., Madhok, J., Matuk, C., & Terashima, H. (2012). CLASS: Continuous learning and automated scoring in science. In *Proceedings of meeting of discovery research K–12 principal investigators.* Arlington, VA: Community for Advancing Discovery Research in Education (CADRE).

Lissitz, R. W. (2006). Longitudinal and value added models of student performance. Maple Grove, MN: JAM Press.

Lovett, I. (2010, November 9). Teacher's death exposes tensions in Los Angeles. *The New York Times*, p. A23 .

Mandinach, E., & Gummer, E. (in press). A systemic view of improving data literacy in educator preparation. *Educational Researcher.*

Mandinach, E. B., & Honey, M. (Eds.). (2008). *Data-driven school improvement: Linking data and learning.* New York: Teachers College Press.

Manyika, J., Chui, M., Brown, B., Bughin, J., Dobbs, R., Roxburgh, C., & Byers, A. H. (2011). *Big data: The next frontier for innovation, competition, and productivity.* McKinsey Global Institute. http://www.mckinsey.com/insights/mgi/research/technology_and_innovation/big_data_the_next_frontier_for_innovation

Markides, C. (2006). Disruptive innovation: In need of better theory. *Journal of Product Innovation Management, 23*(1), 19–25.

Marsh, J., Kerr, K., Ikemoto, G., Darilek, H., Suttorp, M., Zimmer, R., & Barney, H. (2005). *The role of districts in fostering instructional improvement: Lessons from three urban districts partnered with the Institute for Learning.* Santa Monica, CA: RAND Corporation.

Marzano, R. J. (1992). *A different kind of classroom: Teaching with dimensions of learning.* Alexandria, VA: Association for Supervision and Curriculum Development.

Marzano, R. J., Frontier, T., & Livingston, D. (2011). *Effective supervision: Supporting the art and science of teaching.* Alexandria, VA: Association for Supervision and Curriculum Development.

Mathews, J. (2001). Nontraditional thinking in the central office. *School Administrator, 58*(6), 6–11.

Mathews, J. (2009). *Work hard. Be nice: How two inspired teachers created the most promising schools in America.* Chapel Hill, NC: Algonquin Books.

McClellan, C., Atkinson, M. & Danielson, C. (2012). *Teacher evaluator training & certification: Lessons learned from the measures of effective teaching project.* San Francisco: Teachscape, Inc.

McFarlan, F. W. (1984). Information technology changes the way you compete. *Harvard Business Review, 62*(3), 98–103.

McGuinn, P. (2012). Fight club: Are advocacy organizations changing the politics of education? *Education Next, 12*(3). Retrieved from http://educationnext.org/fight-club/

Messick, S. (1989). Meaning and values in test validation: The science and ethics of assessment. *Educational Researcher, 18*(2), 5–11.

MetLife Foundation. (2012). *The MetLife survey of the American teacher: Teachers, parents and the economy.* Retrieved from https://www.metlife.com/assets/cao/contributions/foundation/american-teacher/MetLife-Teacher-Survey-2011.pdf

Meyer, J. W., & Rowan, B. (1977). Institutionalized organizations: Formal structure as myth and ceremony. *American Journal of Sociology, 83* (2), 340–363.

Miles, K., & Frank, S. (2008). *The strategic school: Making the most of people, time, and money.* Thousand Oaks, CA: Corwin Press.

Mislevy, R. J. (1996). Test theory reconceived. *Journal of Educational Measurement, 33*(4), 379–416. doi:10.1111/j.1745-3984.1996.tb00498.x

Mislevy, R. J., Behrens, J. T., DiCerbo, K. E., & Levy, R. (2012). Design and discovery in educational assessment: Evidence centered design, psychometrics, and data mining. *Journal of Educational Data Mining, 4*(1).

Mislevy, R. J., Steinberg, L. S., & Almond, R. G. (1999). *On the roles of task model variables in assessment design* (CSE Technical Report No. 500). Princeton, NJ: Educational Testing Service.

Moody, L., & Dede, C. (2008). Models of data-based decision making: A case study of the Milwaukee public schools. In E. B. Mandinach & M. Honey (Eds.), *Data-driven school improvement: Linking data and learning* (pp. 233–254). New York: Teachers College Press.

Morino, M. (2011). Leap of reason: Managing to outcomes in an era of scarcity. *Innovations: Technology, Governance, Globalization, 6*(3), 167–177.

Moss, P. A., & Piety, P. J. (2007). Chapter 1 introduction: Evidence and decision making. *Yearbook of the National Society for the Study of Education, 106*(1), 1–14.

Moss, P. (2005). Toward "epistemic reflexivity" in educational research: A response to scientific research in education. *Teachers College Record, 107*(1), 19–29.

Moss, P., Girard, B., & Haniford, L. (2006). Validity in educational assessment. *Review of Research in Education, 30,* 109–162.

Mourshed, M., Chijioke, C., & Barber, M. (2010). *How the world's most improved school systems keep getting better.* New York, NY: McKinsey & Company.

National Center for Teaching Quality (2012). *What teacher preparation programs teach about K–12 assessment.* Washington, DC: National Council on Teacher Quality.

National Research Council. (1999). *How people learn: Brain, experience and school.* Washington, DC: Author.

National Research Council. (2002). *Scientific research in education.* Washington, DC: National Academy Press.

National Research Council. (2011). *Incentives and test-based accountability in education.* Retrieved from http://www.nap.edu/openbook.php?record_id=12521&page=1

National Science Foundation. (2007). *NSF's cyberinfrastructure vision for 21st century discovery.* Retrieved from http://www.nsf.gov/pubs/2007/nsf0728/nsf0728_6.pdf

Nichols, S., & Berliner, D. (2007). *Collateral damage: How high-stakes testing corrupts America's schools.* Cambridge, MA: Harvard Education Press.

New York City Department of Education. (2010). *School of One evaluation—2010 spring afterschool and short-term in-school pilot programs.* Retrieved from http://schoolofone.org/resources/so1_final_report_2010.pdf

No Child Left Behind Act of 2001. (2002). Public Law No. 107–110, 115 Statute 1425.

Noell, G., & Gansle, K. (2009, October 27). *Teach for America teachers' contribution to student achievement in Louisiana in grades 4–9: 2004–2005 to 2006–2007* (Technical Report). Louisiana State University, Baton Rouge, LA.

Noell, G., & Gleason, B. (2011, February 25). *The status of the development of the value added assessment model as specified in Act 54* (Report to the Senate Education Committee and the House Education Committee of the Louisiana Legislature). Baton Rouge: Strategic Research and Analysis Louisiana Department of Education.

Obama, B. (2009). *Remarks on education reform.* Retrieved from http://www.gpo.gov/fdsys/pkg/DCPD-200900595/html/DCPD-200900595.htm

O'Day, J., & Smith, M. (1993). Systemic reform and educational opportunity. In S. Fuhrman (Ed.), *Designing coherent education policy* (pp.250–312). San Francisco: Jossey-Bass.

Osguthorpe, R. T., & Graham, C. R. (2003). Blended learning environments: Definitions and directions. *Quarterly Review of Distance Education, 4*(3), 227–233.

Pajak, E. (1993). *Approaches to clinical supervision: Alternatives for improving instruction.* Norwood, MA: Christopher Gordon.

Pallas, A. (2010, July 28). Were some D.C. teachers fired based on flawed calculations? *The Washington Post.* Retrieved from http://voices.washingtonpost.com/answer-sheet/dc-schools/were-some-dc-teacher-dismissal.html

Pea, R. D. (1993). Practices of distributed intelligence and designs for education. In G. Salomon (Ed.), *Distributed cognition: Psychological and educational considerations* (pp. 47–87). New York: Cambridge University Press.

Pellegrino, J. W. (2011). Technology and formative assessment. In E. Baker, B. McGaw, & P. Peterson (Eds.), *International encyclopedia of education* (3rd ed., pp.245–255). Oxford: Elsevier.

Pellegrino, J., Chudowsky, N., & Glaser, R. (2001). *Knowing what students know: The science and design of educational assessment.* Washington, DC: National Academy Press; National Research Council.

Perie, M., Marion, S., & Gong, B. (2009). Moving toward a comprehensive assessment system: A framework for considering interim assessments. *Educational Measurement: Issues and Practice, 28*(3), 5–13.

Peters, L., & Saidin, H. (2000). IT and the mass customization of services: The challenge of implementation. *International Journal of Information Management, 20*(2), 103–119.

Peterson, K. D., Murphy, J., & Hallinger, P. (1987). Superintendents' perceptions of the control and coordination of the technical core in effective school districts. *Educational Administration Quarterly, 23*(1), 79–95.

Peurach, D. J. (2011). *Seeing complexity in public education: Problems, possibilities, and success for all.* New York: Oxford University Press.

Phelps, R. P. (2000). Estimating the cost of standardized student testing in the United States. *Journal of Education Finance, 25*(3), 343–380.

Pianta, R. C., & Hamre, B. K. (2009). Conceptualization, measurement, and improvement of classroom processes: Standardized observation can leverage capacity. *Educational Researcher, 38*(2), 109–119.

Piety, P. J., & Palincsar, A. S. (2006). How do we see?: Information architecture as theory. In *Proceedings of the 7th International Conference on Learning Sciences* (pp. 536–542). Bloomington, IN: International Conference on Learning Sciences.

Ramiller, N., Swanson, E. B., & Wang, P. (2008). Research directions in information systems: Toward an institutional ecology. *Journal of the Association for Information Systems, 9*(1), pp. 1–22.

Raudenbush, S., & Bryk, A. (2002). *Hierarchical linear models: Application and data analysis.* Newberry Park, CA: Sage.

Raudenbush, S., & Willms, J. (1995). The estimation of school effects. *Journal of Educational and Behavioral Statistics, 20*(4), 307–337.

Ravitch, D. (2009). *The death and life of the great American school system: How testing and choice are undermining education.* New York: Basic Books.

Ribes, D., & Finholt, T. (2009). The long now of technology infrastructure: Articulating tensions in development. *Journal of the Association for Information Systems, 10*(5), 377–398.

Roach, S. (1990). *America's technology dilemma: A profile of the information economy.* New York, NY: Morgan Stanley.

Rogers, E. M. (1995). *Diffusion of innovations* (4th ed.). New York: Free Press.

Romero, C., Ventura, S., Pechenizkiy, M., & Baker, R. (Eds.). (2010). *Handbook of educational data mining,* Boca Raton, FL: Chapman & Hall/CRC Data Mining.

Rowan, B. (2002). The ecology of school improvement: Notes on the school improvement industry in the United States. *Journal of Educational Change, 3,* 283–314.

Rupp, A., Templin, J., & Henson, R. (2010). *Diagnostic measurement: Theory, methods, and applications.* Guilford Press.

Sanders, W., & Rivers, J. (1996). *Cumulative and residual effects of teachers on future student academic achievement.* Knoxville: University of Tennessee, Value-Added Research and Assessment Center.

Santos, F., & Gebeloff, R. (2012, February 24). Teacher quality widely diffused, NYC ratings indicate. *The New York Times.* Retrieved from http://www.nytimes.com/2012/02/25/education/teacher-quality-widely-diffused-nyc-ratings-indicate.html

Scholastic and Bill and Melinda Gates Foundation. (2012). *Primary sources: America's teachers on the teaching profession.* Retrieved from http://www.scholastic.com/primarysources/pdfs/Gates2012_full.pdf

Scott, R. (1987). *Organizations: Rational, natural, and open systems* (2nd ed.). Englewood Cliffs, NJ: Prentice Hall.

Shapiro, C., & Varian, H. R. (1998). *Information rules: A strategic guide to the network economy.* Cambridge, MA: Harvard Business Press.

Shelton, J. (2010a). *Gov 2.0 Summit 2010: Next generation models for education.* Retrieved from http://www.youtube.com/watch?v=K1q9bjykbbU

Shelton, J. (2010b, December 17). *The future of education technology.* Remarks to the Brookings Institution, *Leveraging Technology to Reclaim American Educational Leadership Summit.* Retrieved from http://www.brookings.edu/~/media/events/2010/12/17%20education%20technology/20101217_education_technology_transcript_full

Shepard, L. A. (2009). Commentary: Evaluating the validity of formative and interim assessment. *Educational Measurement: Issues and Practice, 28*(3), 32–37.

Shulman, L. S. (1987). Knowledge and teaching: Foundations of the new reform. *Harvard Educational Review, 57*(1), 1–23.

Shute, V. J., Ventura, M., Bauer, M. I., & Zapata-Rivera, D. (2011). Melding the power of serious games and embedded assessment to monitor and foster learning: Flow and grow. In U. Ritterfeld, M. Cody, & P. Vorderer (Eds.), *Serious games: Mechanisms and effects.* Philadelphia: Routledge.

Siedlecki, J. (2012). *Measurement mania: Here to stay until we agree on a clear definition of "teaching."* Retrieved from http://blog.msdf.org/2012/04/measurement-mania-here-to-stay-until-we-agree-on-a-clear-definition-of-teaching/

Simon, H. A. (1996). *The sciences of the artificial.* Cambridge, MA: MIT Press.

Skinner, W. (1986). The productivity paradox. *Management Review, 75*(9), 41–45.

Slavin, R. E. (2002). Evidence-based education policies: Transforming educational practice and research. *Educational Researcher, 31*(7), 15–21.

Slavin, R. E., Cheung, A., Holmes, G. C., Madden, N. A., & Chamberlain, A. (2011). Effects of a data-driven district reform model. *Education, 1*(1), 13–26.

Slavin, R. E., Madden, N. A., Dolan, L. J., Wasik, B. A., Ross, S., Smith, L., & Dianda, M. (1996). Success for All: A summary of research. *Journal of Education for Students Placed at Risk, 1*(1), 41–76.

Slotta, J. D., & Linn, M. C. (2009). *WISE science: Web-based inquiry in the classroom.* New York: Teachers College Press.

Solmon, L. C., & Fagnano, C. L. (1990, Summer). Speculations on the benefits of large-scale teacher assessment programs: How 78 million dollars can be considered a mere pittance. *Journal of Education Finance,* 21–36.

Spencer Foundation. (2009). Data use and educational improvement. Retrieved from http://www.spencer.org/content.cfm/data-use-and-educational-improvement-details

Spillane, J. P. (2005). Distributed leadership. *The Educational Forum, 69,* 143–150.

Spillane, J. P., Halverson, R., & Diamond, J. B. (2001). Investigating school leadership practice: A distributed perspective. *Educational Researcher, 30*(3), 23–28.

Spillane, J. P., Parise, L. M., & Sherer, J. Z. (2011). Organizational routines as coupling mechanisms. *American Educational Research Journal, 48*(3), 586–619.

Staker, H., & Horn, M. (2012). *Classifying K–12 blended learning.* San Mateo, CA: Innosight Institute. Retrieved from http://www.innosightinstitute.org/innosight/wp-content/uploads/2012/05/Classifying-K-12-blended-learning2.pdf

Star, S., & Griesemer, J. (1989). Institutional ecology, translations and boundary objects: Amateurs and professionals in Berkeley's Museum of Vertebrate Zoology, 1907–39. *Social Studies of Science, 19*(3), 387–420.

Streifer, P. A. (2002). *Using data to make better educational decisions.* Lanham, MD: Scarecrow Press.

Streifer, P. A. (2001). The "drill down" process. *School Administrator, 58*(4), 16–19.

Supovitz, J. (2006). *The case for district-based reform: Leading, building, and sustaining school improvement.* Cambridge, MA: Harvard Education Press.

Tate, W. F., King, K. D., & Anderson, C. R. (Eds.). (2011). *Disrupting tradition: Research and practice pathways in mathematics education.* Reston, VA: National Council of Teachers of Mathematics.

The New Teacher Project. (2012). *The irreplaceables: Understanding the real retention crisis in America's urban schools.* Retrieved from http://tntp.org/assets/documents/TNTP_Irreplaceables_2012.pdf

Toppo, G., Gillum, J., & Bello, M. (2011, July 8). Official: Investigation into possible test cheating expands. *USA Today.* Retrieved from http://usatoday30.usatoday.com/news/education/2011-07-08-schools-DC-investigation-cheating_n.htm

Tough, P. (2011, September 14). What if the secret to success is failure? *The New York Times.* Retrieved from http://www.nytimes.com/2011/09/18/magazine/what-if-the-secret-to-success-is-failure.html

Turque, B. (2011, October 25). DC CAS test is coming to second grade. *The Washington Post.* Retrieved from http://www.washingtonpost.com/blogs/dc-schools-insider/post/dc-cas-test-is-coming-to-second-grade/2011/10/25/gIQAe6BbGM_blog.html

Turque, B. (2012, March 7). "Creative . . . motivating" and fired. *The Washington Post.* Retrieved from http://www.washingtonpost.com/local/education/creative-motivating-and-fired/2012/02/04/gIQAwzZpvR_story.html

U.S. Department of Education. (2008). *Teachers' use of student data systems to improve instruction: 2005 to 2007*. Washington, DC: Deparment of Education.

U.S. Department of Education. (2009). *Implementing data-informed decision making in schools: Teacher access, supports and use*. Washington, DC: Deparment of Education.

U.S. Department of Education. (2010). *Transforming American education: Learning powered by technology*. Washington, DC: Deparment of Education.

U.S. Department of Education, Office of Planning, Evaluation, and Policy Development (2010). *Use of education data at the local level from accountability to instructional improvement*. Washington, DC: Deparment of Education.

U.S. Department of Education. (2011). U.S. Education Department launches initiatives to safeguard student privacy [Press release]. Washington, DC: Retrieved from http://www.ed.gov/news/press-releases/us-education-department-launches-initiatives-safeguard-student-privacy

U.S. Department of Education, National Center for Education Statistics. (2003, November). *Financial accounting for local and state school systems: 2003 edition* (Report No. NCES 2004-318). Washington, DC: Deparment of Education.

U.S. Department of Education, Office of Educational Technology. (2004). *Toward a new golden age in American education: How the internet, the law and today's students are revolutionizing expectations*. Washington, DC: Deparment of Education.

U.S. Department of Education, Office of Educational Technology. (2013). *Expanding evidence approaches for learning in a digital world*. Washington, DC: U.S. Department of Education. http://www.ed.gov/edblogs/technology/evidence-framework/

U.S. Department of Education, Office of Postsecondary Education. (2011). *Our future, our teachers: The Obama administration's plan for teacher education reform and improvement*. Washington, DC: U.S. Government Printing Office. Retrieved from http://www.ed.gov/sites/default/files/our-future-our-teachers.pdf

Valli, L., Croninger, R. G., Chambliss, M. J., Graeber, A. O., & Buese, D. (2008). *Test driven: High-stakes accountability in elementary schools*. New York: Teachers College Press.

Walberg, H. J., & Thomas, S. C. (1972). Open education: An operational definition and validation in Great Britain and United States. *American Educational Research Journal*, 197–208.

Wallace Foundation. (2012). *The school principal as leader: Guiding schools to better teaching and learning*. Author.

Wang, P. (2010). Chasing the hottest IT: Effects of information technology fashion on organizations. *MIS Quarterly, 34*(1), 63–85.

Watson, J., Thorn, C., Ponisciak, S., & Boehm, F. (2011, April). *Measuring the impact of team teaching on student–teacher linkage data*. Paper presented at the annual meeting of the American Educational Research Association, Denver, CO.

Wayman, J., Cho, V., Jimerson, J., & Spikes, D. (2012). District-wide effects on data use in the classroom. *Education Policy Analysis Archives, 20*(25). Retrieved from http://epaa.asu.edu/ojs/article/view/979

Wayman, J. C., Conoly, K., Gasko, J., & Stringfield, S. (2008). Supporting equity inquiry with student data computer systems. In E. B. Mandinach & M. Honey (Eds.), *Data-driven school improvement: Linking data and learning* (pp. 171–190). New York: Teachers College Press.

Wayman, J., & Stringfield, S. (2006). Technology-supported involvement of entire faculties in examination of student data for instructional improvement. *American Journal of Education*, 112(4), 549–571.

Weaver-Hightower, M. (2008). An ecology metaphor for educational policy analysis: A call to complexity. *Educational Researcher, 36*, 153–167.

Weingarten, R. (2011, April 25). Comments made at forum titled "The Future of Teaching: New Standards, New Tests, and New Evaluations—What Does It All Mean?" Baltimore, MD.

Weisberg, D., Sexton, S., Mulhern, J., & Keeling, D. (2009). *The widget effect: Our national failure to acknowledge and act on differences in teacher effectiveness*. New York: New Teacher Project.

Weiss, J. (2012, July 11). Keynote address, 2012 NCES STATS-DC Data Conference, Washington, DC.

Wenger, E. (1998). *Communities of practice: Learning, meaning, and identity*. Cambridge, UK: Cambridge University Press.

Wilson, S. M., Miller, C., & Yerkes, C. (1993). Deeply rooted change: A tale of learning to teach adventurously. *Teaching for Understanding: Challenges for Policy and Practice*, 84–129.

Winerip, M. (2011, June 5). Helping teachers help themselves. *The New York Times*, p. A10. Retrieved from: http://www.nytimes.com/2011/06/06/education/06oneducation.html?pagewanted=all

Winerip, M. (2012, April 29). On report cards for N.Y.C. schools, invisible line divides "A" and "F." *The New York Times*. Retrieved from http://www.nytimes.com/2012/04/30/nyregion/on-report-cards-for-nyc-schools-invisible-line-divides-a-and-f.html

Young, V. M. (2006). Teachers' use of data: Loose coupling, agenda setting, and team norms. *American Journal of Education, 112*(4), 521–548.

Index

NAMES

SUBJECTS

About the Author

Philip J. Piety is a national expert in educational data. His expertise draws from professional experience in organizational information technology and a Ph.D. from the University of Michigan titled: *Learning Sciences: Materials, Measurement, and Information Architecture.* His path to being an author is nontraditional. He left high school early to begin working in the information technology revolution that he writes about in this book. After rising through positions of responsibility with multinational software firms, he returned to school and completed all of his degrees as an adult. He now specializes in adapting organizational technology into the complex and varied domain of educational practice, which he also observes as the parent of two elementary school children.